300 CLASSIC RECIPES

THE BEST OF ASIAN COOKING

Arlene Diego
Dhershini Govin Winodan
Heinz von Holzen
Keiko Ishida
Lee Minjung
Nguyen Thanh Diep

Copyright © 2013 Marshall Cavendish International (Asia) Private Limited
This edition with new cover, 2023
The book contains previously published material from the Feast of Flavours series.

Published by Marshall Cavendish Cuisine
An imprint of Marshall Cavendish International

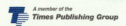

All rights reserved

No part of this publication may be reproduced, stored in a retrieval system or transmitted, in any form or by any means, electronic, mechanical, photocopying, recording or otherwise, without the prior permission of the copyright owner. Request for permission should be addressed to the Publisher, Marshall Cavendish International (Asia) Private Limited, 1 New Industrial Road, Singapore 536196 Tel: (65) 62139300
E-mail: genref@sg.marshallcavendish.com
Website: http://www.marshallcavendish.com

Limits of Liability/Disclaimer of Warranty: The Author and Publisher of this book have used their best efforts in preparing this book. The Publisher makes no representation or warranties with respect to the contents of this book and is not responsible for the outcome of any recipe in this book. While the Publisher has reviewed each recipe carefully, the reader may not always achieve the results desired due to variations in ingredients, cooking temperatures and individual cooking abilities. The Publisher shall in no event be liable for any loss of profit or any other commercial damage, including but not limited to special, incidental, consequential, or other damages.

Other Marshall Cavendish Offices:
Marshall Cavendish Corporation. 99 White Plains Road, Tarrytown NY 10591-9001, USA • Marshall Cavendish International (Thailand) Co Ltd. 253 Asoke, 12th Floor, Sukhumvit 21 Road, Klongtoey Nua, Wattana, Bangkok 10110, Thailand • Marshall Cavendish (Malaysia) Sdn Bhd, Times Subang, Lot 46, Subang Hi-Tech Industrial Park, Batu Tiga, 40000 Shah Alam, Selangor Darul Ehsan, Malaysia

Marshall Cavendish is a trademark of Times Publishing Limited

Printed in Singapore

CONTENTS

COOKING UTENSILS	5
COOKING TECHNIQUES	10
BASIC RECIPES	14
VEGETABLES AND SALADS	22
SOUPS	64
MAIN COURSES	94
RICE	128
NOODLES	164
MEAT	192
POULTRY	222
FISH AND SEAFOOD	248
SNACKS	284
DESSERTS	306
GLOSSARY	344
INDEX	374
A NOTE FROM TIMES	376

COOKING UTENSILS
COOKING TECHNIQUES
BASIC RECIPES

COOKING UTENSILS

Bamboo Mat

Typically measuring about 22 x 20-cm (9 x 8-in), the bamboo mat is a must-have for making sushi rolls. It is better to choose a mat that comprises many small bamboo sticks threaded together to form a flat surface on one side, than one which is made of less, but larger pieces, as the former is more flexible and makes sushi-rolling easier. Bamboo mats, especially those with round bamboo sticks threaded together, can also be used for shaping and creating line patterns on thick-rolled omelettes. After using, ensure that your mat is clean, and completely dry before storing, or it will turn mouldy.

Cleaver

A cleaver is useful for separating bones from meat, tenderising meat, finely shredding vegetables and also smashing garlic. This multi-use kitchen tool is rather heavy, but the weight is inversely proportional to the amount of effort required to use it. That is, the heavier the cleaver, the less effort required in using it. Thus, when buying a cleaver, choose one the heaviest one that you are comfortable with.

Claypot

Nothing beats a claypot for retaining the flavour of stewed meat and chicken. Special care is required in handling a claypot as it breaks easily. To season a claypot: fry grated coconut in the claypot in a little oil for about 10 minutes over low heat.

Earthenware Pot

Made from clay, this pot retains heat well and also allows heat to transfer slowly and gently. It is therefore ideal for cooking hotpot dishes and soups, such as steamboat, *shabu shabu* and *yose nabe*. It is also used for cooking rice and noodle dishes. After using, always cool the earthenware pot completely before washing and do not heat the pot without any liquid in it; the pot may crack.

Grater

Graters are made from a variety of materials including copper, stainless steel, plastic, aluminium and ceramic. Whatever the material the grater is made of, it basically has a flat surface with many fine spikes, or a combination of tiny spikes and holes. While a coarse grater is used for grating hardy vegetables, a fine grater is used for grating dense spices, garlic and ginger.

Mortar and Pestle

The mortar and pestle is an extremely traditional and indispensable kitchen tool in many Asian households. It is primarily used for breaking down various herbs and spices for pastes, bruising aromatic leaves to release flavour, and even skinning toasted peanuts. The time and energy- saving electric blender is fast replacing the mortar and pestle in many Asian homes, but one advantage that the cook has by using a mortar and pestle is that he or she is able to control the texture of the ingredients, which can range from coarse to very fine. A large mortar would be a better consideration, as small ones are inadequate for pounding more than very small quantities of spice paste. Season a new mortar by pounding sand in it until the surface is reasonably smooth.

Scoops and Ladles

Scoops and ladles come in a variety of sizes. In many Asian cultures, they were traditionally made from wood or coconut husks. However, stainless steel varieties are more commonly used today. Short-handled scoops are usually used for serving rice and ladles for dishing out soups and curries.

Spatulas

The spatula is the instrument that the cook uses to stir, flip and move ingredients in a wok. They can be made of metal, wood or plastic, and the material to choose really depends on the type of wok or pan it will be used against. A wooden or plastic spatula is more suitable for non-stick surfaces as it will prevent scratches or similar damage to the non-stick coating. Metal spatulas are better suited to cast iron or stainless steel woks.

Cooking Utensils 7

Steamers

A steamer is a multi-tier container that comes with a lid. Bamboo steamers are the most traditional steamers, and they are usually sold at Chinese sundry shops. They are a common sight in Chinese restaurants that serve *dim sum*. They can also be used in conjunction with any round-based wok. When steaming, ensure that the water in the wok does not surge past the base of the bottom tier upon boiling.

By comparison, metal steamers have several advantages over bamboo steamers. They are durable and are safe from mould growth, which tends to affect bamboo steamers over time. Metal steamers are made up of a bottom section for holding water, a top section for placing perforated trays and a cover on top. They can be placed directly over stove-top heat. When the water boils, steam passes through the holes to cook the food.

Wire Strainer and Sieve

Traditional wire strainers have woven brass handles attached to long bamboo handles, such strainers are better suited to use with woks because of the wide angle at which the mesh baskets are attached to the handles. These strainers can be used to blanch noodles or vegetables in hot water or drain deep-fried food items from hot oil. The more modern wire strainers appear like elongated sieves attached to relatively shorter and vertical handles. These strainers are more convenient because they can be lowered straight down into a normal cooking pot, but they also serve no other purpose aside from blanching.

Wire mesh sieves are used for aerating flours or removing lumps from flour for baking. In cooking, sieves are useful for separating solids from liquids. Sieves are made from a variety of materials—wooden frames and nylon or metal mesh, plastic frames with nylon mesh and fully stainless steel sieves. It is useful to have a few sieves on hand so you will always have a clean, dry sieve available when another is in use or has just been washed.

Wok

The wok is an indispensable tool for cooking stir-fried noodles or deep-fried dishes. Woks were traditionally made of heavy cast iron, with a rounded base, and two small, semi-circular handles at opposing ends. However, modern woks made of aluminium and stainless steel are generally preferred for their light weight and variation in shape and form. The popularity and convenience of non-stick cooking surfaces has since also extended itself to some woks.

When choosing a wok, be mindful of your needs and kitchen conditions over the look and base-material of the utensil. If you have a gas hob, for instance, then a round-based wok will rest more securely on the metal frame of the hob than a wok that is flat-based. This takes into account how the action of stir-frying can cause a flat-based wok to slide along the metal frame and away from the heat source or worse, topple. It is also more practical to purchase a small to medium-size wok, as you can retain better control over the food you are cooking. Although a non-stick wok is more convenient for cooking, a cast-iron wok is more durable as it heats evenly, and is able to withstand high heat on a daily basis for years. Avoid buying woks made of aluminium, as they tend to heat too quickly and unevenly.

In terms of material, cast-iron woks, although not non-stick and heavy, are generally preferred in many Asian households. This is because they are relatively inexpensive and can withstand daily doses of intensely high heat for years without warping. A cast iron or carbon steel wok should be seasoned properly before use. To season, wash the wok and dry it well. Oil the surface by rubbing it with a little cooking oil. Heat up the wok, then leave it to cool down. Repeat these steps for another 2–3 times, then wipe the wok with kitchen paper or a cloth. To clean the wok, place it under running water while it is still hot and brush off dirt. If using a non-stick wok, clean with a soft sponge instead. Avoid using harsh detergents to clean the wok. After cleaning, make sure that the wok is completely dry by wiping dry or heating up the wok.

Cooking Utensils 9

COOKING TECHNIQUES

Blanching

Blanching is a cooking method that helps to soften ingredients, remove any bitter tastes, as well as enable the ingredients to absorb seasoning easily, and retain their colour. Blanching is usually employed for delicate ingredients that require only light cooking, or subject to further cooking. Green vegetables like spinach, asparagus and peas should be cooked briefly in salted water that has been brought to the boil first, then drained and soaked in iced water, or cooled on a flat sieve, using a hand fan to refresh the vegetables.

Boiling

Boiling may seem to be the simplest cooking method, but in Asian cooking, there are three main methods of boiling, namely rapid boiling, slow boiling and prolonged boiling. Knowing when to employ what boiling method is important to achieve a successful dish. Turning up the heat to hurry the boiling process is often not the answer. For example, there are different techniques to cooking noodles. Mastering the appropriate boiling method is crucial, whether for blanching the noodles or preparing the stock for the soup base of the noodle dish. For instance, preparing the stock base for the soup will require prolonged, rigorous boiling, especially if it is derived from bones.

Rapid boiling for a few minutes is applied to ingredients such as tomato wedges or other such vegetables going into a soup. Such a method means that the tomato wedges will be cooked through and just softened but not disintegrating from too much heat. Other ingredients, such as fish pieces, may require slow boiling. This is because the violent motions of rapid boiling will cause the fish pieces to break into bits in the soup. The rolling actions of a slow boil, on the other hand, are gentle enough for the fish pieces to accommodate, so they will cook through while remaining in whole pieces.

Braising and Stewing

This is a long cooking process which takes up to several hours. Meat, seafood and vegetables are slowly simmered together with a variety of sauces and spices to create delicious dishes with rich sauces and wonderful aromas.

The success of braising and stewing depends on the combination of sauces, ingredients and spices used. Light and thick soy sauces are popular base ingredients. Ginger, garlic and shallots give flavour while popular spices used include five-spice powder, cinnamon, clove, star anise, Szechuan and white peppercorns. It is a good idea to wrap all the spices in a muslin bag so that the spices can be easily removed as required and prevent the spices from clouding the sauce.

Before braising, make sure the meat has been marinated for some time so that it can absorb all the seasoning. You can also seal in flavour and juices of meat and vegetables by frying quickly in oil or by blanching in boiling water. Keep the garnishing very simple for braised dishes, some chopped spring onion or topping of coriander or parsley will suffice. Usually, the earthen pot or clay pot is used because of they are better for slow cooking. The wok is also used, especially for whole fowls, fish and large cuts of meat. When braising, applying too much heat will ruin the dish. For ease and convenience, an electric crockpot can also be used for braising and stewing.

Browning

Allowing foods to brown in the pan with or without fat over moderate heat creates greater flavour in the final dish. Allow meats to cook through on one side before flipping over to cook the other side.

Browning onions is a sure way of getting that full-bodied flavour in curries and briyanis. Crisp-fried onions are also great toppings for soups, noodles and even plain rice. To crisp-fry onions, peel, then finely slice. Heat oil until smoking then add the sliced onions. After a minute, reduce the heat and allow the onions to continue to brown. Drain completely on absorbent paper and store away.

Extracting Juices / Milk

In Asian cooking, the extracting of juice or milk mainly refers to coconut milk, citrus fruit juice and tamarind juice. Packets of ready extracted coconut milk are now available from the supermarket, so you don't have to go through the tedious process of extracting the milk from the freshly grated coconut. In some Asian homes, however, the freshly extracted milk is still preferred.

Tamarind juice is not as readily available, but the process is much easier than extracting coconut milk. Take a lime-sized ball of tamarind pulp and place in a small bowl. Add enough water to cover then knead the pulp with your hand until the pulp is separated from the seeds. Strain and discard the seeds. Use the juice according to the recipe.

Frying

Deep-frying

This is a method where food is cooked in a large amount of cooking oil, deep enough to cover it completely. Deep-frying can be done in a wok or in a deep pan. Fill the oil halfway up the wok or pan so that any splattering will be contained. The temperature of the cooking oil is very important when deep-frying. If the oil is not hot enough, the food will absorb all the oil and become greasy; but if too hot, the food will burn. The optimum temperature for deep-frying is at 180°C. Check the temperature with a fat thermometer, or gently lower a morsel of the food for deep-frying and watch how quickly it browns. If it takes about 45 seconds to a minute, the temperature is right.

Continue to monitor the temperature and regulate it by turning the heat down when the oil starts getting hotter. When food is cooked, remove from heat and drain on absorbent paper to remove excess oil. This will also help the food to stay crisp longer.

Shallow-frying

When shallow-frying, the food is cooked with a small amount of oil and the food is hardly moved around so as to produce a crispy outer layer while keeping the inside moist. The natural flavour is also retained. This method is used for cooking fish, eggs, dumplings, stuffed vegetables and any foods that cook easily.

Food prepared this way is usually served with a variety of dips and garnished with colourful vegetables and fruits to make the plain fried dish more attractive. Use a flat pan for shallow-frying so that the oil can be evenly spread out and heated up before adding the food. Control the temperature and watch the timing carefully to prevent overcooking. Start by cooking on high heat for a few seconds, then turn down to medium or low heat, depending on the thickness of the food.

Stir-frying

Stir-frying is one of the most famous methods of Chinese cooking but it is also the most difficult because speed and control is critical in ensuring success. Food is cooked quickly at high temperatures in order to preserve its natural colour and texture, especially vegetables. Stir-frying meat seals in the juices prior to further cooking. It is a healthy method of cooking since very little oil is used. When stir-frying, make sure that you use a good source of heat that can be easily adjusted. The gas cooker is recommended for its ease of control and practicality. On the other hand, electric hot plates are unsuitable for stir-frying because of poor heat control.

Grilling

Grilling is done by setting food above or below a heat source to cook it. This can be done over hot coals, under the electric grill, in the oven or even on the top of the stove using a heavy-based grill pan. In Asian cooking, meat and seafood to be grilled are usually exposed directly to the heat, wrapped in leaves or aluminium foil. Screwpine leaves and banana leaves are commonly used as they impart a lovely fragrance to the cooked food. For successful grilling, the heat must be well-regulated so that the food doesn't burn or blacken on the outside too readily while remaining raw on the inside.

Kneading

Kneading is a technique used in making bread. Once the ingredients have been assembled, use your fingers to gather them together and mix into a smooth, pliable dough. Do this slowly to allow air to be incorporated into the mixture to ensure a light and feathery bread. When you have a ball of dough, rub a little oil (ghee [clarified butter], olive oil or any cooking oil) all over it and place it in a bowl. Cover it with a cloth or some plastic wrap to prevent the dough from drying out.

Marinating

This is a popular technique used all over the world to flavour and tenderize meat prior to cooking it . Marinade ingredients differs across Asian cuisines. For example, in Korea, pineapple syrup and pear juice are commonly used to tenderize beef and pork while marinating. Spring onions are also a common marinating agent in Korean cooking, to lend flavour to the cooked dish. Soy sauce and garlic make a simple but tasty marinade in Chinese cooking, and spices usually form a dry rub or marinade in Indian cooking. Use your hands when marinating; this way, you will be able to effectively rub the marinade into the meat or fish. It is best to marinate meat or fish fresh from the market. If not cooking on the day of purchasing the meat and fish, clean the meat or fish accordingly, marinate, then pack into airtight freezer bags and refrigerate for 2–3 hours to allow the marinade to infuse the meat. Lastly, store in the freezer until required.

Pickling

Pickling is the process of preserving and storing food. It is a method that goes a long way back to the days when refrigeration did not exist, or was not readily available. It was done out of necessity to preserve food for the cold winter months in seasonal Asian countries. Fruit or vegetables are covered in brine, or an alcohol or vinegar solution together with various herbs, spices and seasoning ingredients. They are placed in airtight containers and stored in a cool, dark place for several weeks or months, depending on the requirement.

Roasting

Roasting is usually done to cook whole ducks and chickens or, as in Balinese cooking, whole pigs. Traditionally, roasting is done on a spit over an open fire when food is wrapped in various kinds of leaves, then buried under hot charcoal. In the modern kitchen, use a regular convection oven. For the first 15–20 minutes, roast at high heat or 180–200°C (350–400°F), then reduce the heat to 150–180°C (300–350°F). Frequently baste food with an oil-based basting liquid.

Simmering

Simmering is a cooking technique that involves food cooking in water or liquids kept just below boiling point, at about 94°C (200°F). In Japanese cooking, it is one of the main cooking methods. Ingredients are usually simmered in dashi, to which seasoning has been added. First of all, sugar, sake and mirin are added, followed by soy sauce and salt at a later stage. Salt is always added after sugar; it is believed that salt has a more refined texture than sugar, and is therefore more easily absorbed by ingredients to accentuate their flavours. To make a good simmered Japanese dish, always choose the freshest ingredients and parboil, or precook them, before simmering in a top-quality dashi. However, do note that fish is always simmered in water, and not dashi, since the latter is basically a stock made from fish and seaweed; the fish dish will become overpoweringly fishy if dashi is used.

Smoking

Smoking adds fragrance and flavour to the meat. The meat is often partially cooked first by steaming, then cured in smoke from burning camphor wood, tea leaves or peanut shells. Smoking is usually done in a pot or a wok. Poultry is usually deep-fried after smoking to obtain the crispy skin that is so well-loved by the Chinese in crispy chicken dishes.

Steaming

To steam food, place the food above boiling water and let the heat from the steam cook the food. It is an easy, fast and clean method of cooking. Although the method is simple, the correct marinade has to be carefully chosen to produce the desired flavour and texture. Steaming is good for meat, fish and prawn dishes. When done, add garnishing to bring out the flavour and make the dish more attractive. You can use garnishings such as red chilli flowers, spring onions soaked in cold water for curling effect or a bunch of coriander leaves to make the dish more colourful.

Stewing

Stewing helps to retain all the nutritional goodness and sweetness of the ingredients in the stewing liquid. Tougher cuts of meat can also be used as the cooking process will render them tender. To stew food, the ingredients are usually cut into pieces of similar size and placed into enough liquid to cover them completely. The pot is covered and placed over low heat to cook the ingredients slowly. The stewing liquid is sometimes served as it is to accompany the dish, but it may also be reduced or thickened into gravy.

Tempering

In Indian cooking, tempering refers to the process of heating a little oil, adding your aromatics like cinnamon, cardamom and cloves or, in most cases, mustard seeds, curry leaves, onions and chillies. The general idea is to allow the ingredients to release their flavours and fragrance into the oil. This is then added to the main ingredients for the flavour to be absorbed. The second tempering also uses the same ingredients—oil, mustard seeds, curry leaves, sliced onions, and sometimes dried red chillies and dhal. These are fried to a golden brown and then poured over the prepared curries and sauces to seal in the flavour.

Using Spices

There are dry and wet spices. Dry spices include chilli powder, cilantro, cumin, pepper and turmeric, and these are easily available at the supermarket. Powdered forms of these spices are also available at the supermarket, but as spices do not retain their flavour well, grind them yourself in small batches. Pick out the small stones and sticks that sometimes find their way into the spices and roast in a dry pan over very low heat until the spice is hot to the touch. Leave to cool slightly before grinding in a coffee mill set aside specially for this purpose. Store in a clean, dry jar. Wet spices are generally made only when required with fresh ingredients. To make, dry-roast the dry spices and grind with a little water.

BASIC RECIPES

Basic Spice Paste

Red chillies	300 g (11 oz), large, halved, seeded and sliced
Shallots	500 g (1 lb 1½ oz), peeled and sliced
Garlic	100 g (3½ oz), peeled and sliced
Ginger	70 g (2½ oz), peeled and sliced
Galangal	70 g (2½ oz), peeled and chopped
Lesser galangal	100 g (3½ oz), peeled and sliced
Turmeric	175 g (6¼ oz), peeled and sliced
Candlenuts	70 g (2½ oz)
Dried prawn (shrimp) paste	2 Tbsp, toasted
Coriander seeds	2 Tbsp, crushed
Black peppercorns	1 Tbsp, crushed
Freshly grated nutmeg	¼ tsp
Cloves	8, crushed
Vegetable oil	150 ml (5 fl oz / ⅗ cup)
Lemongrass	2 stalks, bruised
Salam leaves	2
Salt	¾ Tbsp
Water	250 ml (8 fl oz / 1 cup)

1. For each spice paste recipe, combine all ingredients except tamarind pulp, *salam* leaves, lemongrass, salt and water, in a mortar and pestle, blender or ideally, a meat grinder fitted with a medium blade; grind coarsely.

2. Transfer paste to a heavy saucepan. Add remaining ingredients and simmer over medium heat for about 1 hour or until water has evaporated and paste becomes golden in colour.

3. Leave to cool thoroughly before using or storing for future use; one way is to portion into ice cube trays and freeze.

Vegetable Spice Paste

Red chillies	250 g (9 oz), large, halved, seeded and sliced
Bird's eye chillies	25 g (⅘ oz)
Shallots	100 g (3½ oz), peeled and sliced
Garlic	100 g (3½ oz), peeled and sliced
Galangal	100 g (3½ oz), peeled and chopped
Lesser galangal (*kencur*)	100 g (3½ oz), washed and sliced
Turmeric	100 g (3½ oz), peeled and sliced
Candlenuts	200 g (7 oz)
Dried prawn (shrimp) paste	1 Tbsp
Coriander seeds	1 Tbsp, crushed
Black peppercorns	½ Tbsp, crushed
Vegetable oil	150 ml (5 fl oz / ⅗ cup)
Salam leaves	2
Lemongrass	2 stalks, bruised
Water	250 ml (8 fl oz / 1 cup)
Salt	¾ Tbsp

1. For each spice paste recipe, combine all ingredients except those in bold using a mortar and pestle, blender or ideally, a meat grinder fitted with a medium blade; grind coarsely.

2. Transfer paste to a heavy saucepan. Add remaining ingredients and simmer over medium heat for about 1 hour or until water has evaporated and paste becomes golden in colour.

3. Leave to cool thoroughly before using or storing for future use; one way is to portion into ice cube trays and freeze.

Chicken Spice Paste

Bird's eye chillies	50 g (1⅔ oz), finely sliced
Shallots	225 g (8 oz), peeled and sliced
Garlic	125 g (4½ oz), peeled and sliced
Lesser galangal (*kencur*)	50 g (1⅔ oz), peeled and sliced
Turmeric	125 g (4½ oz), peeled and sliced
Candlenuts	100 g (3½ oz)
Palm sugar	50 g (1⅔ oz), chopped
Vegetable oil	**150 ml (5 fl oz / ⅗ cup)**
Lemongrass	**2 stalks, bruised**
***Salam* leaves**	**3**
Salt	**¾ Tbsp**
Water	**250 ml (8 fl oz / 1 cup)**

1. For each spice paste recipe, combine all ingredients except those in bold using a mortar and pestle, blender or ideally, a meat grinder fitted with a medium blade; grind coarsely.

2. Transfer paste to a heavy saucepan. Add remaining ingredients and simmer over medium heat for about 1 hour or until water has evaporated and paste becomes golden in colour.

3. Leave to cool thoroughly before using or storing for future use; one way is to portion into ice cube trays and freeze.

Seafood Spice Paste

Red chillies	450 g (16 oz / 1 lb), large, halved, seeded and sliced
Shallots	225 g (8 oz), peeled and sliced
Garlic	50 g (1⅔ oz), peeled and sliced
Ginger	100 g (3½ oz), peeled and sliced
Turmeric	175 g (6¼ oz), peeled and sliced
Candlenuts	125 g (4½ oz)
Dried prawn (shrimp) paste	2 Tbsp, roasted
Coriander seeds	2 Tbsp, crushed
Tomatoes	200 g (7 oz), halved and seeded
Vegetable oil	**150 ml (5 fl oz / ⅗ cup)**
Tamarind pulp	**2½ Tbsp**
Lemongrass	**2 stalks, bruised**
***Salam* leaves**	**3**
Salt	**¾ Tbsp**
Water	**250 ml (8 fl oz / 1 cup)**

1. For each spice paste recipe, combine all ingredients except those in bold using a mortar and pestle, blender or ideally, a meat grinder fitted with a medium blade; grind coarsely.

2. Transfer paste to a heavy saucepan. Add remaining ingredients and simmer over medium heat for about 1 hour or until water has evaporated and paste becomes golden in colour.

3. Leave to cool thoroughly before using or storing for future use; one way is to portion into ice cube trays and freeze.

East Javanese Yellow Spice Paste

Shallots	180 g (6½ oz), peeled and sliced
Garlic	120 g (4⅓ oz), peeled and sliced
Red chillies	160 g (5¾ oz), halved, seeded and sliced
Turmeric	140 g (5 oz), peeled and sliced
Ginger	40 g (1¼ oz), peeled and sliced
Galangal (*laos*)	40 g (1¼ oz), peeled and sliced
Candlenuts	140 g (5 oz)
Lemongrass	5 stalks, bruised and finely sliced
Coriander seeds	4 Tbsp, toasted and crushed
Cumin	1 Tbsp
Sweet soy sauce	4 Tbsp
Chopped palm sugar	2 Tbsp
Vegetable oil	3 Tbsp
Chicken stock (page 20)	500 ml (16 fl oz / 2 cups)
Salt	1½ Tbsp

1. Combine all ingredients, except oil, stock and salt, in a stone mortar or blender and grind coarsely.
2. Transfer ground ingredients to a heavy saucepan, add oil and sauté over medium heat for 2 minutes or until fragrant.
3. Add stock and simmer over low heat for about 30 minutes or until all the liquid has evaporated and paste is golden in colour. Season with salt.
4. Leave to cool completely before using or storing.

Spiced Tomato Sauce

Vegetable oil	150 ml (5 fl oz / ⅗ cup)
Shallots	200 g (7 oz), peeled and sliced
Garlic	100 g (3½ oz), peeled and sliced
Red chillies	375 g (13⅓ oz), large, seeded and sliced
Bird's eye chillies	375 g (13⅓ oz), left whole
Palm sugar	50 g (1⅔ oz), chopped
Dried prawn (shrimp) paste	1½ Tbsp, roasted
Tomatoes	750 g (1 lb 10 oz), peeled and seeded
Lime juice	1 Tbsp
Salt	to taste

1. Heat oil in a heavy saucepan over moderate high heat. Add shallots and garlic and sauté until golden.
2. Add chillies and sauté until chillies are soft, then add palm sugar and prawn paste. Sauté until sugar caramelises.
3. Add tomatoes and sauté until tomatoes are soft. Remove from heat and leave to cool. Add a little water if mixture is dry.
4. Coarsely grind cooled ingredients using a mortar and pestle or a blender.
5. Adjust sauce to taste with lime juice and salt before serving.

Peanut Sauce

Cooking oil	150 ml (5 fl oz / ⅗ cup)
Coconut milk	1 litre (32 fl oz / 4 cups), extracted from 350 g (12 oz) grated coconut and 1 litre (32 fl oz / 4 cups) water
Sour star fruit	350 g (12 oz), cut into 1-cm (½-in) thick slices and boiled for 1 minute to remove a bit of its sourness
Pineapple	300 g (11 oz), finely chopped
Toasted peanuts	300 g (11 oz), coarsely pounded
Salt	1½ Tbsp
Sugar	220 g (8 oz)

FINELY GROUND PASTE

Dried chillies	25, soaked in water and drained
Shallots	28, peeled
Galangal	2.5-cm (1-in) knob, peeled
Dried prawn (shrimp) paste	1 Tbsp, crushed

1. Heat cooking oil and fry finely ground paste until fragrant. Stir in coconut milk and bring to the boil.
2. Add sour star fruit and pineapple, cook for about 6 minutes. Stir in peanuts and season with salt and sugar.
3. Simmer for 5–10 minutes until sauce thickens, stirring constantly. Serve hot.

Shallot and Lemongrass Dressing

Shallots	40 g (1⅓ oz), peeled, halved and finely sliced
Lemongrass	75 g (2⅔ oz), bruised, finely sliced and chopped
Garlic	20 g (⅔ oz), peeled and finely chopped
Bird's eye chillies	30 g (1 oz), finely sliced
Kaffir lime leaves	2, finely chopped
Dried prawn (shrimp) paste	½ tsp, toasted and finely crumbled
Lime juice	2 Tbsp, freshly squeezed
Vegetable oil	4 Tbsp
Salt	a pinch
Ground black pepper	a pinch

1. Combine all ingredients except salt and pepper in a large bowl. Mix thoroughly for 5 minutes. Season to taste with salt and pepper before using.
2. Alternatively, heat oil in a saucepan and cook all ingredients over medium heat for 5 minutes or until fragrant. Remove from heat. Leave to cool to room temperature before using.

Red Curry Paste

Cumin	2 tsp
Coriander seeds	1 tsp
Dried chillies	8, soaked, drained and coarsely chopped
Kaffir lime zest	½ tsp, finely chopped
Salt	1 tsp
Lemongrass	1 tsp, finely chopped
Garlic	1 Tbsp, peeled and chopped
Galangal	1 Tbsp, peeled and chopped
Dried prawn (shrimp) paste	1 Tbsp

1. Place cumin and coriander seeds in a dry pan. Dry-fry over medium heat for 1–2 minutes until slightly browned and aromatic.
2. Combine all ingredients and pound into a paste. Store refrigerated in an airtight jar. Use as needed.

Dipping Sauce

Fish sauce	1 Tbsp
Coconut juice	2 Tbsp or boiled water
Sugar	1 tsp
Vinegar	1 Tbsp or lemon juice
Garlic	1 clove, peeled and minced
Red chilli (optional)	1 or to taste, minced

1. Combine ingredients and serve in individual dipping saucers.

Beef Spice Paste

Red chillies	250 g (9 oz), large, halved, seeded and sliced
Bird's eye chillies	40 g (1⅓ oz), finely sliced
Shallots	200 g (7 oz), peeled and sliced
Garlic	50 g (1⅔ oz), peeled and sliced
Ginger	50 g (1⅔ oz), peeled and sliced
Galangal	150 g (5⅓ oz), peeled and chopped
Candlenuts	100 g (3½ oz)
Coriander seeds	2 Tbsp, crushed
Black peppercorns	2 Tbsp, crushed
Palm sugar	40 g (1⅓ oz), chopped
Vegetable oil	150 ml (5 fl oz / ⅗ cup)
Salam leaves	3
Salt	¾ Tbsp
Water	250 ml (8 fl oz / 1 cup)

1. Combine all ingredients except *salam* leaves, salt and water using a mortar and pestle, blender or ideally, a meat grinder fitted with a medium blade. Grind coarsely.
2. Transfer paste to a heavy saucepan. Add remaining ingredients and simmer over medium heat for about 1 hour or until water has evaporated and paste is golden in colour.
3. Leave to cool thoroughly before using or storing for future use; one way is to portion into ice cube trays and freeze.

Nasi Goreng Sauce

Vegetable oil	150 ml (5 fl oz / ⅗ cup)
Shallots	200 g (7 oz), peeled and sliced
Garlic	100 g (3½ oz), peeled and sliced
Red chillies	375 g (12½ oz), seeded and sliced
Bird's eye chillies	375 g (12½ oz)
Salam leaves	4
Dried prawn (shrimp) paste	1½ Tbsp, roasted
Palm sugar	75 g (2⅔ oz), chopped
Tomatoes	500 g (1 lb 1½ oz), peeled and seeded
Salt	to taste
Lime juice	1 Tbsp or more to taste

1. Heat oil in heavy saucepan. Add shallots and garlic and sauté until golden.
2. Add chillies and *salam* leaves and sauté until chillies are soft.
3. Add prawn paste and palm sugar and continue to sauté until sugar caramelises. Add tomatoes and sauté until soft, then remove from heat and set aside to cool completely.
4. Grind paste coarsely in a stone mortar or pulse in a blender for a similar effect.
5. Season and adjust to taste with salt and lime juice.

Dashi

Water	as required in recipe
Dried kelp	as required in recipe
Bonito flakes	as required in recipe

1. Prepare dashi. Put water and kelp into a saucepan and leave for 30 minutes. Place over medium heat and when small bubbles appear from the bottom, remove kelp.
2. When water is boiling, add bonito flakes, then reduce heat and simmer for a few seconds. Remove from heat, then leave until bonito flakes sink to the bottom of saucepan. Strain stock and discard solids.

Basic Chicken/Beef/Pork Stock

Chicken, beef or pork bones	2 kg (2 lb 3 oz), skin and fat discarded, then chopped into 2.5-cm (1-in) pieces
Water	2 litres (64 fl oz / 8 cups)

1. Rinse bones until water is clear. Place into a stockpot and add water. Bring to the boil over high heat.
2. Boil for 1–2 hours, skimming off scum that surfaces from time to time.
3. Strain stock and use as required.

Indonesian-style Stock

Chicken, beef, pork or duck bones	5 kg (11 lb), skin and fat discarded, then chopped into 2.5-cm (1-in) pieces
Spice paste (pages 14, 15 or 18, according to type of bones used)	375 g (12½ oz)
Lemongrass	1 stalk, bruised
Kaffir lime leaves	3, torn
Red chillies	2, bruised
Bird's eye chillies	3
Salam leaves	2
Black peppercorns	1 Tbsp, coarsely crushed
Coriander seeds	1 Tbsp, crushed

1. Rinse bones until water is clear. Place into a stockpot and add sufficient cold water to cover. Bring to the boil over high heat.
2. Drain bones and discard liquid. Rinse bones again, then place into a larger stockpot. Add 3 times as much water as there are bones. Bring to the boil, reduce heat and skim off scum.
3. Add remaining ingredients and simmer stock over very low heat for 5–6 hours. If making pork stock, simmer for 2 hours. Use as needed.

Indonesian-style Vegetable Stock

Vegetable oil	2 Tbsp
Shallots	75 g (2⅔ oz), peeled and sliced
Garlic	50 g (1⅔ oz), peeled and sliced
Vegetable spice paste	125 g (4½ oz)
Leek	75 g (2⅔ oz), sliced
Celery	75 g (2⅔ oz), sliced, including stems and leaves
Cabbage	75 g (2⅔ oz), sliced
Spring onions (scallions)	100 g (3½ oz), sliced
Tomatoes	300 g (11 oz), diced
Water	2 litres (64 fl oz / 8 cups)
Bird's eye chillies	2, bruised
Lemongrass	2 stalks, bruised
Kaffir lime leaves	2, torn
Coriander seeds	1 tsp, crushed
Black peppercorns	½ tsp, crushed

1. Heat oil in heavy saucepan. Add shallots and garlic and sauté until fragrant.
2. Add spice paste and sauté again until shallots and garlic are evenly coated and paste is fragrant.
3. Add leek, celery, cabbage, spring onions and tomatoes. Sauté over medium-high heat until vegetables are soft.
4. Add water and all remaining ingredients. Bring to the boil and simmer for 2 hours over medium heat.
5. Strain stock using a cloth or a sieve. Press on vegetables to release as much liquid and flavour as possible. Use as needed.

Compressed Rice Cake (Lontong)

Ginger	30 g (1 oz), peeled, sliced and bruised
Shallots	55 g (2 oz), peeled and sliced
Vegetable oil	3 Tbsp
Screwpine leaf	1
Lemongrass	1 stalk, bruised
Glutinous rice	300 g (11 oz), washed and drained
Coconut milk	600 ml (20 fl oz / 2½ cups)
Salt	a pinch
Banana leaves for wrapping	

1. Grind ginger and shallots finely.
2. Heat oil and sauté ginger and shallots with screwpine leaf and lemongrass until fragrant, then add rice and sauté until evenly coated.
3. Add coconut milk and salt. Bring to the boil, reduce heat and simmer, stirring continuously, until all the liquid has been absorbed. Remove and cool completely.
4. Divide rice into desired serving portions and wrap in banana leaf. Roll up tightly to form a sausage shape, then secure with skewers or string.
5. Steam for 30 minutes or until cooked.

Red Bean Paste

Japanese red beans	500 g (1 lb 1½ oz), washed and drained
Japanese sugar or castor (superfine) sugar	430 g (15⅓ oz)
Salt	½ tsp

1. Prepare red bean paste. Put red beans into a large pot and cover with water. Bring to the boil briefly, then remove from heat and drain.
2. Return drained red beans to pot and add fresh water to fill up three-quarters of pot. Return to the boil, then reduce heat to low and simmer for 2 hours until beans are soft, skimming off any foam that rises to the surface. Remove from heat. Drain well.
3. Return cooked red beans to pot and add sugar. Cook over low heat, stirring constantly for 10 minutes until paste thickens. Add salt and stir to mix well. Remove from heat.
4. Spread out red bean paste on a baking tray and set aside to cool.

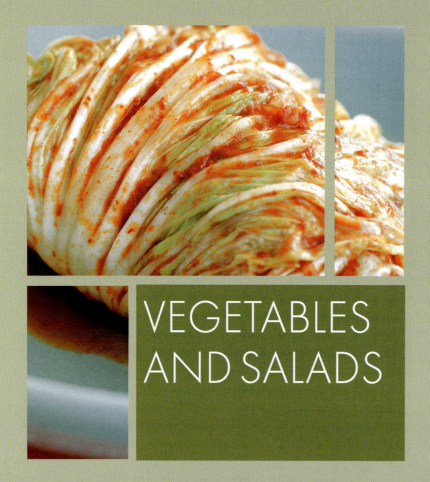

VEGETABLES AND SALADS

BALINESE
24 Corn and Fern Tips with Grated Coconut
25 Mixed Vegetable Salad in Peanut Dressing
26 Creamy Long Bean Salad
27 Pickled Vegetables
28 Fermented Soy Bean Cake in Sweet Soy Sauce

CHINESE
29 Braised Dried Bean Curd with Dried Chinese Mushrooms
30 Bean Sprouts and Carrot with Salted Fish
31 Stir-fried Sweet and Sour Cabbage

FILIPINO
32 Taro Leaves in Spicy Coconut Milk
33 Stewed Vegetables with Prawn Paste
34 Raw Fish Salad
35 Fern Fronds Salad

INDIAN
36 Aubergine in Yoghurt
37 Mixed Vegetables with Dhal
38 Malayalee Stir-fry
39 Cottage Cheese Bhurjee
40 Pumpkin Chutney

INDONESIAN
41 Golden Vegetable Pickle
42 Five-spice Pumpkin Braised in Coconut Milk
43 Fried Bean Curd with Turmeric Sauce

JAPANESE
44 Deep-fried Bean Curd
45 Pan-fried Aubergines with Miso Sauce
46 Simmered Pumpkin
47 Simmered Lotus Root
48 Simmered Radish with Minced Chicken

KOREAN
49 Radish Salad
50 Whole Cabbage Kimchi
51 Bean Sprout Salad
52 Diced Radish Kimchi
53 Seasoned Spinach
54 Pan-fried Stuffed Chillies

THAI
55 Spicy Mackerel Salad
56 Papaya Salad
57 Asparagus in Coconut Cream and Lemongrass Sauce
58 Thai Mushroom Curry
59 Prawn and Mango Salad

VIETNAMESE
60 Water Convolvolus Salad
61 Beef Salad
62 Green Mango Salad
63 Chicken Salad with Polygonum Leaves

BALINESE

Corn and Fern Tips with Grated Coconut

Kaffir lime leaves, palm sugar and lesser galangal make the dressing for this crunchy salad delightfully bold and full of flavour.

Corn kernels	300 g (11 oz), blanched
Fern tips	300 g (11 oz), blanched
Red chillies (optional)	2, large, seeded and sliced
Grated coconut	250 g (9 oz), lightly roasted
Crisp-fried shallots	3 Tbsp

*FRIED CHILLI DRESSING

Vegetable oil	4 Tbsp
Shallots	100 g (3½ oz), peeled and finely sliced
Garlic	75 g (2⅔ oz)
Bird's eye chillies	25 g (⅘ oz), finely sliced
Dried prawn (shrimp) paste	½ tsp, toasted and finely crumbled
Salt	a pinch

DRESSING (COMBINED)

Cooking oil	2 Tbsp
*Fried chilli dressing	4 Tbsp
Kaffir lime leaves	3, finely chopped
Salt	a pinch
Crushed black peppercorns	a pinch
Palm sugar	1 Tbsp, chopped
Lesser galangal	40 g (1⅓ oz), washed and finely ground

1. Combine corn, fern tips, chillies and coconut in a large bowl and mix well.

2. Prepare fried chilli dressing. Heat oil in a frying pan. Add shallots and garlic and sauté for 2 minutes. Add chillies and dried prawn paste and continue to sauté until golden, then season with salt. Remove from heat and leave to cool before use.

3. When ready to serve, add combined dressing ingredients to mixed vegetables and toss to mix. Garnish with crisp-fried shallots and serve immediately.

BALINESE

Mixed Vegetable Salad in Peanut Dressing

This is the Balinese version of the famed Indonesian dish, *Gado-Gado*. In the Balinese version, water is used instead of coconut milk and the peanut sauce is only ground and not cooked.

Long (snake) beans	100 g (3½ oz), cut into 4-cm (1½-in) lengths
Bean sprouts	100 g (3½ oz)
Spinach	100 g (3½ oz)
Cabbage	100 g (3½ oz), thinly sliced
Salt	a pinch or to taste
Ground black pepper	a pinch or to taste
Crisp-fried shallots	2 Tbsp
Shelled peanuts	2 Tbsp, dry-fried, fried in oil or oven-roasted, then crushed
Sweet soy sauce	to taste

PEANUT SAUCE

Peanuts	250 g (9 oz), skins left intact and deep-fried until lightly brown
Garlic	3 cloves, peeled and sliced
Bird's eye chillies	1–3, finely sliced
Lesser galangal	25 g (⁴/₅ oz), finely sliced
Sweet soy sauce	2 Tbsp
Palm sugar	20 g (⅔ oz), chopped
Water	250 ml (8 fl oz / 1 cup)
Salt	a pinch

1. Blanch all vegetables and plunge into iced water to cool. Drain well.
2. Prepare peanut sauce. Combine all ingredients in a stone mortar and grind until very fine. Alternatively, combine in a blender.
3. Combine all vegetables in a large bowl and add peanut sauce. Mix well. Season to taste with salt and pepper.
4. Serve garnished with crisp-fried shallots, crushed peanuts and sweet soy sauce.
5. If desired, serve salad with crispy, deep-fried fermented soy bean cakes (*tempe*) on the side. This dish tastes best when served at room temperature or slightly warm.

BALINESE

Creamy Long Bean Salad

The rich, flavourful coconut cream dressing is a little spicy from the fried bird's eye chillies and deeply aromtic because of the crisp-fried shallots and garlic.

Long (snake) or winged beans	600 g (1 lb 5⅓ oz), or any crisp vegetable
Vegetable spice paste (page 14)	150 g (5⅓ oz)
Coconut cream	125 ml (4 fl oz / ½ cup)
Vegetable or chicken stock (page 20)	125 ml (4 fl oz / ½ cup)
Crisp-fried garlic	2 Tbsp
Bird's eye chillies	3, finely sliced and fried until golden
Lime juice	2 Tbsp
Salt	a pinch or to taste
Ground black pepper	a pinch or to taste
Crisp-fried shallots	2 Tbsp

1 Cut beans of choice into 0.5-cm (¼-inch) pieces, then blanch to soften. Drain and set aside.

2 Combine spice paste and half the coconut cream in a stone mortar or blender (processor) and grind very fine. Transfer to a saucepan.

3 To saucepan, add stock and remaining coconut cream. Bring to a quick boil, ten remove from heat and leave to cool.

4 Put all ingredients except crisp-fried shallots into a large bowl and mix well. Adjust to taste with salt and pepper.

5 Serve garnished with crisp-fried shallots.

Pickled Vegetables

Serving this dish of pickled vegetables requires some planning ahead, but it rewards by refreshing the tongue with zesty, mildly spicy cucumber slices.

Water	250 ml (8 fl oz / 1 cup)
Sugar	250 g (9 oz)
Rice vinegar or white vinegar	250 ml (8 fl oz / 1 cup)
Ginger	55 g (2 oz), peeled and sliced
Lemongrass	1 stalk or more to taste, bruised and tied into a knot
Salt	a pinch
Cucumbers	3, medium, halved lengthways, cored and sliced
Shallots	10, peeled and quartered
Bird's eye chillies	10

1. Combine water, sugar, vinegar, ginger, lemongrass and salt in a saucepan. Bring to the boil and simmer for 1 minute. Remove from heat and leave to cool thoroughly.
2. Combine remaining ingredients and mix well with cooled dressing.
3. Refrigerate for 24 hours before serving at room temperature.

BALINESE

Fermented Soy Bean Cake in Sweet Soy Sauce

Fermented soy bean cakes, or *tempe* to the Indonesians, gain a distinctive nutty flavour when fried and are well complemented by the sweet soy sauce.

Fermented soy bean cake (*tempe*)	400 g (14⅓ oz)
Cooking oil for deep-frying	
Vegetable oil	2 Tbsp
Shallots	60 g (2¼ oz), peeled and sliced
Garlic	40 g (1⅓ oz), peeled and sliced
Red chillies	40 g (1⅓ oz), large, seeded and finely sliced
Galangal	30 g (1 oz), peeled and sliced
Palm sugar	20 g (⅔ oz), chopped
Sweet soy sauce	3 Tbsp
Indonesian-style vegetable stock (page 20)	3 Tbsp
Tomato	1, peeled, seeded and cut into strips
Salt	a pinch
Bird's eye chillies (optional)	4, chopped

1. Slice fermented soy bean cake into equal-size strips. Heat sufficient oil for deep-frying until medium-hot. Lower in soy bean cake pieces and fry until golden and crisp. Drain on absorbent paper towels.

2. Heat 2 Tbsp oil in a frying pan. Add shallots, garlic, chillies and galangal. Sauté for 2–4 minutes.

3. Add palm sugar and sweet soy sauce. Continue to sauté until evenly glazed.

4. Add stock and when it boils, add tomato and sauté for 1 minute. Add fried soy bean cake and stir frequently until sauce has reduced and caramelised.

5. Season to taste with salt and stir in bird's eye chillies, if using, just before serving.

Braised Dried Bean Curd with Dried Chinese Mushrooms

Dried mushrooms and broccoli add a distinctive flavour to this unique bean curd dish.

Dried Chinese mushrooms	8–10, soaked until soft, then drained
Cooking oil	3 Tbsp
Ginger	2 slices, peeled and shredded
Shallot	1, peeled and sliced
Broccoli	85 g (3 oz), cut into small florets and rinsed
Dried bean curd cubes	250 g (9 oz)
Corn flour (cornstarch)	1 tsp, mixed with 1 Tbsp water
Sesame oil	1 tsp
Red chilli	1, sliced
Spring onion (scallion)	1, chopped

SEASONING (COMBINED)

Salt	¼ tsp
Sugar	¼ tsp
Ground white pepper	¼ tsp
Light soy sauce	1 tsp

SAUCE

Basic stock (page 19)	300 ml (10 fl oz / 1¼ cups)
Dark soy sauce	½ Tbsp
Light soy sauce	2 tsp
Sugar	½ tsp
Salt	¼ tsp
Ground white pepper	¼ tsp

1. Combine seasoning ingredients and season mushrooms for 15 minutes.

2. Heat 1½ Tbsp oil in a wok until hot. Stir-fry ginger and shallots until fragrant, then add mushrooms and fry for another 1–2 minutes. Remove and set aside. Stir-fry broccoli for 1 minute, then remove and set aside. Reheat remaining oil in the wok and toss bean curd cubes until crisp and light brown in colour.

3. Add combined sauce ingredients and mushrooms and bring to the boil. Reduce heat and simmer for 10 minutes. Add broccoli and simmer for 2 minutes longer.

4. Thicken with corn flour mixture and sprinkle in sesame oil, red chilli and spring onion. Serve immediately.

CHINESE

Bean Sprouts and Carrot with Salted Fish
Crispy bean sprouts stir-fried with shredded carrots and topped with salted fish.

Salted fish	1 piece, about 5-cm (2-in) square
Cooking oil	4 Tbsp
Garlic	1 clove, peeled and chopped
Bean sprouts	450 g (1 lb)
Small carrot	1, peeled and shredded
Light soy sauce	½ Tbsp

1. Soak salted fish in water for a few minutes, then drain and slice thinly.
2. Heat oil in a wok. Brown garlic, then add salted fish. Fry until fragrant, then dish out and set aside.
3. Use the same oil to stir-fry bean sprouts and shredded carrot for about 2 minutes. Season with light soy sauce.
4. Garnish with salted fish and serve immediately before bean sprouts go limp.

Stir-fried Sweet and Sour Cabbage

A simple stir-fry of cabbage with chilli and peanut oil.

Chinese cabbage	1 head, about 900 g (2 lb)
Rice vinegar or wine vinegar	4–6 tsp
Sugar	4–6 tsp
Light soy sauce	4–6 tsp
Salt	a large pinch
Tapioca or potato flour	1–1½ tsp
Peanut or corn oil	4–5 Tbsp
Red chillies	1 large or 2 small, seeded and cut into thin strips
Sesame oil	2–3 tsp for sprinkling

1 Remove any tough leaves from Chinese cabbage, then halve the rest lengthways and slice across into 5-cm (2-in) strips. Mix vinegar, sugar, soy sauce, salt and tapioca or potato flour. Reserve.

2 Heat a wok until hot. Add 2–3 Tbsp oil and swirl it around. Add cabbage and stir-fry continuously for 5–6 minutes. If cabbage begins to burn, lower heat. The cabbage bulk will decrease. Transfer cabbage to a colander and drain.

3 Wipe wok dry and reheat it. Add remaining oil and swirl it around, then add chilli strips and sauce. When sauce bubbles, add cabbage.

4 Stir and toss to let cabbage absorb sauce. When thoroughly hot, transfer to a serving dish. Sprinkle sesame oil over cabbage and serve immediately.

FILIPINO

Taro Leaves in Spicy Coconut Milk

This spicy dish of taro leaves simmered in coconut milk comes from Bicol Region in the southern part of Luzon, where coconut milk and chillies feature as main ingredients in the cuisine.

Dried taro leaves	1 kg (2 lb 3 oz)
Fermented prawn (shrimp) paste	100 g (3½ oz) or use 45 g (1½ oz) dried prawn (shrimp) paste
Chicken thighs or drumsticks	300 g (11 oz), deboned and cut into 1-cm (½-in) cubes
Red chillies	85 g (3 oz), sliced diagonally
Green chillies	100 g (3½ oz), sliced diagonally
Red bird's eye chillies	25 g (⁴⁄₅ oz), sliced
Onions	2, medium, peeled and sliced
Garlic	5 cloves, peeled and finely chopped
Ginger	20 g (⅔ oz), peeled and sliced
Thick coconut milk	480 ml (16 fl oz / 2 cups) + 250 ml (8 fl oz) / 1 cup), mixed with 125 ml (4 fl oz / ½ cup) water into a smooth paste
Water	625 ml (20 fl oz / 2½ cups)
Salt	to taste (optional)

1. Using your hands, shred taro leaves and discard hard stalks. Set aside. Heat a wok over medium heat and combine prawn paste, chicken, chillies, onions, garlic and ginger.

2. Gradually add taro leaves and stir to mix well. Add concentrated coconut milk and water and bring mixture to the boil. Reduce heat to medium low and leave to simmer for 10–15 minutes, or until taro leaves are soft and chicken is cooked. Stir mixture occasionally to prevent sticking.

3. Add diluted coconut milk and simmer until oil starts to exude from mixture and liquid is almost completely evaporated. Add salt to taste, if desired.

4. Dish out and serve immediately with plain rice.

Stewed Vegetables with Prawn Paste

This simple but nourishing dish originates from the Ilocos province in Northern Luzon. Flavoured with fermented prawns, *pinakbet tagalog* is popular all over the Philippines.

Cooking oil	2 Tbsp
Garlic	5 cloves, peeled and crushed
Onion	1, medium, peeled and sliced
Fermented prawn (shrimp) paste	55 g (2 oz) or use 30 g (1 oz) dried prawn (shrimp) paste, mixed with some water into a smooth paste
Tomato	1, medium, sliced
Chicken thighs or drumsticks	200 g (7 oz), deboned and cut into 1-cm (½-in) cubes
Prawns (shrimps)	150 g (5⅓ oz), small, peeled
Water	750 ml (24 fl oz / 3 cups)
Pumpkin	400 g (14⅓ oz), peeled and cut into 3-cm (1½-in) cubes
Aubergines (brinjals/eggplants)	400 g (14⅓ oz), sliced on the diagonal into 1-cm (½-in) slices
Bitter gourds	400 g (14⅓ oz), seeded and sliced on the diagonal into 1-cm (½-in) thick slices
Ladies fingers (okra)	150 g (5⅓ oz), stems discarded
Salt	to taste

1. In a large frying pan or wok, heat oil over medium heat. Fry garlic until light brown, then add onion and fry until soft.
2. Add prawn paste and fry for 1 minute, then add tomato and fry for another 1 minute.
3. Add chicken pieces and fry for 1 minute, then add prawns and stir to mix well. Cook until prawns turn pink and are cooked, then add water and bring to the boil.
4. Add pumpkin and cover pan or wok. Reduce heat to low and leave mixture to simmer for 5 minutes, or until pumpkin is tender.
5. Add aubergines, bitter gourds and ladies fingers and toss with ingredients to mix well. Cover and leave to simmer for another 5–7 minutes or until vegetables are tender. Stir occasionally to prevent burning. Season with salt, if desired.
6. Dish out and serve immediately with plain rice.

FILIPINO

Raw Fish Salad

A popular appetiser that goes well with cold drinks and features at the table during special family occasions, this dish is similar to the Latin American ceviche. This Visayan version features coconut milk that gives this dish a fuller, richer flavour. For maximum flavour, ensure each mouthful is made up of a little of every single ingredient.

White fish fillets (mackerel, red snapper, yellow fin tuna or anchovy)	500 g (1 lb 1½ oz)
Apple cider vinegar	125 ml (4 fl oz / ½ cup)
Calamansi or lemon juice	90 ml (3 fl oz / ⅜ cup)
Shallots	110 g (4 oz), peeled and thinly sliced
Young ginger	15 g (½ oz), peeled and thinly sliced
Tomato	1, medium, cut into 8 wedges
Red capsicum (bell pepper)	1, cored, seeded and sliced into strips
Coriander leaves (cilantro)	3 sprigs, finely chopped
Salt	to taste
Ground black pepper	1 tsp
Bird's eye chillies	3, sliced
Sugar	2 tsp
Thick coconut milk	85 ml (2½ fl oz / ⅓ cup)
Red onion	1, large, peeled and finely sliced

1. Clean fish and remove all bones. Using a sharp knife, cut into bite-size pieces or strips.
2. In a glass mixing bowl, place fish pieces and add vinegar. Leave aside to marinate for 30 minutes. Fish should turn slightly opaque in colour after marinating.
3. Drain vinegar and add calamansi or lemon juice and mix well. Add remaining ingredients except for coconut milk and onion. Toss to mix well. Place in the refrigerator to chill for 2 hours.
4. Just before serving, add coconut milk and stir to mix well. Transfer salad to a serving bowl and garnish with red onion. Serve immediately.

FILIPINO

Fern Fronds Salad

This unique Filipino salad features fiddlehead fern fronds, a local vegetable that grows in abundance in the woods and along the banks of streams in local villages. Use water convolvolus (*kang kong*) as a substitute, if fern fronds are unavailable.

Fiddlehead fern fronds	1 kg (2 lb 3 oz)
Fermented anchovies	85 g (3 oz), or fermented anchovy sauce (*budu*)
Tomatoes	200 g (7 oz), diced
Spanish onion	1, large, peeled and diced
Calamansi or lime juice	2 tsp

1. Choose tender young shoots and fronds that are firm and unblemished. Discard the hard part of the stems.
2. Bring a pot of water to the boil and blanch ferns for 1 minute. Remove and place in a colander to drain thoroughly.
3. Transfer ferns to a serving plate. Add remaining ingredients and toss well. Leave salad to cool to room temperature.
4. Serve as an accompaniment to fried or grilled meat or fish, and plain rice.

Vegetables and Salads 35

INDIAN

Aubergine in Yoghurt

This dish is perfect as a dip with crackers or as a side dish.

Cooking oil for deep-frying	
Purple aubergines (brinjals/eggplants), long variety	3
Yoghurt	250 ml (8 fl oz / 1 cup)
Green chillies	3
Cumin	½ tsp
Grated coconut	85 ml (2½ fl oz / ⅓ cup)
White peppercorns	1 tsp
Salt	to taste
Curry leaves	2 stalks

1. Heat oil for deep-frying.
2. Cut aubergines into thin discs and fry immediately. Fry discs until golden brown then drain well and set aside.
3. Blend remaining ingredients except for 1 stalk of curry leaves together in a blender.
4. Pour mixture into a wok and add in remaining stalk of curry leaves. Allow mixture to come to the boil slowly.
5. Add aubergines, dish out and serve immediately.

Mixed Vegetables with Dhal

This mild curry goes well with other spicy meat dishes or fried fish.

Channa dhal	180 g (6½ oz)
Water	700 ml (25 fl oz / 2⅘ cups)
Potatoes	2, peeled and diced
Pumpkin	100 g (3½ oz), peeled and diced
Winter melon	100 g (3½ oz), cut into dices
Carrot	1, peeled and diced
Yam	1, small, peeled and diced
Snake gourd	1, peeled and diced
Green chillies	3, chopped
Onion	1, peeled and chopped
Turmeric powder	1 tsp
Chilli powder	½ Tbsp
Salt	to taste
Coconut milk	125 ml (4 fl oz / ½ cup)

PASTE

Grated coconut	55 g (1⅔ oz)
Cumin	1 tsp
Garlic	2 cloves, peeled
Water	125 ml (4 fl oz / ½ cup)

TEMPERING

Cooking oil	1½ Tbsp
Mustard seeds	1 tsp
Uncooked rice	1 tsp
Dried red chillies	2, each cut into 3 sections
Curry leaves	2 stalks

1. Prepare paste. Combine ingredients and grind into a paste. Set aside.
2. Boil dhal in water until soft. Add vegetables, turmeric and chilli powders and salt. Mix well.
3. Add half the coconut milk and cook until vegetables are almost done.
4. Add paste and stir. Simmer for about 10 minutes before adding remaining coconut milk.
5. Heat oil for tempering and add mustard seeds, rice, chillies and curry leaves. Heat until mustard seeds start to splutter. Pour into curry.
6. Serve hot with white rice or bread or crispy poppadom.

INDIAN

Malayalee Stir-Fry

This is a colourful vegetarian dish. It uses both dried red chillies and green chillies, so it can be rather spicy even though it looks mild.

Green bananas	2, peeled and diced
Sweet potato	1, peeled and diced
Long beans	10, cut into 2.5-cm (1-inch) lengths
Cooking oil	2 Tbsp
Mustard seeds	1 tsp
Curry leaves	1 stalk
Dried red chillies	2, chopped
Onion	1, peeled and chopped
Green chillies	2, sliced
Salt	to taste

TURMERIC SOLUTION

Turmeric powder	1 tsp
Water	125 ml (4 fl oz / ½ cup)

1 Prepare turmeric solution. Mix water and turmeric powder and soak bananas, sweet potato and long beans to prevent oxidation.

2 Rub hands and a knife with some cooking oil. This makes it easier to wash away the sap from the green bananas. Peel and dice green bananas. Place into turmeric solution to prevent oxidation.

3 Peel and dice sweet potato. Cut long beans into 1-cm (½-in) lengths. Place into the same turmeric solution.

4 Heat oil in a wok and add mustard seeds, curry leaves and dried red chillies. Allow mustard seeds to splutter before adding onion and green chillies.

5 Drain bananas, sweet potato and long beans. Rinse and add to wok. Season to taste with salt then toss and cover. Leave to cook until water has completely evaporated.

6 Cook over low heat for another 10 minutes until vegetables are tender. Serve hot.

INDIAN

Cottage Cheese Bhurjee

You can eat this dish with rice or Indian breads or use it as a sauce with spaghetti or lasagna.

Cooking oil	125 ml (4 fl oz / ½ cup)
Onions	2, peeled and minced
Tomatoes	2, minced
Green chillies	3, minced
Red chillies	2, minced
Garlic	4 cloves, peeled and minced
Cottage cheese	1 kg (2 lb / 3 oz), crumbled
Chilli powder	3 tsp
Toasted cumin powder	1 tsp
Kitchen king masala	1 tsp
Salt	to taste
Water	125 ml (4 fl oz / ½ cup)
Tomato paste	125 ml (4 fl oz / ½ cup)
Cream	125 ml (4 fl oz / ½ cup)
Coriander leaves (cilantro)	1 sprig, minced
Sugar	1 tsp
Diced red and yellow capsicums (bell peppers)	a handful

1. Heat oil in a wok. Add onions, tomatoes, green and red chillies and garlic. Cook until onions begin to brown.
2. Add cottage cheese and stir. Add chilli and cumin powders and masala. Add salt and mix well, then pour in water and add tomato paste. Mix well.
3. Cover and allow cottage cheese to cook in the sauce and absorb all the flavours.
4. Slowly pour in cream and add coriander and sugar. Stir and taste to adjust seasoning.
5. Allow flavours to infuse for at least 15 minutes before serving. Garnish with diced capsicums and serve.

INDIAN

Pumpkin Chutney

Chutneys add flavour and dimension to plain and simple meals. This chutney can also be used as a dip.

Pumpkin	800 g (1¾ lb)
Cooking oil	1½ Tbsp
Mustard seeds	2 tsp
Curry leaves	2 stalks
Garlic	3 cloves, peeled and minced
Water	60 ml (2 fl oz / ¼ cup)
Chilli powder	1 tsp
Toasted cumin powder	1 tsp
Turmeric powder	1 tsp
Salt	to taste
Brown sugar	1½ Tbsp
Ghee (clarified butter)	½ tsp

1. Cut pumpkin in half and remove pith and seeds. Cut into large chunks and steam until tender.
2. Heat oil in a wok and add mustard seeds, curry leaves and garlic. Sauté quickly, then add pumpkin. Stir to mix well.
3. Add water, chilli, cumin and turmeric powders and salt. Keep stirring to mix.
4. Add brown sugar and keep stirring until flavours are well mixed.
5. Add ghee and adjust seasoning to taste. Serve hot with Indian breads.

Golden Vegetable Pickle

In northern Sulawesi, this delightful and tasty vegetable dish is often served with seafood or pork dishes and generous helpings of rice.

Bamboo shoots	200 g (7 oz), cleaned and finely sliced
Green (French) beans	55 g (2 oz), sliced
Carrots	55 g (2 oz), peeled and finely sliced
Raw skinned peanuts	100 g (3½ oz)
Shallots	55 g (2 oz), peeled and left whole
Bird's eye chillies	15 g (½ oz), left whole
Cucumber	55 g (2 oz), halved, cored and sliced
Sugar	55 g (2 oz)
Coconut milk	175 ml (6 fl oz)
Rice vinegar	2 Tbsp
Salt	to taste

SPICE PASTE

Shallots	55 g (2 oz), peeled and sliced
Garlic	30 g (1 oz), peeled and sliced
Turmeric	20 g (⅔ oz), peeled and sliced
Ginger	20 g (⅔ oz), peeled and sliced
Vegetable oil	3 Tbsp
Lemongrass	2 stalks, bruised and knotted
Indonesian-style chicken stock (page 20)	200 ml (7 fl oz / ¾ cup)

1. Blanch bamboo shoots for 1 minute, then plunge into iced water to cool and drain. Repeat step with beans and carrots.
2. Prepare spice paste. Combine all ingredients, except oil, lemongrass and stock, in a stone mortar or blender. Grind into a very fine paste.
3. Heat oil in a heavy saucepan. Add spice paste and lemongrass. Sauté over low heat for 2 minutes or until fragrant.
4. Add stock, stir through and simmer until half the liquid has evaporated.
5. Add blanched vegetables, peanuts, shallots, chillies and cucumber. Gently mix in ingredients until they are evenly coated with spice paste.
6. Add sugar, coconut milk and vinegar. Stir through and return to the boil, then simmer until sauce is slightly thickened.
7. Season to taste with salt. Remove from heat and leave to cool to room temperature before serving.

INDONESIAN

Five-spice Pumpkin Braised in Coconut Milk

Simple to prepare, this dish of braised pumpkin is rich with coconut milk and mildly spicy. Paired with plain, steamed rice, it makes a heartwarming meal.

Shallots	50 g (1⅔ oz), peeled and sliced
Ginger	15 g (½ oz), peeled and sliced
Vegetable oil	3 Tbsp
Vegetable or chicken stock (page 20)	150 ml (5 fl oz / ⅗ cup)
Pumpkin	600 g (1 lb 5⅓ oz), peeled and cubed
Screwpine (pandan) leaf	1, sliced
Turmeric leaf	1, sliced
Kaffir lime leaves	3, bruised
Lemon grass	1 stalk, bruised and knotted
Bird's eye chillies	10, seeded if desired
Coconut milk	350 ml (11½ fl oz)
Lemon basil	10 g (⅓ oz), sliced
Spring onions (scallions)	75 g (2⅔ oz), sliced
Salt	to taste

1. Combine shallots and ginger in a stone mortar and grind into a very fine paste.
2. Heat oil in a saucepan. Add paste and 3 Tbsp of stock and sauté over medium heat until fragrant.
3. Add pumpkin cubes and stir until they are evenly coated with spice paste.
4. Add all remaining ingredients, except lemon basil, spring onions and salt. Bring to the boil, reduce heat and simmer until pumpkin is almost soft.
5. Add lemon basil and spring onions and simmer 2 minutes more.
6. Season to taste with salt, then dish out and serve.

INDONESIAN

Fried Bean Curd with Turmeric Sauce

Fried bean curd in a spicy turmeric-infused, coconut-based sauce, this dish makes a great appetiser or a side dish in a more extensive Indonesian meal.

Vegetable oil	2 Tbsp
East Javanese yellow spice paste (page 16)	125 g (4½ oz)
Kaffir lime leaves	2, bruised
Lemongrass	1 stalk, bruised
Bird's eye chillies	1–3, chopped
Celery	55 g (2 oz), sliced
Young leek	55 g (2 oz), sliced
Indonesian-style chicken stock or vegetable stock (page 20)	375 ml (12 fl oz / 1½ cups)
Coconut cream	180 ml (6 fl oz / ¾ cups)
Firm bean curd	4, each 100 g (3½ oz), dusted with rice flour and deep-fried
Salt	a pinch or to taste
Freshly crushed white peppercorns	a pinch or to taste

1. Heat oil in a saucepan. Add spice paste and sauté until fragrant. Add *salam* and kaffir lime leaves, lemongrass and bird's eye chillies. Sauté until fragrant.

2. Add celery and leek and sauté for 1 minute. Add stock, bring to the boil and simmer for 1 minute before adding coconut cream. Return to a simmer.

3. Add fried bean curd and simmer over very low heat for 2 minutes, turning bean curd frequently. Add a splash of stock if sauce thickens too much. Season to taste with salt and pepper, then remove from heat.

4. Prepare some garnishing, if desired. Finely slice some leek, celery and red chilli so there is a handful of each and place in a mixing bowl. Toss with 1 Tbsp lime juice and 2 Tbsp vegetable oil until well mixed. Season to taste, if desired. Serve bean curd as desired and topped with garnishing ingredients, if using.

Vegetables and Salads

JAPANESE

Deep-fried Bean Curd

Known as *agedashi tofu* in Japanese, this bean curd dish is a popular appetiser.

Bean curd (soft or firm)	2 slabs, each 300 g (11 oz), cut into large pieces and pat dry
Egg	1, lightly beaten
Potato flour for coating	
Cooking oil for deep-frying	
Green *shishito* chillies	12, washed, pat dry and pierced
Japanese light soy sauce	1 Tbsp
Mirin	1 tsp

DASHI

Water	150 ml (5 fl oz / $3/5$ cup)
Dried kelp	5-cm (2-in) piece
Bonito flakes	10 g (⅓ oz)

GARNISHING

Finely sliced Japanese spring onion (scallion)	to taste
Grated mature ginger	to taste
Fine dried bonito flakes	to taste

1. Prepare dashi (page 19).

2. Dip bean curd pieces in beaten egg and coat with potato flour. Heat oil to 170°C (350°F). Deep-fry bean curd until golden. Remove and drain on absorbent paper. Scald *shishito* chillies in hot oil to preserve colour. Remove immediately and drain on absorbent paper.

3. Prepare sauce. Heat 100 ml (3½ fl oz / ⅖ cup) dashi, light soy sauce and mirin in a small saucepan and bring to the boil. Remove from heat. Arrange deep-fried bean curd and *shishito* chillies in individual serving dishes. Pour sauce over. Serve hot, garnished with spring onions, grated ginger and bonito flakes to taste.

JAPANESE

Pan-fried Aubergines with Miso Sauce

A simple dish of aubergines coated in a sweet, slightly sticky miso sauce makes for a tasty appetiser.

Cooking oil	3 Tbsp
Sesame oil	3 Tbsp
Japanese aubergines (brinjals /eggplants)	6, washed, ends trimmed and cut into 1-cm (½-in) thick rounds
Toasted white sesame seeds	to taste

SEASONING

Soy bean paste (*miso*)	3 Tbsp
Sugar	3 Tbsp
Mirin	2 Tbsp
Sake	3 Tbsp
Water	2 Tbsp

1. Combine seasoning ingredients in a small bowl and blend well. Set aside.
2. Heat both types of oil in a frying pan. Add aubergines and pan-fry for 3–5 minutes on both sides until brown.
3. Pour seasoning mixture over aubergine slices, stirring gently to mix well. Simmer over low heat for 2–3 minutes until sauce has thickened and aubergines are well-coated. Remove from heat.
4. Dish out onto a plate. Sprinkle sesame seeds on top, if desired, before serving.

Vegetables and Salads

JAPANESE

Simmered Pumpkin

Pumpkin is a summer vegetable with lots of vitamins. When buying pumpkins, choose those with bright orange-coloured flesh as they are sweeter. The vegetable is cooked very simply in this recipe, creating a very refreshing dish.

Japanese pumpkin	600 g (1 lb 5⅓ oz), seeded, washed and left unpeeled
Water	200 ml (7 fl oz / ¾ cup)
Sugar	2 Tbsp
Mirin	1 Tbsp
Japanese light soy sauce	1 tsp
Salt	a pinch
Toasted white sesame seeds	to taste

1. Cut pumpkin into 5 x 6-cm (2 x 2½-in) pieces. Bevel the edges of each piece on the skin side.
2. Put pumpkin, water and sugar in a medium saucepan, then cover with a drop-in lid, or a sheet of baking paper trimmed to fit pan. Simmer over medium heat for 2–3 minutes.
3. Add mirin, light soy sauce and salt. Reduce heat to low and simmer for 5–10 minutes until pumpkin has softened. Remove from heat.
4. Dish out, then sprinkle sesame seeds on top and serve.

JAPANESE

Simmered Lotus Root

A popular character in Joruri, a traditional Japanese play set during the Edo period, Kimpira is renowned for his superhuman strength. It is believed that eating this healthy dish will keep one strong like Kimpira, hence its name. If lotus roots are unavailable, substitute with burdock, carrots, potatoes or white radish.

Lotus root	200 g (7 oz), washed and peeled
Sesame oil	1 Tbsp
Dried red chilli	1, finely cut with a pair of scissors
Toasted white sesame seeds	1 Tbsp

SEASONING

Japanese dark soy sauce	1½ Tbsp
Sugar	1 Tbsp
Sake	1 Tbsp
Mirin	1 Tbsp

1. Roll cut lotus root into wedges, then soak in water. Drain when ready to use. Bring a pot of water to the boil, then add drained lotus root and boil for about 5 minutes. Drain and set aside.
2. Combine seasoning ingredients in a small bowl. Blend well until sugar has dissolved. Set aside.
3. Heat sesame oil in a frying pan over medium heat, then add chilli and lotus. Stir-fry for 1 minute.
4. Pour seasoning mixture over lotus root and stir to mix well. Simmer for 1–2 minutes until most of the liquid is absorbed, and lotus root is well-coated with a glossy sauce. Remove from heat.
5. Transfer to a plate and sprinkle sesame seeds on top before serving.

JAPANESE

Simmered Radish with Minced Chicken

Radish is great for simmering in dishes with meat or poultry, as it can absorb the flavours of the other ingredients fully during the slow-cooking process. Turnips and pumpkins are also good substitutes for radish in this recipe.

White radish (*daikon*)	600 g (1 lb 5⅓ oz), peeled and cut into 2.5-cm (1-in) thick rounds
Raw rice grains (any kind except Basmati or fragrant Thai)	1 Tbsp
Salt	½ tsp
Light soy sauce (*usukuchi shoyu*)	½ tsp
Minced chicken	150 g (5⅓ oz)
Mirin	1 Tbsp
Sugar	1 Tbsp
Dark soy sauce (*koikuchi shoyu*)	1 Tbsp
Ginger juice	1 tsp
Potato flour (potato starch)	½ Tbsp, mixed with 1 Tbsp water
Old ginger	4-cm (1¾-in) knob, peeled, finely shredded, then soaked and drained before use

DASHI

Water	500 ml (16 fl oz / 2 cups)
Dried kelp (*konbu*)	10-cm (4-in) piece
Bonito flakes	20 g (⅔ oz)

1. Prepare dashi (page 19).
2. Bevel the edge of each round of radish on both sides. Make a cross-shape incision on one side of each round. Put radish and rice into a large pot, cover with water. Boil over medium heat for 20 minutes, until radish is cooked and just tender.
3. Drain and discard rice and water, then rinse radish under tap water lightly to remove all bitter juices and rice starch. Drain.
4. Add 400 ml (13⅓ fl oz / 1⅔ cups) dashi, salt and light soy sauce into a large pot. Bring to the boil, then add cooked radish and simmer over low heat for 5 minutes. Remove radish from stock and set aside.
5. Add minced chicken, mirin, sugar, dark soy sauce and ginger juice to stock. Mix well. Bring to the boil and stir in potato flour mixture to thicken sauce. Remove from heat.
6. Divide radish among individual serving bowls and ladle sauce over. Garnish with shredded ginger and serve hot.

Radish Salad

This radish salad is both sweet and sour, with the use of sugar and vinegar.

White radish	200 g (7 oz), shredded or julienned
Salt	1 tsp
Sugar	1 Tbsp
White sesame seeds	½ tsp, roasted
Vinegar	2 Tbsp
Crushed garlic	1 tsp
Ginger juice	1 tsp
Chopped spring onion (scallion)	1 Tbsp
Red chilli slices	

1. Mix radish with salt and sugar to preserve it. Refrigerate for 3–4 hours.
2. Drain radish of any juices and mix with sesame seeds, vinegar, crushed garlic, ginger juice and spring onion.
3. Taste and add more salt and sugar as preferred. Serve cold, garnished with red chilli slices as desired.

KOREAN

Whole Cabbage Kimchi

This classic Korean kimchi is made with Chinese cabbage. It is served with almost every meal in Korea.

Chinese cabbage	2 heads, cut lengthwise in half
Coarse salt	300 g (11 oz)
Korean preserved prawns (shrimps)	85 g (3 oz)
Chilli powder	70 g (2½ oz)
Onion	100 g, peeled and chopped
Salt	2 Tbsp
Sugar	2 Tbsp
Garlic	7 cloves, peeled and minced
Ginger	1-in (2.5-cm) knob, peeled and minced
White radish	1, medium, sliced into thin strips
Spring onions (scallions)	5, chopped or 2 stalks leeks, chopped

1 Wilt cabbage by sprinkling liberally with coarse salt and letting it sit for 4 hours. Rinse cabbage thoroughly and drain well.
2 Blend preserved prawns with chilli powder, onion, salt, sugar, garlic and ginger.
3 Remove from blender and mix in radish and scallions or leeks. Mix well.
4 Pack mixture between leaves of wilted cabbage.
5 Place cabbage into airtight plastic containers or kimchi jars. Store at room temperature for 1–2 days before refrigerating. Use as required.

Bean Sprout Salad

This is a refreshing dish of crisp and nutritious soy bean sprouts.

Water	3 Tbsp
Soy bean sprouts	300 g (11 oz), tailed and cleaned
Salt	as needed
Crushed garlic	1 tsp
White sesame seeds	½ Tbsp, roasted and finely ground
Spring onion (scallion)	1, chopped
Sesame oil	to taste

1. Place water and bean sprouts in a pan and sprinkle 1 tsp salt over. Place over medium heat, cover and leave bean sprouts to steam for 5–7 minutes.

2. Mix steamed bean sprouts with crushed garlic, ground sesame seeds and spring onion. Adjust to taste with more salt and sesame oil. Serve cold.

Vegetables and Salads

KOREAN

Diced Radish Kimchi

A kimchi made with radish and seasoned with chilli powder and fish sauce.

White radish	1, large, peeled and cut into 2 x 1.5-cm (1 x ¾-in) dice
Salt	55 g (2 oz)
Artificial sweetener	1 tsp
Spring onions (scallions)	2, cut into 2-cm (1-in) lengths
Ginger	2 slices, chopped
Garlic	3 cloves, peeled and crushed
Chilli powder	120 g (4⅓ oz)
Fish sauce	2 Tbsp

1. Rinse radish dices and drain well. Toss with salt and sweetener then leave for 30 minutes. Drain off any excess water from radish. Do not rinse.

2. Mix together spring onions, ginger, garlic, chilli powder and fish sauce. Add a pinch of salt if preferred.

3. Combine with radish and store in an airtight container for 1 day before serving.

KOREAN

Seasoned Spinach

This simple side dish is made with boiled spinach. You can use any type of spinach for this recipe.

Spinach	150 g (5⅓ oz), roots discarded and cut into 2 parts, stalks and leaves
Garlic	½ tsp, peeled and crushed
Salt	½ tsp
Sesame oil	½ tsp
Toasted white sesame seeds	½ tsp

1. Bring a pot of water to the boil and sprinkle in some salt. Place spinach in, stalks first. When stalks are almost cooked, add leaves. Remove from heat as soon as water comes to the boil again.
2. Rinse spinach in ice-cold water and drain. Squeeze out any excess water with your hands.
3. Cut spinach into shorter sections and mix with crushed garlic, salt and sesame oil. Toss well then sprinkle sesame seeds over.
4. Serve or store for up to a day in the refrigerator.

Vegetables and Salads

KOREAN

Pan-fried Stuffed Chillies

Stuffed chillies dipped in beaten egg and lightly fried until golden.

Green chillies	10
Red chillies	1–2 (optional)
Salt	¾ Tbsp
Minced beef	55 g (2 oz)
Minced pork	55 g (2 oz)
Egg	1
Plain (all-purpose) flour	65 g (2⅓ oz)
Cooking oil	as needed
Ground white pepper	to taste

SEASONING

Light soy sauce	½ Tbsp
Sugar	½ Tbsp
Spring onion (scallion)	½ Tbsp, chopped
Crushed garlic	1 Tbsp
Sesame oil	1 Tbsp
Ground white pepper	

DIPPING SAUCE

Light soy sauce	1 Tbsp
Water	1 Tbsp
Vinegar	½ Tbsp
Sugar	½ Tbsp

1 Cut tops off chillies, then cut into half lengthways. Remove seeds and sprinkle with salt. Set aside for 30 minutes. Pat dry with absorbent paper.
2 Combine seasoning ingredients. Divide into 2 portions and separately mix into minced beef and pork.
3 Mix dipping sauce ingredients together. Set aside.
4 Remove excess moisture from chillies and rub flour into the cavity. Fill with seasoned beef or pork.
5 Heat a pan with some oil. Dip stuffed chillies in beaten egg and pan-fry. Do not flip chillies over too often. When meat is slightly browned, remove from heat.
6 Serve hot with dipping sauce.

THAI

Spicy Mackerel Salad

A light but tasty fried fish salad with crushed chillies, peanuts and green apple strips.

Mackerels	4, medium, gutted and cleaned
Cooking oil for frying	
Shallots	4–5, peeled and chopped
Ginger	2.5-cm (1-in) knob, peeled and grated
Red chillies	4, lightly crushed
Green chillies	4, lightly crushed
Peanuts	3 Tbsp, crushed
Green apple	½, cut into fine strips
Lemon juice	3 Tbsp
Lemon zest	1 Tbsp, grated
Salt	to taste
Freshly ground black pepper	to taste
Lettuce leaves	5

GARNISH
Coriander leaves (cilantro)

1. Steam fish for 5–7 minutes. Before they are completely cooked, remove fish from steamer and lightly pat dry.
2. Heat cooking oil and fry steamed fish until golden. Drain and leave to cool. Debone and skin, then flake the flesh.
3. In a bowl, mix fish meat with shallots, ginger, chillies, peanuts and apple. Add lemon juice and zest. Season with salt and pepper. Mix well.
4. Dish out onto a plate lined with lettuce leaves. Garnish with coriander leaves.

Vegetables and Salads 55

THAI

Papaya Salad

The sourness of the raw papaya makes this salad an ideal way to cleanse the palate and excite the taste buds before or during a meal.

Raw papaya	4–5 cups, peeled and coarsely grated
Garlic	3 cloves, peeled and chopped
Bird's eye chilies	3, chopped
Fish sauce	1 Tbsp
Lemon juice	2 Tbsp
Peanuts	2 Tbsp, crushed
Ground white pepper	to taste
Lettuce and cabbage leaves	

GARNISH
Tomatoes	3, thinly sliced

1. Mix grated papaya with garlic, chillies, fish sauce, lemon juice and peanuts. Season with pepper.
2. Serve on a bed of lettuce and cabbage leaves. Garnish with tomato slices.

Asparagus in Coconut Cream and Lemongrass Sauce

Stir-fried asparagus and prawns in a creamy coconut sauce.

Cooking oil	2 Tbsp
Lemongrass	2 stalks, finely sliced
Garlic	2 cloves, peeled and finely sliced
Young ginger	1.5-cm (¾-in) knob, peeled and finely sliced
Asparagus spears	500 g (1 lb ½ oz), cut into 5-cm (2½-in) lengths
Prawns (shrimps)	150 g (5⅓ oz), shelled and deveined
Coconut milk	250 ml (8 fl oz / 1 cup)
Bean sprouts	250 g (9 oz), tailed, blanched and drained

1. Heat cooking oil and fry lemongrass, garlic and ginger until fragrant.
2. Add asparagus, prawns and coconut milk and bring to the boil. Simmer for 5 minutes or until asparagus is tender.
3. Arrange blanched bean sprouts on a serving plate, top with asparagus and garnish with red chilli slices.

Thai Mushroom Curry

A spicy oyster mushroom curry that goes well with white rice. For a milder curry, use fewer or omit the bird's eye chillies completely when making the paste.

Cooking oil	90 ml (3 fl oz / ⅜ cup)
Fresh oyster mushrooms	500 g (1 lb 1½ oz)
Water	435 ml (14 fl oz / 1¾ cups)
Kaffir lime leaves	4
Polygonum leaves	1 stalk
Red bird's eye chillies	10
Coconut milk	500 ml (16 fl oz / 2 cups)
Fish sauce	2½ Tbsp
Salt	2 tsp
Ground white pepper	½ tsp

PASTE

Green chillies	4
Bird's eye chillies	20
Shallots	8, peeled
Garlic	5 cloves, peeled
Coriander (cilantro) roots	2
Kaffir lime zest	grated from 1 small lime
Ground cumin	2½ tsp
Lemongrass	4 stalks, finely sliced
Galangal	1-cm (½-in) knob, peeled and sliced
Dried prawn (shrimp) paste	1-cm (½-in) square

1. Combine paste ingredients and grind into a fine paste. Heat oil and sauté finely ground paste until fragrant.
2. Stir in mushrooms and water. Bring to the boil for 10 minutes.
3. Add kaffir lime leaves, polygonum leaves and bird's eye chillies. Stir in coconut milk, fish sauce, salt and pepper. Simmer for another 10 minutes and serve hot.

THAI

Prawn and Mango Salad

Peanuts are sprinkled on top of this salad dish for a crunchy texture.

Freshwater prawns (shrimps)	500 g (1 lb 1½ oz), blanched and drained
Unripe mangoes	2, peeled and finely sliced
Kaffir lime leaves	2, finely sliced
Coriander leaves (cilantro)	15 g (½ oz), chopped
Mint leaves	2 Tbsp, chopped
Fish sauce	4 Tbsp
Calamansi limes	2, juiced
Salt	to taste
Sugar	to taste
Glass noodles	200 g (7 oz), blanched and drained
Crisp-fried shallots	55 g (2 oz)
Salad greens	as desired
Peanuts	85 g (3 oz), toasted and pounded

PASTE

Red chillies	3
Bird's eye chillies	3
Dried prawns (shrimps)	45 g (1½ oz), soaked in water and drained
Garlic	3 cloves, peeled
Grated palm sugar or brown sugar	3 Tbsp
Tomatoes	2, quartered

1. Combine ingredients for paste in a blender and process until fine. Transfer to a mixing bowl.
2. Add all other ingredients except salad greens and peanuts to the mixing bowl and toss well with finely pounded paste.
3. Line a serving dish with salad greens, spoon salad over and sprinkle with peanuts. Serve immediately.

Vegetables and Salads 59

VIETNAMESE

Water Convolvulus Salad

Water convolvulus, or water spinach, is very rich in iron and is paired with a basic Vietnamese salad dressing here.

Water convolvulus	1 kg (2 lb 3 oz), use stalks only
Salt	2 Tbsp
Sesame oil	2 tsp
Pork thigh	200 g (7 oz), with a bit of skin and fat intact, boiled and thinly sliced
Prawns (shrimps)	300 g (11 oz), boiled and peeled but with tails intact
Polygonum leaves	20 g (2/3 oz), stalks discarded and leaves coarsely chopped
Skinned peanuts	55 g (2 oz), toasted and coarsely pounded
Shallots	30 g (1 oz), peeled, sliced and crisp-fried

DRESSING

Sugar	6 Tbsp
Lime juice	6 Tbsp
Chicken seasoning powder	4 tsp
Fish sauce	2 Tbsp

DIPPING SAUCE (COMBINED)

Fish sauce	1 Tbsp
Coconut juice	2 Tbsp, or boiled water
Sugar	1 tsp
Vinegar	1 Tbsp, or lemon juice
Garlic	1 clove, peeled and minced
Red chilli (optional)	1 or to taste, minced

1. Cut water convolvulus stalks into 8-cm (3-in) lengths, then halve each length lengthways.
2. Add salt to stalks and knead for a few minutes to extract the juice which tastes of tannins. Discard juice and rinse stalks well.
3. Combine all dressing ingredients in a mixing bowl. Stir until sugar dissolves. Add stalks and toss together with sesame seed oil until well mixed.
4. Transfer salad to a serving plate or bowl. Arrange pork slices and prawns on top.
5. Garnish with chopped polygonum leaves, pounded peanuts and fried shallots. Serve with dipping sauce.

VIETNAMESE

Beef Salad

Star fruit slices make this salad refreshingly juicy, banana slices give it substance, while onion rings give bite and zing.

Beef fillet	600 g (1 lb 5 oz)
Vinegar	as required
Water	as required
Green banana	1, peeled and thinly sliced
Unripe sour star fruit	2, peeled and thinly sliced
Onions	2, peeled and cut into thin rings
Cooking oil	1–2 Tbsp
Coriander leaves (cilantro)	20 g (2/3 oz)
Skinned peanuts	55 g (2 oz), toasted and coarsely pounded
Red chilli	1, finely sliced
Shallots	30 g (1 oz), peeled, sliced and crisp-fried
Prawn (shrimp) crackers	20, deep-fried

SEASONING

Chopped garlic	2 tsp, pan-fried in oil until golden brown
Ground black pepper	2 tsp
Sugar	2 tsp
Sesame oil	2 tsp

1. Slice beef thinly and across grain to ensure tenderness. Put beef slices into a bowl. Add seasoning ingredients and mix well. Set aside for 10 minutes.
2. Make sufficient vinegar-water mixture (3 parts water to 1 part vinegar) to soak cut banana and star fruit slices, as well as onion rings separately.
3. Heat oil in a frying pan over high heat for 30 seconds. Add beef slices and stir-fry quickly, then remove from heat.
4. Drain all soaked ingredients well. Then, combine with cooked beef in a mixing bowl and toss.
5. Transfer tossed ingredients to a serving plate or bowl. Garnish as desired with coriander leaves, pounded peanuts, red chilli slices and fried shallots.
6. Serve with prawn crackers and dipping sauce.

Vegetables and Salads

VIETNAMESE

Green Mango Salad

Also known as Vietnamese mint, polygonum leaves impart an intense and inimitable aroma that uniquely brings out the flavour of prawns.

Green mangoes	1 kg (2 lb 3 oz), peeled, seeds discarded and flesh finely sliced into strips
Prawns (shrimps)	300 g (11 oz), barbecued or grilled, then peeled with tails left intact
Polygonum leaves	20 g (2/3 oz), stalks discarded and leaves coarsely chopped
Skinned peanuts	55 g (2 oz), toasted and coarsely pounded
Prawn (shrimp) crackers	20, deep-fried

DRESSING (COMBINED)

Chilli sauce	4 Tbsp
Sugar	3 Tbsp or more to taste
Light soy sauce	2 Tbsp

DIPPING SAUCE (COMBINED)

Fish sauce	1 Tbsp
Coconut juice	2 Tbsp, or boiled water
Sugar	1 tsp
Vinegar	1 Tbsp, or lemon juice
Garlic	1 clove, peeled and minced
Red chilli (optional)	1 or to taste, minced

1. In a large bowl, toss green mango shreds in combined dressing ingredients. Do not squeeze mango shreds or crispness will be lost. Adjust to taste with some sugar if mango is too sour.
2. Transfer salad to a serving plate, then arrange cooked, peeled prawns on top.
3. Garnish with chopped polygonum leaves and pounded peanuts.
4. Serve salad with prawn crackers and dipping sauce.

VIETNAMESE

Chicken Salad with Polygonum Leaves

A tangy and peppery salad of tender chicken, aromatic polygonum leaves and crisp onion strips will whet any sluggish appetite.

Vinegar	as required
Water	as required
Onions	2, peeled and cut into half-moon slices
Chicken	1, about 1.5 kg (3 lb 4½ oz)
Rice wine or vodka	2 Tbsp
Polygonum leaves	55 g (2 oz), washed and stalks discarded
Red chillies	1–2, sliced

SEASONING

Ground black pepper	1 tsp
Chicken seasoning powder	3 tsp
Sugar	1½ Tbsp
Salt	2 tsp
Lime juice	3 Tbsp

DIPPING SAUCE (COMBINED)

Lime juice	1 Tbsp
Salt	2 tsp
Ground black pepper	1 tsp

1. Make sufficient vinegar-water mixture (3 parts water to 1 part vinegar) to soak onion slices. Drain onion slices well before use.
2. Steam chicken for 20 minutes or until cooked through. Remove chicken from steamer and sprinkle rice wine or vodka all over. Return chicken to steamer and replace lid. Leave for 5 minutes, then remove from heat.
3. Debone slightly cooled chicken and cut flesh into desired bite-size pieces. Alternatively, shred chicken meat by hand.
4. Put chicken pieces into a mixing bowl. Add polygonum leaves, drained onion slices and seasoning ingredients and mix.
5. Transfer salad to a serving plate or bowl. Add chilli slices on top.
6. Serve with dipping sauce.

Vegetables and Salads

SOUPS

BALINESE
- 66 Green Papaya Soup
- 67 Balinese Seafood Soup

CHINESE
- 68 Duck and Salted Vegetable Soup
- 69 Old Cucumber and Pork Soup
- 70 Hot Sour Soup
- 71 Bean Curd Hot Pot

FILIPINO
- 72 Chicken and Young Coconut Soup
- 73 Chicken Broth with Ginger and Green Papaya
- 74 Beef Shank Broth
- 75 Prawns in Sour Broth

INDONESIAN
- 76 Hot and Sour Seafood Soup
- 77 Mixed Vegetables in Clear Soup

JAPANESE
- 78 Miso Soup with Pork and Vegetables
- 79 Bean Curd and Seaweed Miso Soup
- 80 Tokyo-style New Year's Soup
- 81 Short-neck Clam Clear Soup

KOREAN
- 82 Kimchi Stew
- 83 Spicy Soft Bean Curd Stew
- 84 Spicy Fish Stew
- 85 Soy Bean Paste Stew

STRAITS CHINESE
- 86 Dried Fish Bladder Soup
- 87 Papaya in Peppery Soup

THAI
- 88 Chicken Soup with Galangal
- 89 Thai Fish Chowder
- 90 Thai Vegetable Soup
- 91 Pumpkin Soup with Coconut Cream

VIETNAMESE
- 92 Vietnamese Sour Fish Soup
- 93 Pumpkin Soup with Coconut Milk

BALINESE

Green Papaya Soup

Aromatic and deliciously creamy, this soup is suitable for vegetarians but not vegans because of the dried prawn paste in the vegetable spice paste.

Green papaya	1, about 750 g (1 lb 10 oz)
Vegetable oil	1 Tbsp
Vegetable spice paste (page 14)	250 g (9 oz)
Lemongrass	1 stalk, bruised
Salam leaves	2
Indonesian-style vegetable stock (page 20)	1 litre (32 fl oz / 4 cups)
Coconut milk	250 ml (8 fl oz / 1 cup)
Salt	a pinch or to taste
Crushed black peppercorns	a pinch or to taste

GARNISH
Crisp-fried shallots
Chopped kaffir lime leaves

1. Peel and deseed papaya, then dice into 0.5-cm (¼-in) thick pieces.
2. Heat oil in a stock pot. Add spice paste, lemongrass and *salam* leaves. Sauté until fragrant.
3. Add papaya and continue to sauté until papaya is evenly coated with spice paste and changes colour. Pour in stock and mix well. Bring to the boil and simmer until papaya is almost cooked.
4. Add coconut milk and simmer until papaya is tender. If liquid reduces too much, add more stock. Season to taste with salt and pepper.
5. Garnish and serve immediately.

Balinese Seafood Soup

The mixed seafood imparts a certain sweetness to this light and refreshing soup, while the sour star fruit adds hints of tartness and zest.

Prawns (shrimps)	400 g (13⅓ oz), cleaned and deveined
Fish fillets	8, cut into 50 g (1⅔ oz) pieces
Clams or mussels	4
Salt	a pinch or to taste
Ground black pepper	a pinch or to taste
Seafood spice paste (page 15)	4 Tbsp
Lime juice	2 Tbsp
Vegetable oil	1–2 Tbsp
Indonesian-style vegetable stock (page 20)	1 litre (32 fl oz / 4 cups)
Salam leaves	3
Kaffir lime leaves	2
Sour star fruit	2
Tomatoes	4, peeled, seeded and cut into wedges

1. Season seafood with salt and pepper, then add spice paste and lime juice. Mix well.
2. Heat oil in a heavy saucepan. Add seafood and sauté quickly until colour changes on both sides of prawns and fish.
3. Add stock, *salam* and lime leaves and sour star fruit. Bring to the boil, then braise over very low heat until seafood is almost cooked and mussels open.
4. Add tomato wedges and simmer until seafood is tender and tomatoes are warmed through.
5. Season to taste with salt and pepper. Serve.

CHINESE

Duck and Salted Vegetable Soup

A simple savoury soup with duck and pickled plums.

Duck	½
Salted cabbage	250 g (9 oz), cut into 5-cm (2-in) squares
Cooking oil	1 Tbsp
Ginger	5-cm (2-in) knob, crushed
Water	2.5 litres (80 fl oz / 10 cups)
Pickled sour plums	2
Tomatoes	2, quartered
Ground white pepper	¼ tsp

1. Cut duck into 4 pieces and set aside.
2. Soak salted cabbage in water for 1 hour. Drain and lightly squeeze out excess water.
3. Heat oil in a pot and sauté ginger for 1–2 minutes until aromatic. Add duck and stir-fry for 5 minutes until the duck changes colour.
4. Pour water into the pot and add salted stems and sour plums. Bring to the boil, reduce heat to low, cover and simmer for 2½ hours or until duck is tender.
5. Add tomatoes and pepper and simmer for a further 10 minutes. Serve.

CHINESE

Old Cucumber and Pork Soup

A refreshing clear soup with a definite crunch to it.

Old cucumber with skin	1 large
Lean pork with some fat	360 g (12 oz), whole piece, uncut and rinsed
Dried Chinese red dates	6, seeded and rinsed
Water	1.25 litres (40 fl oz / 5 cups)
Salt	1½ tsp
Light soy sauce	2 Tbsp

1. Cut old cucumber in half lengthways. Scoop out seeds with a spoon and cut each half into 5-cm (2-in) pieces.
2. Place cucumber, pork and water in a large pot. Add dates to the pot. Cover and bring to the boil.
3. Add salt, reduce heat and simmer for 45–60 minutes. Skim off the surface scum from time to time.
4. When pork is tender, remove and cut into 2.5-cm (1-in) thick slices. Return pork to soup.
5. Serve with a small dish of light soy sauce as a dip for pork.

Soups

CHINESE

Hot Sour Soup

Chicken and prawns are added to this peppery chicken stock-based vegetable soup.

Chicken drumstick	1, boned and cut into small cubes
Small prawns (shrimps)	300 g (11 oz), peeled and diced (optional)
Basic chicken stock (page 19)	2.25 litres (75 fl oz / 9 cups)
Sichuan vegetable	1 large piece, unwashed and diced
Carrot	1, peeled and diced
Dried Chinese mushrooms	4, soaked and diced
Button mushrooms	½ can, quartered
Straw mushrooms	½ can, quartered
Fresh baby corn	10 cobs, diced
Red chillies	3, split to remove seeds
Chinese black vinegar	165 ml (5½ fl oz / ⅔ cup)
Bean curd	1 square piece, diced
Frozen green peas	100 g (3½ oz), rinsed
Sweet potato flour	4 Tbsp, mixed with 125 ml (4 fl oz / ½ cup) chicken stock, strained
Eggs	2, lightly beaten

SEASONING

Ground white pepper	1 tsp
Salt	1 tsp
Corn flour (cornstarch)	1 tsp

1 Marinate chicken and prawns with seasoning ingredients for 15 minutes.

2 Pour strained stock into a deep cooking pot and bring to the boil. Add Sichuan vegetable, carrot, all the mushrooms, corn, chillies and black vinegar. Allow to simmer for 10 minutes.

3 Put in chicken and prawns and when mixture begins to boil, add bean curd and green peas. Simmer for another 5 minutes, then stir in sweet potato flour mixture and eggs. Serve.

CHINESE

Bean Curd Hot Pot

This popular Chinese soup is made with minced chicken, bean curd and bamboo shoots.

Soft bean curd	6 pieces or 6 packets silken bean curd
Chicken	60 g (2¼ oz), minced
Egg yolks	3
Salt	to taste
Ground white pepper	to taste
Cooking oil	2 tsp
Tender tips of winter bamboo shoot	30 g (1 oz)
Salt	to taste
Lettuce leaves	3–4

CHICKEN STOCK

Chicken bones	2 kg (4 lb 6 oz), skin and fat discarded
Water	2 litres (64 fl oz / 8 cups)

1. Prepare chicken stock. Rinse bones until water is clear. Place into a stockpot and add water. Bring to the boil over high heat. Boil for 1–2 hours skimming off scum that surfaces from time to time. Strain to get about 1.5 litres (48 fl oz / 6 cups) stock.
2. Pass bean curd through a sieve. Mix with minced chicken.
3. Beat egg yolks with salt and pepper. Add to bean curd and chicken mixture and blend well.
4. Pour mixture into a mould lightly greased with cooking oil. Steam over high heat for 7 minutes before serving.
5. Meanwhile, reheat chicken stock and add bamboo shoot. Boil for 10 minutes. Season to taste with salt.
6. Put steamed bean curd mixture into a big soup bowl and pour boiling stock over. Add lettuce leaves, garnish and serve immediately.

Chicken and Young Coconut Soup

An aromatic combination of young coconut, chicken and lemongrass, this dish originates from the southern provinces of Luzon, where there is an abundance of coconut plantations.

Cooking oil	4 Tbsp
Garlic	5 cloves, peeled and crushed
Onion	1, large, peeled and chopped
Young ginger	2.5-cm (1-in) knob, peeled and sliced
Fish sauce	3 Tbsp
Lemongrass	3 stalks, bruised and cut into 5-cm (2-in) pieces
Chicken	1, about 1 kg (2 lb 3 oz), deboned and cut into bite-size pieces
Screwpine leaves	2, knotted
Basic chicken stock (page 19)	1.5 litres (48 fl oz / 6 cups)
Young coconut	1, flesh scooped out and water reserved
Ground black pepper	½ tsp
Salt	to taste

1 In a saucepan, heat oil over medium heat and fry garlic until golden brown. Add onion and fry until slightly translucent.

2 Add ginger and fry until fragrant. Stir in fish sauce and mix well. Add lemongrass, chicken pieces and screwpine leaves and continue to fry for another 5 minutes.

3 Add chicken stock and bring mixture to the boil. Reduce heat to low and leave to simmer for 25 minutes, or until chicken is cooked and tender.

4 Add coconut flesh and stir in reserved coconut water. Season with pepper and salt and remove from heat.

5 Ladle into serving bowls. Serve on its own as a starter, or as a main dish with rice.

Chicken Broth with Ginger and Green Papaya

Flavoured with ginger, green papaya and drumstick leaves, Filipinos consider this soup as a one-pot meal. Serve it as a starter, on its own or a main dish accompanied with white rice.

Cooking oil	4 Tbsp
Garlic	8 cloves, peeled and chopped
Onion	1, large, peeled and sliced
Young ginger	50 g (1⅔ oz), peeled and thinly sliced
Fish sauce	4 Tbsp
Chicken	1, about 1 kg (2 lb 3 oz), cut into 12 pieces or bite-size pieces
Water	2 litres (64 fl oz / 8 cups)
Green papaya	1, medium, skinned, cut into half lengthwise and sliced into 2.5-cm (1-in) thick wedges
Salt	to taste
Drumstick leaves	10 g (⅓ oz)

1. In a saucepan, heat oil over medium heat. Fry garlic until golden brown. Add onion and fry until soft and translucent.

2. Add ginger and fry until fragrant, then stir in fish sauce and mix well.

3. Add chicken pieces and stir to mix well. Fry for 5 minutes, then add water and bring to the boil. Reduce to low heat, cover saucepan and leave mixture to simmer for 25 minutes. Add more water, if necessary.

4. Add papaya and increase heat. Bring soup to the boil and cook until papaya slices are tender. Add salt and drumstick leaves and stir to mix well.

5. Dish out and serve immediately.

FILIPINO

Beef Shank Broth

This clear, tasty soup derives its flavour from the bone marrow of beef shank. This dish originates from the Southern province of Batangas where cattle is raised and herded. Similar to Italy's *bollito misto* and France's *pot au feau*, it is a dish that is definitive of Filipino cuisine. The beef shank should be cooked until the meat, ligaments and tendons are almost gelatinous. For variety, add slices of cabbage and Chinese cabbage to turn it into a one-pot meal.

Beef shank with bone marrow	about 2 kg (4 lb 6 oz), cut 8-cm (3-in) thick across the bone
Water	3 litres (96 fl oz / 12 cups) or more
Fish sauce	4 Tbsp, or to taste
Black peppercorns	1 Tbsp, coarsely crushed
Salt	to taste
Spring onions (scallions)	2, sliced

1. Place beef shank in a stock pot large enough to hold all ingredients. Add water to completely cover beef shank.
2. Bring to the boil over high heat. Skim off any scum that rises to the surface. Reduce heat to low, cover pot and leave to simmer for 2 hours or until beef shank is tender and falls off easily from the bone.
3. Season with fish sauce, black peppercorns and salt. Stir to mix well.
4. Garnish with spring onions. Dish out and serve immediately.

Prawns in Sour Broth

This broth acquires its tangy flavour from tamarind, tomatoes and lemon juice used in the recipe. It may be served as a starter on its own or as a one-pot dish, accompanied with rice.

Prawns (shrimps)	500 g (1 lb 1½ oz), medium-sized
Taro	10, small, peeled
Rice-rinsing water or water	2 litres (64 fl oz / 8 cups)
Onion	1, peeled and sliced
Tomato	1, medium, sliced
White radish	1, about 300 g (11 oz), peeled and sliced on the diagonal into 1-cm (½-in) thick slices
Fish sauce	4 Tbsp
Water convolvolus (*kang kong*)	500 g (1 lb 1½ oz), washed and drained
Sour star fruit	200 g (7 oz), boiled until soft, then mashed, or use 65 g (2⅓ oz) tamarind pulp, mixed with 250 ml (8 fl oz / 1 cup) water and strained
Green chillies	2–3, bruised
Salt	to taste (optional)

1. Clean prawns. Trim whiskers and keep prawn shell intact.
2. Place taro in a pot and add enough water to cover yam completely. Bring to the boil and cook until taro is tender. Remove from heat, drain and set aside.
3. In a large saucepan, pour in rice-rinsing water or water, bring to the boil over high heat and add onion and tomato. Reduce heat to low and leave to simmer for 10 minutes.
4. Add radish and increase heat. Return mixture to boil for 5 minutes, or until radish is just tender.
5. Reduce heat to low and add tamarind pulp and fish sauce. Stir to mix well. When mixture has reached a gentle simmer, add boiled taro, prawns and return mixture to the boil for 3 minutes.
6. Add water convolvolus, sour star fruit and chillies. Return mixture to the boil for 3 minutes and add salt to taste, if desired, before removing from heat.
7. Dish out and serve immediately with plain white rice.

Note: Rice rinsing water refers to the second or third rinse of water from washing rice before cooking. Traditionally, it is the preferred choice of liquid for cooking this soup.

INDONESIAN

Hot and Sour Seafood Soup

This recipe can be prepared with assorted seafood instead of a whole fish. If using assorted seafood, prepare about 800 g (1¾ lb). Use firm fish fillets, prawns (shrimps) and clams.

Whole fish	1, about 1 kg (2 lb 3 oz), cleaned and cut into roughly equal slices, use red mullet, snapper or mackerel
Salt	to taste
Freshly crushed black pepper	to taste
Indonesian-style stock (page 20)	1 litre (32 fl oz / 4 cups)
Tomatoes	4, medium, skinned, seeded and cut into wedges
Salam leaves	2, finely sliced

SPICE MIXTURE

Vegetable oil	3 Tbsp
Red chillies	55 g (2 oz), halved, seeded and sliced
Shallots	85 g (3 oz), peeled and sliced
Garlic	40 g (1⅓ oz), peeled and sliced
Lemongrass	2 stalks, bruised and finely sliced
Galangal	30 g (1 oz), peeled and cut into fine strips
Turmeric	30 g (1 oz), peeled and finely sliced
Ginger	30 g (1 oz), peeled and finely sliced
Lemon basil	12 sprigs, roughly sliced
Sour star fruit	10, halved and sliced

1. Season fish with salt and pepper to taste, then refrigerate or set aside in a cool place until needed.
2. Prepare spice mixture. Heat oil in a heavy saucepan. Add all ingredients and sauté over medium heat for 2 minutes or until fragrant.
3. Season spice mixture to taste with salt and pepper, then add stock. Bring to the boil and simmer for 1 minute.
4. Lower fish into stock mixture, return to a simmer and poach fish at just below 80°C (180°F) for 5 minutes.
5. Carefully remove fish from saucepan and arrange in one large serving bowl or divide among individual serving ones.
6. Finally, add tomatoes to soup and return to a simmer. Adjust seasoning to taste with more salt and pepper, if necessary.
7. Ladle soup over fish, sprinkle *salam* leaves over to garnish and serve.

INDONESIAN

Mixed Vegetables in Clear Soup

Chicken croquettes are added to this chicken stock-based soup.

Shallots	8, peeled
Garlic	4 cloves, peeled
White peppercorns	1 tsp
Margarine	1 Tbsp
Galangal	5 thin slices, peeled
Lemongrass	1 stalk, bruised
Basic chicken stock (page 19)	1.25 litres (40 fl oz / 5 cups)
Cooked bamboo shoots	250 g (9 oz), cut into fine strips
Spring onions (scallions)	3, cut into 1-cm (½-in) pieces
Bean sprouts	250 g (9 oz), tailed
Glass noodles	25 g (⅘ oz), cut into 10-cm (4-in) lengths, soaked in water until tender, drained
Chinese parsley	1 sprig, chopped

CHICKEN CROQUETTES

Minced chicken	150 g (5⅓ oz)
Almonds	50 g (1⅔ oz), ground
Egg	1, with yolk separated
Ground white pepper	¼ tsp
Plain (all-purpose) flour	1 Tbsp
Salt	½ tsp

1. Prepare chicken croquettes. Mix all ingredients, except egg white, thoroughly. Shape mixture into small balls.
2. Bring a pot of water to the boil. Coat each ball with lightly beaten egg white, then toss into boiling water. Remove when croquettes start to float. Drain and set aside.
3. Combine shallots, garlic and peppercorns and grind until fine. Heat margarine in a pot, then add ground spices, galangal and lemongrass and fry until fragrant.
4. Add chicken stock and bring to the boil. Stir in cooked bamboo shoots and spring onions. Add bean sprouts, glass noodles, croquettes and Chinese parsley.
5. Dish out and serve immediately.

Soups 77

JAPANESE

Miso Soup with Pork and Vegetables

In Japanese, *ton* refers to pork. Substantial enough to be served as a main dish, this speciality originates from northern Japan, and is traditionally served at festivities held by the riverside during autumn.

Sesame oil	2 Tbsp
Thinly-sliced pork belly or pork shoulder	150 g (5⅓ oz), cut into bite-size pieces
Potatoes	2, small, peeled, cut into cubes, then soaked and drained just before use
Carrot	½, peeled and thinly sliced
White radish	6-cm (2½-in) length, peeled and thinly sliced
White devil's tongue jelly (*konnyaku*), packed in water	130 g (4⅔ oz), drained, cut into thick matchsticks, then blanched and drained
Burdock	70 g (2½ oz), scrubbed clean and cut into small pieces
Fresh shiitake mushrooms	2, stems discarded and thinly sliced
Deep-dried bean curd	1, cut into thin strips
Sake	2 Tbsp
Soy bean paste	60–70 g (2–2½ oz)
Japanese spring onion (*naga negi* / scallion)	1, finely sliced

DASHI

Water	1 litre (32 fl oz / 4 cups)
Dried kelp (*konbu*)	12-cm (4¾-in) piece
Bonito flakes	30 g (1 oz)

GARNISHING

Chopped Japanese spring onion (scallion)
Japanese seven-spice seasoning (optional)

1 Prepare dashi (page 19).

2 Heat sesame oil in a saucepan and stir-fry pork, potatoes, carrot, white radish, devil's tongue jelly and burdock over medium heat for 2–3 minutes. Pour in dashi and simmer for about 10 minutes, then add shiitake mushrooms and bean curd.

3 Simmer for 2–3 minutes, and skim off any foam that rises to the surface. Turn off heat, add sake and strain soy bean paste into soup, then stir until paste has dissolved.

4 Add spring onion and reheat. When soup is almost boiling, remove from heat. Ladle soup into individual serving bowls. Garnish with sliced spring onion.

5 Sprinkle seven-spice seasoning on top, if desired. Serve hot.

JAPANESE

Bean Curd and Seaweed Miso Soup

Served at most meals, steamed rice and miso soup are the traditional staples of Japanese cuisine. For an interesting variation to this recipe, substitute the dried seaweed with vegetables such as ladies fingers, mushrooms, snow peas or chives, or, use deep-fried bean curd, potatoes, bamboo shoots or white radish to replace regular bean curd.

Bean curd (soft or firm)	200 g (7 oz), cut into small cubes
Dried cut seaweed (wakame)	1 Tbsp
Soy bean paste (miso)	60 g (2¼ oz)
Japanese spring onion (naga negi / scallion)	¼, finely sliced

DASHI

Water	800 ml (26 fl oz / 3¼ cups)
Dried kelp (konbu)	10-cm (4-in) piece
Bonito flakes	25 g (⁴⁄₅ oz)

1. Prepare dashi (page 19).
2. Return strained dashi to the saucepan and add bean curd and seaweed. Bring to the boil, then remove from heat. Strain soy bean paste into soup, then stir until bean paste has dissolved.
3. Reheat soup and return to the boil, then remove from heat immediately. Garnish with sliced spring onion and serve hot.

Soups

JAPANESE

Tokyo-style New Year's Soup

While rice cake soup is traditionally served on 1st January to celebrate the New Year in Japan, the recipe for the soup differs from region to region. This recipe hails from Tokyo, hence, its name.

Chicken thigh	120 g (4⅓ oz), skinned, fat removed and deboned, then cut into small pieces
Sake	1 tsp
White radish	6-cm (2½-in) length, thinly sliced
Carrot	¼, peeled and cut into shapes with a vegetable cutter
Fresh shiitake mushrooms	2, stems discarded, shallow cuts made on mushroom caps to form desired pattern
Pink-swirled fish paste cake	8 thick slices, each about 0.5-cm (¼-in)
Rice cakes	4, each about 55 g (2 oz)
DASHI	
Water	1 litre (32 fl oz / 4 cups)
Dried kelp (*konbu*)	12-cm (5-in) piece
Bonito flakes	30 g (1 oz)
SEASONING	
Sake	1 Tbsp
Salt	½–⅔ tsp
Japanese light soy sauce	¼ tsp
GARNISHING	
Trefoil (*mitsuba*)	1 small bunch, cut into 2-cm (¾-in) lengths
Yuzu zest	1 small piece, cut into fine strips

1. Prepare dashi (page 19).
2. Marinate chicken with sake and leave for about 10 minutes. Pour dashi into a medium-size pot and bring to the boil. Add chicken, radish, carrot, shiitake mushrooms and fish paste cake. Cook for about 10 minutes.
3. While soup is boiling, grill rice cakes in a preheated oven at 200°C (400°F), or toaster for 5–10 minutes, until slightly puffy and light brown in colour.
4. Mix seasoning ingredients together and stir into soup. Remove from heat.
5. Place a grilled or toasted rice cake into each individual serving bowl and ladle soup over. Garnish with trefoil and yuzu zest. Serve hot.

JAPANESE

Short-neck Clam Clear Soup

Enjoy this clear soup with a rich-tasting stock, sweetened by the natural juices of the clams. You can also add seaweed, mushrooms and fish paste to the soup for a more substantial dish. If short-neck clams are unavailable, substitute with any other kind of clams.

Salt	1¼ tsp
Water	250 ml (8 fl oz / 1 cup)
Short-neck clams	300 g (11 oz)
Sake	1 Tbsp
Japanese light soy sauce	1 Tbsp
Myoga ginger flower buds	2, thinly sliced

STOCK
Water	700 ml (22 fl oz / 2¾ cups)
Dried kelp (*konbu*)	10-cm (4-in) piece

1. Dissolve 1 tsp salt in water and soak clams for about 30 minutes to remove any grit. Rinse well, then drain and set aside.
2. Prepare stock. Put water and kelp into a saucepan and leave for 30 minutes. Cook over medium heat and when small bubbles appear from the bottom, remove kelp.
3. Heat stock in a medium saucepan and when boiling, add clams. Return to the boil, then reduce heat and skim off any foam that rises to the surface.
4. Season with remaining salt, sake and light soy sauce. Simmer for 3 minutes, until clams open and discard any that remain closed.
5. Ladle into individual serving bowls and garnish with sliced myoga ginger flower buds. Serve hot.

Soups 81

KOREAN

Kimchi Stew

This spicy and sour kimchi stew is made more substantial with the addition of pork.

Pork	100 g (3½ oz), thinly sliced
Ginger juice	1 tsp
Light soy sauce	2 tsp
Ground black pepper	1 tsp
Sugar	1 tsp
Kimchi brine	250 ml (8 fl oz / 1 cup)
Sour kimchi	200 g (7 oz), cut into 2-cm (1-in) cubes
Water	375 ml (12 fl oz / 1½ cups)
Soft bean curd	1 square, sliced
Leek slices	

1. Season pork with ginger juice, soy sauce, pepper, sugar and kimchi brine for 20 minutes.
2. Place seasoned pork with sour kimchi in a pot. Pour in water and bring to the boil.
3. Reduce heat and add bean curd. Simmer for 20 minutes.
4. Garnish with leek slices and serve hot.

Note: Kimchi comes soaked in brine. Drain the brine for use in recipes such as this one.

Spicy Soft Bean Curd Stew

A hot and spicy bean curd stew with kimchi and egg.

Red chilli oil	1 Tbsp
Crushed garlic	1 Tbsp
Chilli powder	1 Tbsp
Light soy sauce	1 tsp
Beef seasoning powder	½ Tbsp
Onion	50 g (1⅔ oz), peeled and diced
Kimchi	30 g (1 oz), chopped
Pork	50 g (1⅔ oz), sliced
Water	250 ml (8 fl oz / 1 cup)
Silken or egg bean curd	140 g (5 oz / 1 tube), sliced into rounds
Egg	1
Spring onion (scallion)	1, sliced or leek slices

1. Heat an empty earthen bowl or clay pot until it becomes very hot. Reduce heat and add in chilli oil, crushed garlic, chilli powder, soy sauce, beef seasoning powder, onion, kimchi and pork. Stir-fry for 5 minutes.
2. Pour in water and bring to the boil. Carefully slide in bean curd rounds without breaking them. Simmer over low heat for 10–15 minutes.
3. Crack egg into stew and remove from heat. Sprinkle spring onion or leek slices on top and serve.

KOREAN

Spicy Fish Stew

A spicy fish and vegetable stew that goes well with white rice.

Ginger juice	2 tsp
Salt	1 tsp
Ground white pepper	1 tsp
Red snapper or cod	1, medium-size, cut into large pieces
Courgette (zucchini)	30 g (1 oz), cut into 2-cm (1-in) squares
Carrot	30 g (1 oz), cut into 2-cm (1-in) squares
Red chilli	1, sliced
Chrysanthemum leaves	2 small stalks, cut into 3-cm (1½-in) lengths (optional)

STOCK

Dried anchovies	30 g (1 oz)
Dried kelp (*konbu*)	10 x 10-cm (5 x 5-in) piece
White radish	100 g (3½ oz)
Onion	100 g (3½ oz)
Water	2.5 litres (80 fl oz / 10 cups)

SEASONING

Red chilli paste	2 Tbsp
Chilli powder	1 Tbsp
Crushed garlic	1 Tbsp
Salt	1 tsp
Ground white pepper	1 tsp
Sugar	1 tsp

1. Prepare stock. Combine stock ingredients and cook over medium heat for 40 minutes. Strain stock and discard solids.
2. Sprinkle ginger juice, salt and pepper over fish. Leave for 30 minutes.
3. Combine seasoning ingredients and mix well.
4. Return stock to the boil and add zucchini, carrot, chilli, fish and seasoning. Cook for 10 minutes.
5. Serve hot with chrysanthemum leaves, if using.

Soy Bean Paste Stew

This lightly spicy stew is flavored with dried anchovies and fermented soy bean paste.

Water	435 ml (14⅔ fl oz / 1¾ cups)
Dried anchovies	100 g (3½ oz)
Korean soy bean paste	3 Tbsp
Firm bean curd	180 g (6½ oz), cut into 1-cm (½-in) cubes
Green chilli	1, sliced and seeded
Crushed garlic	½ Tbsp
Courgette (zucchini)	1, small, sliced
Potatoes	150 g (5⅓ oz), peeled and sliced
Chilli powder	1 tsp
Spring onions (scallions)	2, sliced

1. Bring water to the boil and add dried anchovies. Leave to boil for 20 minutes to make a stock.
2. Remove dried anchovies and pour stock into an earthen bowl or clay pot.
3. Add fermented soy bean paste and stir to dissolve.
4. Reduce heat to medium then add all remaining ingredients except chilli powder and scallions.
5. Cook for about 10 minutes then stir in chilli powder.
6. Garnish with spring onions and serve hot.

Straits Chinese

Dried Fish Bladder Soup

This is a popular Chinese soup made with chicken balls, fish bladder and fish rolls.

FISH ROLLS
Fish paste	200 g (7 oz), see recipe
Omelettes	3, each 15-cm (6-in) in diameter, made from 3 large beaten eggs

CHICKEN BALLS
Minced chicken	150 g (5⅓ oz)
Salt	¼ tsp
Corn flour (cornstarch)	1 Tbsp
Sesame oil	1 tsp
Ground white pepper	¼ tsp
Beaten egg	1½ Tbsp
Black (woodear) fungus	1 Tbsp, soaked in water until expanded, hard centre part discarded and finely chopped
Carrot	2½ Tbsp, peeled and finely chopped
Turnip	2 Tbsp, peeled and finely chopped

SOUP
Chicken bones	from 3 chickens
Water	2.5 litres (80 fl oz / 10 cups)
Dried fish bladder	40 g (1⅓ oz), soaked in hot water for 10 minutes, drained and excess water squeezed out
Carrot	½, peeled and sliced
Fishballs	20, made from 175 g (6¼ oz) fish paste
Cabbage	350 g (12 oz), cut into big pieces
Cooked chicken meat	70 g (2½ oz), sliced to 5-mm (¼-in) thickness
Salt	2 tsp
Ground white pepper	¼ tsp

FISH PASTE
Salt	1½ tsp
Iced water	180 ml (6 fl oz / ¾ cup)
Spanish mackerel fillet	600 g (1 lb 5 ⅓ oz)
Ground white pepper	½ tsp
Corn flour (cornstarch)	4 tsp
Seasoning powder	⅛ tsp

1. Make fish paste. Dissolve salt in iced water. Pound fish fillet in a mortar and pestle or blend it in an electric blender. Add salted iced water slowly until it becomes a smooth paste. Divide into 3 portions.

2. Using 1 portion of paste, make fish rolls. Spread and smoothen paste evenly on each omelette with a wet butter knife. Roll tightly for a beautiful firm pattern when sliced. Steam rolls for 8 minutes over rapidly boiling water. Set aside to cool. When cool, slice rolls at 0.5-cm (¼-in) thickness. Set aside. Prepare chicken balls. Mix all the ingredients well and with wet hands, shape mixture into small balls. Arrange on greased baking tray.

3. Use remaining 2 portions of paste to make fishballs. Add pepper and tapioca flour or corn flour and seasoning powder. Stir paste in one direction using a metal spoon. Throw paste against side of the mortar or a mixing bowl several times until it becomes sticky and elastic which gives a springy texture when cooked. Wet or oil your hands, depending on the recipe, and take a handful of paste. Squeeze it through the thumb and forefinger to form a walnut-sized lump of fish paste. Scrape off with wet teaspoon and roll into a ball. Put fishballs in bowl of water which is mixed with ⅛ tsp salt.

4. Prepare soup. Boil chicken bones in water, strain, and bring to the boil. Add dried fish bladder and chicken balls. Bring to the boil and add carrot, fishballs, cabbage and chicken meat. Season with salt and pepper. Add sliced fish rolls. Switch off heat. Garnish and serve hot.

STRAITS CHINESE

Papaya in Peppery Soup

This papaya soup is both spicy and peppery.

Almost-ripe papaya	600 g (1 lb 5 ⅓ oz), peeled, seeded, cut lengthways into 8 pieces and sliced into 0.5-cm (¼-in) thick pieces
Water	1.5 litres (48 fl oz / 6 cups)
Young turmeric leaf	1
Prawns (shrimps)	300 g (11 oz), peeled and deveined
Salt	1¾ tsp
Sugar	3 Tbsp
Seasoning powder	⅛ tsp

FINELY GROUND PASTE (COMBINED)

Red chillies	2
Shallots	8, peeled
Candlenuts	6
White peppercorns	15 or ½ tsp ground white pepper
Dried prawn (shrimp) paste	1½ tsp, crushed

1. Prepare finely ground paste. Combine ingredients in a blender and blend into a fine paste.
2. Combine papaya, finely ground paste and water in a saucepan and bring to the boil. Simmer for 7 minutes. Add turmeric leaf and continue to simmer for 1 minute.
3. Add prawns, salt, sugar and seasoning powder. Cook for 3 minutes until prawns are done and papaya is tender.
4. Serve hot with spicy prawn paste.

THAI

Chicken Soup with Galangal

A wholesome chicken soup with the unique peppery flavour of galangal and the refreshing taste of lemongrass and kaffir lime leaves.

Water	250 ml (8 fl oz / 1 cup)
Coconut milk	1 litre (32 fl oz / 4 cups)
Chicken thighs	8, sliced or 600 g (1 lb 5⅓ oz) chicken breast, diced
Lemongrass	2 stalks, cut into 2.5-cm (1-in) lengths
Galangal	1-cm (½-in) knob, peeled and finely sliced
Fish sauce	2 Tbsp
Bird's eye chillies	3
Kaffir lime leaves	3
Lemon juice	2 Tbsp

GARNISH

Red chilli	1, shredded
Spring onion (scallion)	1, chopped

1. Bring water to the boil with half the coconut milk.
2. Add chicken, lemongrass, galangal and 1 Tbsp fish sauce. Simmer for about 20 minutes or until chicken is cooked. Less cooking time will be required for diced chicken breast.
3. Stir in remaining coconut milk and turn up heat. As soon as it begins to boil, toss in whole chillies and kaffir lime leaves. Stir and remove from heat.
4. Serve in individual bowls. Sprinkle with lemon juice and fish sauce to taste. Garnish with chilli and spring onion.

Thai Fish Chowder

A hot and spicy fish soup with a distinct lemony flavour of lemongrass and kaffir lime leaves.

Cooking oil	2 Tbsp
Dried chillies	15
Garlic	6 cloves, peeled
Shallots	8, peeled
Basic stock (page 19)	1 litre (32 fl oz / 4 cups)
Coriander (cilantro) roots	3, bruised
Lemongrass	3 stalks, bruised and halved
Kaffir lime leaves	5
Galangal	5-cm (2-in) knob, peeled and finely sliced
Fish sauce	4 Tbsp
Bird's eye chillies	8, bruised
Salt	1 tsp
Spanish mackerel fillet	500 g (1 lb 1½ oz), cut into 2.5-cm (1-in) pieces

1. Heat cooking oil and stir-fry dried chillies until crisp. Remove and drain well.
2. In the same oil, fry garlic and shallots for about 2–3 minutes or until light brown. Remove and drain well.
3. Combine fried dried chillies, garlic and shallots and grind together into a fine paste.
4. Bring chicken stock to the boil. Add coriander roots, lemongrass, kaffir lime leaves, galangal, fish sauce, bird's eye chillies and salt. Stir well and continue to boil for about 5 minutes.
5. Add ground paste and mackerel and cook for another 5 minutes. Spoon into bowls and garnish as desired. Serve hot.

Thai Vegetable Soup

A spicy vegetable soup filled with the wholesome goodness of carrot, sponge gourd, oyster mushrooms and baby corn cobs.

Water	1.25 litres (40 fl oz / 5 cups)
Lemongrass	1 stalk, bruised
Fish sauce	4 Tbsp
Carrot	1, peeled and cut into 3.5-cm (1½-in) lengths
Bird's eye chillies	4
Sponge (bottle) gourd	500 g (1 lb 1½ oz), peeled and cut into 3.5-cm (1½-in) strips
Fresh oyster mushrooms	150 g (5⅓ oz)
Baby corn cobs	8, cut into 3.5-cm (1½-in) lengths
Thai sweet basil	2 sprigs, plucked
Salt	to taste

PASTE

White peppercorns	10
Dried prawn (shrimp) paste	2.5-cm (1-in) square
Fish sauce	3 Tbsp
Shallots	10, peeled
Dried prawns (shrimps)	150 g (5⅓ oz), soaked and drained

GARNISH

Crisp-fried shallots	1 Tbsp
Bird's eye chillies	3–4
Red chilli	1, chopped

1. Combine paste ingredients and grind until fine.
2. Bring water to the boil, then add finely ground paste and lemongrass. Simmer for 15 minutes.
3. Add fish sauce, carrot and bird's eye chillies and boil for 3 minutes.
4. Add sponge gourd, mushrooms and baby corn. Boil for another 5 minutes.
5. Stir in basil leaves and season with salt.
6. Serve hot, garnished with crisp-fried shallots, bird's eye chillies and chopped red chillies.

Pumpkin Soup with Coconut Cream

A coconut milk-based soup laced with prawns and pumpkin pieces.

Pumpkin	350 g (12 oz)
Lemon juice	1 Tbsp
Prawns (shrimps)	125 g (4½ oz), shelled
Shallots	2, peeled and chopped
Dried prawn (shrimp) paste	1 Tbsp
Bird's eye chillies	2
Water	250 ml (8 fl oz / 1 cup)
Coconut cream	750 ml (24 fl oz / 3 cups)
Ground white pepper	to taste
Thai sweet basil	a handful

1. Slice pumpkin in half and scoop out seeds. Skin and cut flesh into rectangular pieces. Sprinkle pumpkin flesh with lemon juice. Set aside.

2. Pound prawns with shallots, prawn paste and chillies, adding a little of the water if necessary, to form a well-mixed paste.

3. Pour half the coconut cream into a pan. Add prawn mixture and bring to the boil. Reduce heat and stir with a wooden spoon to ensure a smooth consistency.

4. Add pumpkin flesh and cook gently for 10 minutes. Pour in remaining coconut cream and water. Season with pepper. Cover pan and leave to simmer for a further 10 minutes until pumpkin flesh is tender but not mushy. Stir in basil leaves and serve immediately.

VIETNAMESE

Vietnamese Sour Fish Soup

Brightly colourful and appetisingly tangy, this nutritious soup of fish, pineapple and vegetables is full of crunch and a pleasure to the senses.

Mackerel	1, about 1 kg (2 lb 3 oz), or use mudfish (snakehead) or other freshwater fish
Basic pork stock (page 19)	1 litre (32 fl oz / 4 cups)
Salt	1 tsp or to taste
Tamarind juice	20 g (⅔ oz) tamarind pulp mixed with 250 ml (8 fl oz / 1 cup) hot water and strained
Pineapple	½, peeled, quartered lengthways then cut across into 0.5-cm (¼-in) thick slices
Tomatoes	2, each cut into 8 wedges
Bean sprouts	55 g (2 oz), tailed
Chinese celery	55 g (2 oz), leaves separated and stems cut into 3-cm (1½-in) lengths
Minced garlic	1 tsp, crisp-fried
Fish sauce	2 Tbsp
Sliced red chilli	2 Tbsp

SEASONING

Chicken seasoning powder	½ tsp
Fish sauce	½ tsp
Sugar	½ tsp

1. Wash and clean fish. Make 3 diagonal cuts on each side of body. Set aside.

2. Bring stock to the boil. Season with salt. Add fish and allow liquid to return to the boil, then add tamarind juice. Regularly remove scum from liquid surface.

3. When fish is almost cooked, add seasoning ingredients. The soup should taste a bit sour and sweet. Adjust soup to taste, then add pineapple and tomato pieces, bean sprouts and Chinese celery stems. Return liquid to the boil before removing from heat.

4. Transfer all or a portion of fish soup to a serving bowl, then garnish with fried garlic and Chinese celery leaves.

5. Serve fish soup with fish sauce in a small saucer and chilli slices in another.

VIETNAMESE

Pumpkin Soup with Coconut Milk

Sweet pumpkin, creamy coconut milk, and tiny but pungent dried prawns combine to produce a richly flavoured soup.

Coconut milk	300 ml (10 fl oz / 1¼ cups)
Water	800 ml (26 fl oz / 3¼ cups)
Dried prawns (shrimps)	55 g (2 oz), soaked in warm water for 15 minutes then drained well and roughly pounded
Pumpkin	1 kg (2 lb 3 oz), peeled and cut into bite-sized pieces
Straw mushrooms	300 g (11 oz)
Silken bean curd cubes	20, each 5 x 5-cm (2 x 2-in), deep-fried
Chicken seasoning powder	3 tsp
Salt	2 tsp
Ground black pepper	2 tsp

1 Bring coconut milk and water to the boil. Add dried prawns and pumpkin pieces. Cook for 10 minutes over medium heat.

2 Add mushrooms and fried bean curd pieces. Cook for 5 minutes more. Then, season with seasoning powder and salt.

3 Transfer soup into a large serving bowl and season with pepper.

4 Serve with steamed rice.

Soups 93

MAIN COURSES

BALINESE
- *96* Marinated Mahi-mahi Steamed in Bamboo
- *97* Chicken Soup with Vegetables and Eggs
- *98* Mushrooms and Chicken in Banana Leaf
- *99* Pork in Sweet Soy Sauce
- *100* Grilled Chicken
- *101* Roast Chicken in Banana Leaf

CHINESE
- *102* Claypot Fish Head
- *103* Roast Pork Ribs
- *104* Butter Prawns with Toasted Coconut

FILIPINO
- *105* Seafood Chowder
- *106* Vegetable and Chicken Pot Pie
- *107* Macaroni Soup
- *108* Chicken Asado

INDIAN
- *109* Claypot Rice with Spicy Pepper Chicken
- *110* Creamy Mutton Stew
- *111* Indian Shepherd's Pie
- *112* Chilli Sausage on Creamy Potato Mash
- *113* Easy Chicken Tanjine
- *114* Tandoori Chicken

INDONESIAN
- *115* Braised Lamb Shanks in Spiced Coconut Sauce
- *116* Grilled Pork Ribs with Sautéed Vegetables
- *117* Grilled Fish with Tomatoes and Chillies
- *118* Chicken with Tomato Sambal
- *119* Creamy Duck Curry

JAPANESE
- *120* Braised Beef and Potatoes
- *121* Teriyaki Chicken
- *122* Pan-fried Ginger Pork
- *123* Grilled Spanish Mackerel with White Miso Paste

KOREAN
- *124* Mushroom Stew with Vegetables
- *125* Grilled Salmon

THAI
- *126* Duck with Curry
- *127* Crabs with Glass Noodles

BALINESE

Marinated Mahi-mahi steamed in Bamboo

For this dish, the Balinese often replace fish with eel, crab or prawns (shrimps). If bamboo is unavailable, use banana leaves or corn husks as wrappers, then steam or charcoal-grill parcels to cook.

Firm fish fillet	600 g (1 lb 5 ⅓ oz), skinned, cleaned and diced, use mahi-mahi, snapper or mackerel
Seafood spice paste (see pg 20)	125 g (4½ oz)
Lime juice	1 Tbsp
Salt	a pinch
Crushed black peppercorns	a pinch
Grated coconut	100 g (3½ oz)
Coconut cream	125 ml (4 fl oz / ½ cup)
Crisp-fried shallots	2 Tbsp
Crisp-fried garlic	2 Tbsp
Bird's eye chillies	2, finely chopped
Chopped palm sugar	1 tsp
Chopped kaffir lime leaves	½ tsp

STUFFING

Salam leaves	4
Tomatoes	2, halved and sliced
Lemon basil	8 sprigs
Bamboo segments	1 large, or 4 small, scrubbed clean and steamed empty for 30 minutes

1 Combine fish, spice paste, lime juice, salt and pepper in a bowl. Mix well and leave to marinate for 10 minutes in the refrigerator.

2 Add all remaining ingredients to fish and mix well.

3 Place 1 *salam* leaf at one end of a bamboo segment. Add on some fish followed by a slice of tomato and basil, then repeat order of ingredients until cavity is filled.

4 If using 4 small bamboo segments, repeat stuffing process with remaining three segments.

5 Replace bamboo cover and steam for about 15 minutes. Alternatively, place bamboo directly onto hot charcoal and cook for 10 minutes.

BALINESE

Chicken Soup with Vegetables and Eggs

With noodles, assorted vegetables and eggs added, this chicken soup makes a hearty meal.

Indonesian-style stock (page 20)	3 litres (96 fl oz / 12 cups)
Chicken	1, about 1.5 kg (3 lb 4½ oz)
Chicken spice paste (page 15)	2 Tbsp
Kaffir lime leaves	2, torn
Salam leaves	2
Red chillies	2, large, bruised
Bird's eye chillies	2, bruised
Crushed black peppercorns	a pinch
Cabbage	200 g (7 oz), finely shredded
Bean sprouts	200 g (7 oz), cleaned
Chinese celery leaves	50 g (1⅔ oz), finely sliced
Spring onions (scallions)	50 g (1⅔ oz), finely sliced
Glass noodles	100 g (3½ oz), blanched to soften, then cooled in iced water
Salt	to taste
Hard-boiled eggs	4, shelled and cut into wedges
Crisp-fried shallots	

1. Prepare chicken stock. When stock has simmered for 4 hours, add chicken. Simmer for 1 hour, or until chicken is very tender and meat almost falls off the bone.
2. Remove chicken from stock and place into a deep container. Strain chicken stock over chicken. Leave chicken to cool.
3. Drain chicken from cold stock. Separate meat from bones and shred very finely. Discard bones.
4. Return stock to the boil. Add spice paste, lime and salam leaves, chillies and pepper. Simmer until liquid is reduced to about 1.5 litres (48 fl oz / 6 cups).
5. Add cabbage, bean sprouts, celery and spring onions. Simmer for 2 minutes.
6. Add shredded chicken and glass noodles. Return to the boil and simmer for 2 minutes. Season to taste with salt.
7. To serve, ladle soup into individual bowls and garnish with eggs and crisp-fried shallots.

BALINESE

Mushrooms and Chicken in Banana Leaf

Deeply aromatic and flavourful, these steamed parcels are equally delightful eaten on their own or with rice.

Chicken thighs (legs)	500 g (1 lb 1½ oz), boned and cut into 1.5-cm (¾-in) cubes
Shiitake mushrooms	125 g (4½ oz), stems removed and diced
Eggs	2, well beaten
Coconut cream	4 Tbsp
Spring onions (scallions)	50 g (1⅔ oz), finely sliced
Salt	a pinch or to taste
Crushed white peppercorns	a pinch or to taste
Salam leaves	8
Banana leaf wrappers	8, each about 25 x 18-cm (10 x 7-in)

SPICE PASTE

Garlic	30 g (1 oz), peeled and sliced
Shallots	50 g (1⅔ oz), peeled and sliced
Ginger	30 g (1 oz), peeled and sliced
Red chillies	40 g (1⅓ oz), halved, seeded and sliced
Candlenuts	30 g (1 oz), toasted and crushed
Salt	a pinch or to taste
Vegetable oil	3 Tbsp

1. Prepare spice paste. Combine all ingredients, except oil, in a stone mortar or blender and grind until very fine.
2. Heat oil in heavy saucepan. Add spice paste and sauté over medium heat until fragrant, then remove from heat and leave to cool to room temperature.
3. Combine all remaining ingredients, except *salam* and banana leaves, in a large bowl and mix until chicken and mushrooms are well coated.
4. Soften each banana leaf wrapper by either holding it over a gas flame or soaking in boiling water for about 3 seconds.
5. Place a *salam* leaf at the centre of a banana leaf wrapper and top with 2 Tbsp chicken and mushroom mixture.
6. Take one long edge of the wrapper and fold it in towards the centre to cover the ingredients, then roll up tightly. Secure open ends with bamboo skewers or cocktail sticks. Repeat until ingredients are used up.
7. Steam parcels for 4 minutes, then charcoal- or oven-grill for 3 minutes using very low heat. Turn parcels over at least once.
8. Serve as desired.

BALINESE

Pork in Sweet Soy Sauce

Tender cubes of pork are smothered in a thick, lip-smacking sauce that is mildly spicy but definitely whets the appetite.

Vegetable oil	2 Tbsp
Shallots	70 g (2½ oz), peeled and sliced
Garlic	50 g (1⅔ oz), peeled and sliced
Boned pork shoulder or neck	800 g (1¾ lb), cut into 2-cm (1-in) cubes
Ginger	50 g (1⅔ oz), peeled and sliced
Indonesian sweet soy sauce	4 Tbsp
Indonesian salty soy sauce	2 Tbsp
Crushed black peppercorns	a pinch
Indonesian-style stock (page 20)	1 litre (32 fl oz / 4 cups)
Bird's eye chillies	6–10, left whole
Red chillies	2–3, large, left whole

1. Heat oil in a heavy saucepan. Add shallots and garlic and sauté over medium heat for 2 minutes or until lightly coloured.
2. Add pork and ginger. Sauté for 2 minutes.
3. Add both soy sauces and black pepper. Sauté for 1 minute.
4. Pour in half the chicken stock, add chillies and simmer over medium heat for about 1 hour. Top up with more stock as it evaporates.
5. When done, there should be very little sauce left and the meat should be shiny and dark brown in colour.

Main Courses

BALINESE

Grilled Chicken

The smoky flavour of charcoal-grilled meat is inimitably inviting and appetising, but even without it, the chicken here is flavoursome enough to be gripping.

Spring chickens	4, each about 800 g (1¾ lb)
Chicken spice paste (page 15)	250 g (9 oz)
Salt	a pinch or to taste
Crushed black peppercorns	a pinch or to taste
Vegetable oil	2 Tbsp
Lemongrass	2 stalks, bruised
Salam leaves	3
Bird's eye chillies	3–4, bruised
Kaffir lime leaves	2, bruised
Indonesian-style stock (page 20)	1 litre (32 fl oz / 4 cups)
Coconut cream	250 ml (8 fl oz / 1 cup)

BASTING LIQUID (COMBINED)

Chicken spice paste (page 15)	125 g (4½ oz)
Vegetable oil	125 ml (4 fl oz / ½ cup)

1. Cut chicken up into evenly-sized, smaller pieces.
2. Season chicken with half the spice paste, salt and pepper. Cover and leave to marinate in refrigerator.
3. Heat oil in a heavy saucepan. Add remaining spice paste, lemongrass, *salam* leaves, bird's eye chillies and kaffir lime leaves. Sauté over medium heat for 2 minutes.
4. Pour in chicken stock and bring to the boil, then add coconut cream and bring to a simmer.
5. Add chicken, reduce heat and simmer until 75 per cent cooked. Turn chicken frequently when cooking.
6. Leave chicken in sauce to cool to room temperature, then remove and drain well. Reserve sauce.
7. Grill chicken either in the oven or over very hot, glowing charcoal until cooked and golden brown. To make basting liquid, combine all ingredients. Baste frequently.
8. Heat up reserved sauce and simmer until all the liquid is evaporated. Serve as a dipping sauce to go with the grilled chicken.

BALINESE

Roast Chicken in Banana Leaf

Traditionally, the chicken was wrapped in layers of banana stem, not leaves. The thicker stem layers protected the chicken from searing hot coals and cooked the chicken with steam instead of charcoal heat.

Chicken	1, about 1.2 kg (2 lb 10 oz)
Salt	a pinch + more for seasoning
Crushed black peppercorns	a pinch + more for seasoning
Shallots	55 g (2 oz), peeled and sliced
Garlic	25 g (⁴/₅ oz), peeled and chopped
Turmeric	55 g (2 oz), peeled and chopped
Lesser galangal	25 g (⁴/₅ oz), cleaned and sliced
Galangal	25 g (⁴/₅ oz), peeled and sliced
Candlenuts	25 g (⁴/₅ oz), chopped
Bird's eye chillies	5, finely sliced
Red chillies	2, large, seeded and sliced
Lemongrass	4 stalks, bruised, finely sliced and minced
Palm sugar	25 g (⁴/₅ oz), chopped
Cooking oil	2 Tbsp
Tapioca (cassava) leaves	200 g (7 oz), cleaned, blanched for 5 minutes and roughly chopped
Salam leaves	2, left whole
Banana leaves for wrapping	as needed
Bamboo or saté skewers	as needed

1. Clean chicken thoroughly, then season inside and out with salt and pepper. Combine all ingredients except tapioca, *salam* and banana leaves, as well as skewers in a bowl. Mix well. Reserve and set aside one-quarter of mixture.

2. To remaining three-quarters, add tapioca and *salam* leaves. Mix well again. Fill chicken's cavity with mixture, then seal opening with a bamboo or saté skewer. Stuff reserved mixture under chicken's skin, then wrap in several layers of banana leaves and secure with bamboo or saté skewers.

3. Steam parcel for 35 minutes, then remove and open top layers of banana leaves. Transfer open parcel to an oven preheated to 180°C (350°F) and roast for 30–40 minutes. Unwrap to serve.

Main Courses

Claypot Fish Head

Crunchy fish head served with a sweet and tangy sauce in a claypot.

Fish head (garoupa, threadfin, red snapper)	1, about 800 g (1¾ lb), chopped into large pieces
Chinese rice wine	½ Tbsp
Light soy sauce	½ Tbsp
Ginger juice	½ Tbsp
Ground white pepper	½ tsp
Cooking oil	for deep-frying + 3 Tbsp
Soft bean curd	1 square piece, cut into 2.5-cm (1-in) cubes
Ginger	2.5-cm (1-in) knob, peeled and sliced
Onion	1, peeled and cut into 6 wedges
Dried Chinese mushrooms	4
Canned button mushrooms	6–8
Red chillies	2, sliced
Spring onions (scallions)	2, cut into 2.5-cm (1-in) sections
Corn flour (cornstarch)	½ Tbsp, mixed with 1 Tbsp water
Lettuce leaves	6–8, washed

BATTER

Egg	1, beaten
Corn flour (cornstarch)	2 Tbsp
Water	2 Tbsp

SAUCE

Chicken stock (page 20)	250 ml (8 fl oz / 1 cup)
Oyster sauce	1 Tbsp
Light soy sauce	½ Tbsp
Chinese rice wine	2 tsp
Sesame oil	1 tsp
Sugar	1 tsp
Ground white pepper	½ tsp

1. Clean fish head and marinate with rice wine, soy sauce, ginger juice and pepper for 30 minutes.
2. Heat wok with oil for deep-frying until hot. Coat fish head with batter and deep-fry fish head for 5–8 minutes on each side until golden brown and cooked. Set aside.
3. Put in bean curd and deep-fry for 2 minutes. Drain from oil and leave aside.
4. Heat claypot with 3 Tbsp cooking oil and sauté ginger and onion until fragrant.
5. Put in mushrooms and stir-fry for 1 minute. Add button mushrooms and chillies and toss briskly.
6. Pour in combined sauce ingredients and bring to the boil.
7. Put in fish head and bean curd. Reduce heat a little, cover and simmer for 5–8 minutes. Add spring onions and thicken with corn flour mixture.
8. Arrange lettuce leaves around sides of claypot and serve immediately.

Roast Pork Ribs

Pork ribs marinated in garlic and ginger and roasted over a slow fire.

Pork ribs	1.2 kg (2 lb 10 oz), kept in whole panels about 10–12-cm (4–5-in) long
Garlic	4 cloves, peeled and finely chopped
Ginger	2 thin slices, peeled
Star anise	1 piece
Maltose	1 Tbsp

SEASONING

Coarse sugar	110 g (4 oz)
Light soy sauce	3 Tbsp
Thick soy sauce	1 tsp
Oyster sauce	2 Tbsp
Hoisin sauce	1½ Tbsp
Plum sauce	1½ Tbsp
Chinese rice wine	1 Tbsp
Ginger powder	½ tsp
Five-spice powder	1 tsp
Sesame oil	1 Tbsp
Ground white pepper	¼ tsp
Red colouring	¼ tsp

1. Rinse panels of ribs. Dry well with kitchen paper.
2. Mix seasoning ingredients in a bowl. Put in garlic, ginger and star anise. Mix well. Pour mixture over ribs and marinate for at least 8–10 hours (preferably overnight) in the refrigerator.
3. Preheat oven to 220°C (440°F) for 15 minutes. Place ribs on a wire rack and roast for at least 1 hour, basting ribs with marinade occasionally and turning ribs over every 15 minutes.
4. Pour remaining marinade into a small saucepan and add maltose. Stir over low heat until maltose dissolves.
5. To coat ribs, dip them one by one into maltose mixture. Grill on each side for 3–5 minutes or until well roasted.

CHINESE

Butter Prawns with Toasted Coconut

Buttered shrimps tossed with toasted coconut is an unmistakably luscious dish.

Large prawns (shrimps)	500 g (1 lb 1½ oz), feelers trimmed
Salt	1 tsp
Ground white pepper	½ tsp
Cooking oil	as needed
Butter	85 g (3 oz)
Pan-toasted grated coconut	55 g (2 oz), blended until fine
Sugar	2 tsp
Bird's eye chillies	10, finely sliced
Chopped spring onion (scallion)	as desired
Chopped coriander leaves (cilantro)	as desired
Small lime	1, juice extracted

OMELETTE

Eggs	2, beaten
Light soy sauce	1 tsp
Salt	¼ tsp
Ground white pepper	½ tsp

1. Season prawns with ½ tsp salt and pepper for 30 minutes.
2. Combine omelette ingredients. Heat 1 Tbsp oil in a pan and pour in omelette mixture. Swirl mixture around to form a thin omelette. When omelette sets, flip it over carefully to cook on the other side.
3. Leave omelette to cool before slicing into fine strips. Set aside.
4. Heat oil for deep-frying and fry seasoned prawns until just cooked. Drain from oil.
5. Heat butter over low heat and put in toasted coconut, sugar, ½ tsp salt and bird's eye chillies. Toss well until fragrant. Add finely chopped omelette, spring onion, coriander leaves and lime juice.
6. Dish out and serve immediately.

Seafood Chowder

Also known as bouillabaisse or Fisherman's soup, this is a medley of seafood that is simmered in a rich broth of tomatoes and fish stock. It is the Filipino adaptation of a Spanish recipe that is served on special occasions.

Water	2 litres (64 fl oz / 8 cups)
Onions	2, large, peeled and sliced + 1, peeled and minced
Leeks	100 g (3½ oz), ends trimmed and finely sliced
Bay leaf	½
Clams	200 g (7 oz), scrubbed, then soaked in cold water for 30 minutes
Fish fillets	250 g (9 oz), sliced
Ground black pepper	1 tsp
Chicken or beef stock cube	½
Olive oil	4 Tbsp
Garlic	1 head, peeled and minced
Canned whole tomatoes	1 can, 440 g (15¾ oz), drain and chopped
Red capsicums (bell peppers)	125 g (4½ oz), cored, seeded and sliced into strips
Prawns (shrimps)	6, large, peeled and deveined, leaving tail intact
Squid	250 g (9 oz), sliced into 1-cm (½-in) thick rings
Sugar	2 Tbsp
Salt	to taste
Dried thyme	1 tsp

1. In a large pot, add water, sliced onions, leeks, bay leaf, clams, fish, pepper and chicken or beef stock cube. Bring mixture to the boil, then leave to simmer over medium heat for 15 minutes. Discard any clams that do not open. Remove from heat and set aside.
2. Meanwhile, heat oil in a large saucepan over medium heat and fry garlic and minced onion until fragrant and onion is translucent. Add tomatoes and capsicums and stir to mix well.
3. Add prawns, squid and broth mixture. Increase heat and bring to the boil, then reduce heat to medium and leave to simmer for 5 minutes.
4. Season with sugar and salt and leave mixture to simmer for another 3 minutes.
5. Sprinkle with thyme and remove from heat. Dish out and serve immediately.

FILIPINO

Vegetable and Chicken Pot Pie

The rich and creamy mixture of chicken and vegetables goes well with the light and flaky puff pastry crust, making this hearty dish a welcome treat!

Chicken breast	750 g (1 lb 10½ oz), skinned
Water	750 ml (24 fl oz / 3 cups) or more if necessary
Butter	110 g (4 oz)
Garlic	5 cloves, peeled and minced
Spanish onion	1, medium, peeled and sliced
Chorizo	85 g (3 oz), sliced diagonally
Potatoes	300 g (11 oz), peeled and cut into 2.5-cm (1-in) cubes
Carrots	100 g (3½ oz), peeled and cut into 2.5-cm (1-in) cubes
Broccoli florets	250 g (9 oz), blanched
Red capsicum (bell pepper)	85 g (3 oz), cored, seeded and sliced
Fresh or canned button mushrooms	100 g (3½ oz), sliced
Green olives	85 g (3 oz), pitted and halved
Grated Cheddar cheese	100 g (3½ oz)
Plain (all-purpose) flour	55 g (2 oz)
Milk	125 ml (4 fl oz / ½ cup)
Salt	1 tsp
Ground white pepper	½ tsp
Dried Italian herb mix or dried basil leaves	½ tsp
Egg wash	1 egg yolk beaten with 1 Tbsp fresh milk
Frozen puff pastry	200 g (7 oz), leave to thaw for 1 hour at room temperature

1. Place chicken in a saucepan and add enough water to cover. Bring to the boil over high heat, then reduce heat and simmer for 25 minutes or until chicken is cooked and tender. Remove chicken and reserve 625 ml (20 fl oz / 2½ cups) boiling liquid.

2. Cut chicken into 1-cm (½-in) pieces and set aside.

3. In a saucepan, melt 55 g (2 oz) butter. Fry garlic until fragrant, then add onion and fry until soft. Add chicken pieces and chorizo and fry for 2 minutes.

4. Add potatoes, carrots, broccoli, capsicum and mushrooms and fry for 5 minutes.

5. Add 250 ml (8 fl oz / 1 cup) reserved boiling liquid and olives. Reduce heat to simmer until vegetables are tender. Add cheese and stir to mix well. Cook for another 2 minutes and remove from heat.

6. In a separate saucepan, melt remaining butter over medium heat. Gradually add flour, stirring constantly until a smooth paste is formed.

7. Remove from heat and add remaining boiling liquid and milk, stirring continuously with a whisk to avoid lumps from forming.

8. Return flour mixture to stove and cook over low heat until sauce thickens. Season with salt, pepper and Italian herb mix. Add chicken and vegetable mixture and stir to mix well. Remove from heat and transfer mixture to a large ovenproof baking dish.

9. Preheat oven to 190°C (370°F). Lightly dust a clean work surface with flour. Roll out puff pastry to a suitable size for baking dish. Place over baking dish, seal and crimp edges to seal. Brush pastry with egg wash and prick with a fork to allow steam to escape while baking.

10. Bake for 30 minutes or until pastry is puffed and golden brown. Serve immediately.

FILIPINO

Macaroni Soup

This well-loved Filipino comfort food is imbued with the rich taste of chicken and milk, and the refreshing flavours of carrots and celery. In the Philippines, stock made from ham hock is used to give this soup a rich and smoky flavour.

Cooking oil	4 Tbsp
Garlic	2 cloves, peeled and finely chopped
Onion	1, large, peeled and minced
Chicken breast or fillet	200 g (7 oz), skin removed and cut into 2.5-cm (1-in) pieces
Carrot	55 g (2 oz), peeled and finely diced
Celery	30 g (1 oz), peeled and finely diced
Basic chicken stock (page 19) or water	1.5 litres (48 fl oz / 6 cups)
Elbow macaroni	200 g (7 oz)
Milk	375 ml (12 fl oz / 1½ cups)
Butter	40 g (1⅓ oz)
Ground white pepper	½ tsp
Salt	to taste

1. In a large saucepan, heat oil over medium heat. Fry garlic until light brown, then add onion and fry until soft.
2. Add chicken, carrot and celery and stir-fry for 3 minutes. Add chicken stock or water and bring mixture to the boil.
3. Add macaroni and cook for 8–10 minutes or until al dente. Reduce heat to low and add milk while stirring continuously. Add butter, then season with pepper and salt to taste. Leave mixture to simmer for 5–7 minutes or until soup is of desired consistency.
4. Dish out into serving bowls and serve immediately.

FILIPINO

Chicken Asado

Unlike the Spanish *asado*, where meat is roasted or grilled over a fire, This Filipino version braises the chicken in a tangy marinade before deep-frying it for a crispy, mouth-watering texture. If possible, marinate the chicken a day in advance to achieve a fuller, richer flavour.

Pineapple juice	375 ml (12 fl oz / 1½ cups)
Lemon juice	1 Tbsp
Light soy sauce	3 Tbsp
Dark soy sauce	3 Tbsp
Salt	to taste
Ground black pepper	to taste
Chicken	1, about 1.2 kg (2 lb 10 oz)
Brown sugar	55 g (2 oz)
Garlic	3 cloves, peeled and crushed
Bay leaf	1
Water	500 ml (16 fl oz / 2 cups) or more if necessary
Cooking oil	for deep-frying

ASADO SAUCE

Cooking oil	4 Tbsp
Garlic	2 cloves, peeled and minced
Spanish onions	2, large, peeled and sliced into rings
Tomato	1, medium, seeded and minced
Reserved marinade from boiling chicken	
Salt	½ tsp
Ground black pepper	1 tsp

1. Combine pineapple and lemon juice and soy sauces in a large bowl. Add salt and pepper and stir to mix well. Place chicken in to steep in the marinade. Refrigerate for 3 hours or overnight, if preparing a day in advance. Reserve marinade.

2. Transfer chicken to a large wok with marinade. Add sugar, garlic, bay leaf and enough water to cover chicken. Bring to the boil over high heat.

3. Reduce heat to medium, cover wok and leave to simmer until chicken is cooked and tender and liquid has reduced by half. Remove chicken and set aside to cool. Discard bay leaf and reserve boiling liquid.

4. Prepare asado sauce. In a saucepan, heat oil over medium heat and fry garlic until golden brown. Add onion and fry until soft, then add tomato and stir to mix well.

5. Add reserved boiling liquid and bring to the boil. Reduce heat and leave to simmer for 5 minutes. Season with salt and pepper. Taste and adjust seasoning, if necessary. Remove from heat, transfer to a bowl and set aside.

6. Using the same wok, heat oil for deep-frying over medium to high heat. Gently lower in chicken and deep-fry until chicken is crisp and golden brown. To achieve an even colour and crispness, ladle oil all over chicken for 10–15 minutes. Remove chicken and leave to drain on absorbent paper. Transfer chicken to a serving platter and spoon asado sauce over. Serve immediately.

INDIAN

Claypot Rice with Spicy Pepper Chicken

This is an easy one-dish meal, inspired by the popular Chinese claypot recipe. Here, spices are added to excite the taste buds.

Chicken	1, about 1 kg (2 lb 3 oz)
Cooking oil	1½ Tbsp
Onion	1, peeled and sliced
Garlic	3 cloves, peeled and minced
Ground white pepper	1 Tbsp
Ground black pepper	1 Tbsp
Salt	1 tsp
Curry leaves	1 stalk
Cumin powder	1 tsp
Chilli powder	½ Tbsp
Dark soy sauce	1 Tbsp

GINGER AND GARLIC PASTE

Rice	
Long grain or Basmati rice	370 g (13¼ oz)
Water	750 ml (24 fl oz / 3 cups)
Ginger	1-cm (½-in) knob, peeled and chopped
Garlic	5 cloves, peeled and chopped
Salt	½ tsp
Screwpine leaves	2, crushed and tied into a knot

GARNISH

Fried shallots	1½ Tbsp
Spring onions (scallions)	55 g (2 oz), chopped
Cashew nuts	a handful, toasted
Raisins or sultanas	a handful, fried
Red and green chilli	1 each, sliced

1. Cut chicken into 12–14 equal-size pieces. Smaller pieces will cook faster. Heat oil in a wok and add onion and garlic. Allow to brown slightly then add chicken and keep frying until colour changes.

2. Add in all remaining ingredients. (Do not add any water to the wok.) Mix well then lower heat and prepare rice.

3. Blend ingredients for ginger and garlic paste. Wash and drain rice completely. Put rice, water, ginger and garlic, salt and screwpine leaves into a clay pot. Bring to the boil and stir. Reduce heat, cover and cook for a further 5 minutes.

4. Uncover pot and place chicken over rice. Replace cover and cook for 10–12 minutes over very low heat to prevent burning. Garnish and serve immediately.

INDIAN

Creamy Mutton Stew

This dish goes well with Indian breads such as *appoms*, *dosas* or crusty French bread.

Potatoes	6, halved and boiled in their skins
Onions	2, peeled and sliced
Green chillies	5, split in half lengthwise
Ginger	2.5-cm (1-in) knob, peeled and sliced
Curry leaves	4 stalks
Mutton	300 g (11 oz), diced and boiled until tender, stock reserved
Salt	to taste
Coconut milk	125 ml (4 fl oz / ½ cup)
Fresh milk	125 ml (4 fl oz / ½ cup)
Cooking oil	1 Tbsp
Ground white pepper	1–2 tsp

1. Peel and mash potatoes. Place in a pan and add enough water to cover mashed potatoes.
2. Add onions, green chillies, ginger and 2 stalks of curry leaves. Bring to a slow boil and stir to mix.
3. Add cooked mutton and stock. Add salt and stir in coconut milk and fresh milk. Cook for 15 minutes.
4. Put in remaining curry leaves, drizzle in oil and swirl the pot to mix. Add pepper to taste.
5. Set aside for at least 30 minutes before serving with bread.

Indian Shepherd's Pie

The use of chilli powder in this version of shepherd's pie makes it lightly spicy.

FILLING

Cooking oil	
Onion	1, peeled and minced
Garlic	5 cloves, peeled and minced
Mutton or lamb	500 g (1 lb 1½ oz), minced
Canned stewed tomatoes	1 can, 411 g (14⅔ oz)
Chilli powder	1 Tbsp
Cumin powder	1 tsp, toasted
Freshly ground black pepper	1 Tbsp
Tomato paste	1 Tbsp
Coriander leaves (cilantro)	25 g (⅘ oz), chopped
Salt	to taste

TOPPING

Potatoes	6–7, boiled in skins until soft then peeled
Fresh milk	125 ml (4 fl oz / ½ cup)
Salt	to taste
Ground black pepper	to taste
Bread crumbs	55 g (2 oz)
Carrots	55 g (2 oz), peeled and shredded
Coriander leaves (cilantro)	25 g (⅘ oz), minced
Cheddar cheese	55 g (2 oz), grated
Mozzarella cheese	55 g (2 oz), grated

1. Heat some oil and sauté onions and garlic until fragrant. Add meat and cook until colour changes.
2. Add all remaining filling ingredients and mix well. Cook until meat is done and liquid has almost dried up.
3. Roughly mash potatoes and mix in milk, salt and pepper.
4. Spoon meat into an ovenproof dish and level it out. Top with mashed potatoes, then sprinkle bread crumbs, carrots, coriander leaves and cheeses over.
5. Bake in a preheated oven at 180°C (350°F) until top is golden brown. Remove from oven and leave to cool slightly before serving.

INDIAN

Chilli Sausage on Creamy Potato Mash

Olive oil	
Garlic	5 cloves, peeled and minced
Onion	1, peeled and minced
Streaky bacon	4 rashers, chopped into small pieces
Canned kidney beans	450 g (1 lb), reserve can for use later
Water	as needed
Chilli powder	2 tsp
Toasted cumin powder	1 tsp
Ground black pepper	1 tsp
Salt	to taste
Canned condensed tomato soup	250 g (9 oz)
Fat, juicy sausages	6, scored

MASH

Potatoes	4, boiled in skins until soft then peeled
Butter	2 tsp
Salt	to taste
Black peppercorns	1 Tbsp, crushed
Milk	180 ml (6 fl oz / ¾ cup)

GARNISH

Onions	2, peeled and thinly sliced
Coriander leaves (cilantro)	1 sprig, chopped

1. In a saucepan, sauté minced garlic and onion in 1 Tbsp olive oil until golden brown.
2. Add bacon and fry until slightly crisp.
3. Pour in kidney beans. Fill empty kidney beans can with water and set aside.
4. Add chilli and cumin powders, pepper and salt. Mix well then pour in tomato soup. Mix again before adding water from kidney beans can. Simmer over low heat. Meanwhile, on a griddle, slow cook sausages with 1 tsp olive oil until skin becomes crispy.
5. Put sausages into the pot with kidney beans and cook for another 15 minutes. Add some chopped coriander leaves.
6. Caramelise onions in a pan and set aside for garnishing. Prepare mash. Mash potatoes while still hot. Add butter, salt and pepper. Add milk and mix until creamy and light.
7. Add half the fried onions and remaining coriander leaves to mash and mix.
8. Serve sausages and beans topped with caramelised onions and coriander. Serve with mash.

INDIAN

Easy Chicken Tajine

A tajine is a deep-glazed earthenware dish with a conical lid used throughout North Africa. Meals cooked using a tajine are usually slow-braised, and are also known as tajines. This recipe, however, does not require a tajine.

Stewed tomatoes	400 g (14⅓ oz)
Garlic	4 cloves, peeled
Meat curry powder	½ Tbsp
Cumin powder	½ Tbsp, toasted
Kitchen king masala	1 tsp (optional)
Black peppercorns	1 tsp
Salt	to taste
Sugar	1 tsp
Boneless chicken meat	400 g (14⅓ oz), diced
Canned chickpeas	55 g (2 oz), with brine
Dried apricots	10, sliced
Raisins or sultanas	20 g (⅔ oz)

GARNISH
Red, yellow and green capsicum (bell pepper) cubes
Sliced dried apricots
Chopped coriander leaves (cilantro)

1. Puree stewed tomatoes with garlic. Pour into a saucepan. Bring to a slow boil.

2. Add meat curry powder, cumin powder, kitchen king masala, pepper, salt and sugar. Return to the boil then add chicken, chickpeas, apricots and raisins or sultanas. Simmer until chicken is cooked and tender.

3. Taste and adjust seasoning if necessary. Garnish with capsicum cubes, sliced apricots and chopped coriander leaves or as desired. Serve with bread, rice or couscous.

Main Courses

INDIAN

Tandoori Chicken

Although there are many ingredients to this recipe, it is not difficult to do. You only have to blend the ingredients together and marinate the chicken.

Chicken breasts	10 (with bones), washed and drained
Ghee (clarified butter)	55 g (2 oz)
Mango powder	3 Tbsp (optional)
Coarse chilli powder	2 Tbsp

MARINADE
Shallots	10, peeled
Garlic	6 cloves, peeled
Ginger	2.5-cm (1-in) knob, peeled
Sugar	1 tsp
Salt	1½ tsp
Chilli paste or powder	1½ Tbsp
Tomato paste	1½ Tbsp
Dijon mustard	2 tsp
Yoghurt	125 g (4½ oz)
Cumin	½ tsp, dry-toasted and finely ground
Garam masala	½ tsp
Saffron	10 strands
Red food colouring	¼ tsp
Mango chutney	2 Tbsp
Lemon juice	2 Tbsp

GARNISH
Lemon wedges
Sliced onions
Coriander leaves (cilantro)

1. Combine and grind ingredients for marinade. Pat chicken dry with absorbent paper and prick chicken or make shallow cuts on chicken to allow marinade to penetrate.

2. Rub marinade into meat thoroughly. Cover and refrigerate for at least 1 hour. Preheat oven to 200°C (400°F). Place chicken on a tray lined with greaseproof paper or aluminium foil and bake for 30 minutes until done.

3. Sprinkle half the ghee, mango and chilli powders all over chicken. Turn chicken over and sprinkle remaining ghee, mango and chilli powders over. Bake for another 15 minutes. Garnish and serve.

INDONESIAN

Braised Lamb Shanks in Spiced Coconut Sauce

Like many Indonesian stews and braised dishes, the sauce here is fantastically delicious. Offal and tripe can also be used in this recipe.

Lamb shanks	800 g (1¾ lb), use whole and trimmed or cut into 3-cm (1½-in) slices
Lamb shoulder	400 g (14⅓ oz), cut into 2-cm (1-in) cubes
Vegetable oil	3 Tbsp
East Javanese yellow spice paste (page 16)	250 g (9 oz)
Cardamom pods	1 Tbsp, crushed
Cinnamon	2 sticks, each about 10-cm (4-in) long, bruised
Cloves	10, crushed
Grated palm sugar	1 Tbsp
Lemongrass	3 stalks, bruised
Kaffir lime leaves	3, bruised
Indonesian-style stock (page 20)	500 ml (16 fl oz / 2 cups)
Coconut milk or milk	250 ml (8 fl oz / 1 cup)
Salt	to taste
Freshly ground black pepper	to taste
Celery leaves	25 g (⅘ oz), sliced
Leek or spring onions (scallions)	25 g (⅘ oz), sliced
Tomatoes	50 g (1⅔ oz), halved, seeded and diced
Crisp-fried shallots	2 Tbsp
Melinjo nut crackers	50 g (1⅔ oz), deep-fried
Lime	1, cut into wedges
Nasi goreng sauce (page 19)	3 Tbsp

1. Bring 3 litres (96 fl oz / 12 cups) water to the boil in a large pot. Add lamb shanks and meat and return to the boil.
2. Remove lamb and rinse under running water. Discard boiling liquid and set meat aside to drain well. Heat oil in a large, heavy saucepan.
3. Add spice paste, cardamoms, cinnamon, cloves, palm sugar, lemongrass and kaffir lime leaves. Sauté for 2 minutes or until fragrant.
4. Add lamb and stir over medium heat until it is evenly covered with spice paste.
5. Add half the stock or just enough to cover meat. Bring to the boil and simmer over medium-low heat until meat is nearly cooked. Regularly check liquid level and add small amounts of stock as it reduces.
6. Add coconut milk or milk, return to the boil and simmer until meat is tender and comes away from the bone easily.
7. Season to taste with salt and pepper, then stir in celery, leek, tomatoes and fried shallots. Serve with crackers, lime and *nasi goreng* sauce on the side.

INDONESIAN

Grilled Pork Ribs with Sautéed Vegetables

This recipe requires the meat to be steamed before grilling, but the extra step taken is well worth it as the meat remains succulent.

Pork ribs	500 g (1 lb 1½ oz), cut into 100 g (3½ oz) portions
Shallots	85 g (3 oz), peeled and sliced
Ginger	20 g (⅔ oz), peeled and finely sliced
Vegetable oil	3 Tbsp + enough for grilling
Indonesian-style stock (page 20)	150 ml (5 fl oz / ⅗ cup)
Lemongrass	2 stalks, bruised
Water convolvulus (kang kong)	75 g (2⅔ oz), cleaned and sliced
Spring onions (scallions)	75 g (2⅔ oz), cut into 4-cm (2-in) lengths
Green (French) beans	75 g (2⅔ oz), sliced
Tomatoes	75 g (2⅔ oz), peeled, seeded and sliced
Salt	to taste

MARINADE (COMBINED)
Lime juice	3 Tbsp
Vegetable oil	3 Tbsp
Salt	1 tsp
Ground white pepper	½ Tbsp

1. Steam pork ribs for 45 minutes, then remove and cool to room temperature. Mix ribs with marinade and set aside for 30 minutes so flavours can penetrate meat.

2. Grill ribs either in the oven or over medium charcoal heat, basting frequently with oil. When done, set ribs aside to rest. Combine shallots and ginger in a stone mortar or blender and grind into a fine paste.

3. Heat 3 Tbsp oil in heavy saucepan, add paste and lemongrass and sauté over low heat until fragrant. Add splashes of stock to prevent burning. Add all vegetables, increase heat and sauté vegetables with 3 Tbsp stock for 2 minutes or until vegetables are cooked.

4. Season to taste with salt, then add pork ribs and mix well. Dish out. Garnish, if desired, with crisp-fried shallots and serve.

INDONESIAN

Grilled Fish with Tomatoes and Chillies

Instead of using a whole fish, this recipe can also be prepared with firm fish fillets, such as snapper, mahi-mahi or mackerel. Use approximately 600 g (1 lb 5 oz) in place of whole fish.

Whole fish (snapper or other firm-fleshed fish)	4, each about 500 g (1 lb 1½ oz)
SEASONING	
Salt	to taste
Freshly crushed white pepper	¼ tsp
Lime juice	2 Tbsp
Vegetable oil	2 Tbsp + more for basting
SAUCE	
Tomatoes	200 g (7 oz), peeled, halved, seeded and diced
Bird's eye chillies	5–10, sliced, use more or less according to taste
Shallots	50 g (1⅔ oz), peeled and sliced
Lime juice	2 Tbsp
Salt	a pinch
Vegetable oil	3 Tbsp

1. Use a sharp knife to make 4 slits, each about 2-cm (1-in) deep, on both sides of fish. This not only helps the seasoning to better penetrate the fish, but also helps the fish to cook more evenly.
2. Rub fish with seasoning ingredients, then refrigerate or leave in a cool place for 30 minutes to marinate.
3. Meanwhile, prepare sauce. Combine all ingredients and mix well, then set aside in a cool place for 30 minutes.
4. Grill fish over hot charcoal for a few minutes on each side, basting frequently with vegetable oil. This prevents the fish from sticking to the grill and helps the seasoning to penetrate the fish. Alternatively, oven-grill until cooked.
5. Remove grilled fish and place on a serving platter. Serve with sauce spooned on top or on the side.

Main Courses 117

INDONESIAN

Chicken with Tomato Sambal

This dish of tender chicken with an appetising sauce that is mildly spicy and tangy goes brilliantly with plain, steamed rice.

Spring chickens	4, each about 750 g (1 lb 11 oz), quartered
Salt	1 Tbsp
Freshly crushed black pepper	½ Tbsp
Lime juice	2 Tbsp
Vegetable oil	4 Tbsp
Indonesian-style stock (page 20)	500 ml (16 fl oz / 2 cups)
Shallots	40 g (1⅓ oz), peeled and chopped
Garlic	30 g (1 oz), peeled and chopped
Tomatoes	10 g (⅓ oz), peeled, halved, seeded and diced
Lemon basil	2 Tbsp, sliced
Lime juice	4 Tbsp
Indonesian sweet soy sauce	2 Tbsp
Salt	a pinch or to taste
Freshly crushed black pepper	a pinch or to taste

SPICE PASTE

Red chillies	100 g (3½ oz), halved, seeded and sliced
Bird's eye chillies	25 g (⅘ oz), sliced
Shallots	55 g (2 oz), peeled and sliced
Garlic	40 g (1⅓ oz), peeled and sliced
Dried prawn (shrimp) paste	½ Tbsp, toasted

1. Season chicken with salt, pepper and lime juice. Refrigerate or leave in a cool place for 30 minutes.
2. Meanwhile, prepare spice paste. Combine all ingredients in a stone mortar or blender and grind into a very fine paste.
3. Heat half the oil in a large, heavy saucepan and sauté spice paste over medium heat until fragrant. Add chicken pieces and sauté until they are evenly coated with spice paste.
4. Stir in stock and bring to the boil, then reduce heat, cover and simmer until chicken is tender and most of the liquid has evaporated.
5. Remove chicken from saucepan and keep warm, then add remaining oil to saucepan and heat.
6. Add all remaining ingredients and sauté for 1 minute or until they are warmed through. Adjust seasoning to taste before serving. Garnish, if desired, with a sprig of lemon basil.

INDONESIAN

Creamy Duck Curry

The robust flavour of duck is complemented beautifully in this recipe by the generous use of spices, both dry and fresh.

Duck	1, about 2 kg (4 lb 6 oz), cleaned
Salt	to taste
Vegetable oil	2 Tbsp
Indonesian-style stock (page 20)	1 litre (32 fl oz / 4 cups)
Coconut milk	400 ml (13 fl oz / 1⅔ cups)
Crisp-fried shallots	2 Tbsp

SPICE PASTE

Red chillies	55 g (2 oz), seeded and sliced
Bird's eye chillies	2–4, sliced
Shallots	100 g (3½ oz), peeled and sliced
Garlic	20 g (⅔ oz), peeled and sliced
Galangal	25 g (⅘ oz), peeled and chopped
Lesser galangal	20 g (⅔ oz), washed and sliced
Turmeric	35 g (1 oz), peeled and sliced
Candlenuts	15 g (½ oz)
Dried prawn (shrimp) paste	½ tsp
Coriander seeds	½ tsp, crushed
Crushed black pepper	¼ tsp
Grated nutmeg	¼ tsp
Cloves	2
Vegetable oil	2 Tbsp
Lemongrass	2 stalks, bruised and knotted
Salam leaves	2

1. Cut duck into 12 pieces and set aside. Prepare spice paste. Combine all ingredients, except lemongrass and salam leaves, in a blender and grind coarsely.

2. Transfer blended ingredients to a heavy saucepan. Add remaining spice paste ingredients, 125 ml (4 fl oz / ½ cup) water and a pinch of salt or to taste.

3. Simmer over medium heat for 1 hour or until all the liquid has evaporated and paste is golden. Remove from heat and leave to cool completely before using.

4. Mix duck with one-third of the spice paste and refrigerate for 1 hour to marinate.

5. Heat oil in a stewing pan and sauté remaining spice paste until fragrant. Add duck and continue to sauté until meat changes colour. Add half the stock or just enough to cover duck pieces. Bring to the boil, reduce heat and simmer until meat is cooked. Regularly check liquid level and add more stock as it evaporates during cooking.

6. Continue until duck is tender to your liking, adding coconut milk near the end. When sauce has reduced to a creamy consistency, adjust seasoning to taste and dish out. Garnish as desired with crisp-fried shallots and serve.

Main Courses 119

JAPANESE

Braised Beef and Potatoes

Ask your local butcher for thinly sliced beef of a tender cut that is suitable for a simmered *sukiyaki* dish. Packaged sukiyaki-style beef is also available at the chilled section of most Japanese supermarkets.

Sesame oil	1½ Tbsp
White onions	1½, peeled and cut into wedges along the grain
Thinly sliced beef	200 g (7 oz), cut into bite-size pieces
Potatoes	4, medium, peeled and cut into chunks, soaked, then drained before use
Carrot	1, medium, peeled and roll cut into wedges
Hot water	300 ml (10 fl oz / 1¼ cups)
French beans	85 g (3 oz), trimmed and cut into 4-cm (1¾-in) lengths, then blanched

SEASONING

Sugar	1½ Tbsp
Mirin	1½ Tbsp
Japanese dark soy sauce	2½–3 Tbsp

1. Combine seasoning ingredients in a small bowl. Mix well and set aside. Heat oil in a pot over high heat, then add onions and beef and stir-fry for 1–2 minutes.

2. Add seasoning and simmer briefly until all liquid is absorbed. Add potatoes, carrot and hot water.

3. Cover and simmer over medium-high heat for about 15 minutes, until sauce is mostly absorbed.

4. Stir in French beans and simmer for 1 minute to heat through. Remove from heat.

5. Transfer to a serving bowl and serve hot with rice, if desired.

Teriyaki Chicken

This simple Japanese dish of pan-fried chicken coated in a sweet soy sauce marinade is a popular favourite among children and adults alike.

Boneless chicken thighs	400 g (14⅓ oz)
Cooking oil	2 Tbsp
Japanese dark soy sauce	2 Tbsp
Mirin	2 Tbsp
Sake	2 Tbsp
Mayonnaise	to taste
Ground Japanese pepper	to taste

GARNISHING

White radish (daikon)	¼, peeled and finely julienned
White radish sprouts	1 small bunch, cut into 3-cm (1¼-in) lengths, soaked in ice water and drained before use

1. Trim and discard excess fat from chicken thighs. Make a few deep cuts in the thickest part of the flesh.
2. Heat oil in a frying pan over high heat. Place chicken in, skin side first. Cover and pan-fry for about 2 minutes.
3. Remove lid, turn chicken over and cover to pan-fry other side over medium heat for about 5 minutes, until brown and cooked.
4. Combine soy sauce, mirin and sake in a small bowl, then pour sauce over chicken in pan. Cook for about 1 minute until chicken is well-coated, and sauce is reduced. Remove from heat.
5. Arrange chicken on a serving plate. Garnish with shredded white radish and radish sprouts as desired.
6. Serve with mayonnaise on the side. Sprinkle chicken with ground Japanese pepper, if desired.

JAPANESE

Pan-fried Ginger Pork

This is one of my favourite quick-and-easy recipes—I prepare it whenever I am pressed for time.

Pork tenderloin (fillet)	500 g (1 lb 1½ oz), cut into 0.5-cm (¼-in) thick slices
Sake	1 Tbsp
Dark soy sauce (*koikuchi shoyu*)	2 Tbsp
Mirin	2 Tbsp
Sake	2 Tbsp
Sesame oil	2 tsp
Sugar	2 tsp
Grated old ginger	2 Tbsp
Grated garlic	2 tsp
Cooking oil	1 Tbsp

PARSLEY POTATOES

Potatoes	2, medium, peeled and cubed
Finely chopped parsley	1 tsp
Ground black pepper	to taste
Salt	to taste

GARNISHING

White radish sprouts	a small bunch, soaked in ice water and drained before use
Cherry tomatoes	2–3, halved

1 Prepare parsley potatoes. Boil potato cubes for 10–15 minutes until soft and cooked. Drain thoroughly and place in a mixing bowl. Sprinkle with chopped parsley, pepper and salt, then toss to mix well. Set aside.

2 Marinate pork in sake for 5 minutes. In a small bowl, whisk together soy sauce, mirin, sake, sesame oil, sugar, ginger and garlic until well-blended. Set aside.

3 Heat oil in a frying pan over high heat. Stir-fry pork briefly for 1–2 minutes, until meat changes colour.

4 Add seasoning mixture to pan and simmer briefly for 1–2 minutes until pork is cooked. Remove from heat.

5 Transfer to a serving plate. Arrange potatoes on the side and garnish with radish sprouts and cherry tomatoes. Serve with rice and a simple green salad, if desired.

JAPANESE

Grilled Spanish Mackerel with White Miso Paste

A local dish in Kyoto, the main seasoning ingredient used is white soy bean paste, or *saikyo miso*, a local speciality of the prefecture. Substitute Spanish mackerel with yellowtail, sea bream, salmon, squid, scallop or white pomfret, if preferred.

Spanish mackerel fillets	2, each about 100 g (3½ oz)
Salt	¼ tsp

PICKLED LOTUS ROOT

Rice vinegar	75 ml (2½ fl oz / ⅓ cup)
Water	500 ml (16 fl oz / 2 cups)
Lotus root	200 g (7 oz)
Sugar	1½ Tbsp
Salt	⅓ tsp

MARINADE

White soy bean paste	50 g (1⅔ oz)
Brown soy bean paste	15 g (½ oz)
Mirin	½ Tbsp
Sake	½ Tbsp
Sugar	½ Tbsp

1 Prepare pickled lotus root. Combine 1 Tbsp vinegar with water and set aside. Wash and peel lotus root, then slice into 0.3-cm (1/10-in) rounds. Trim into flower shapes if desired. Soak in vinegar solution immediately for about 5 minutes to prevent discolouration. Drain and blanch lotus root in boiling water for 1–2 minutes until tender but still crisp. Remove and drain well.

2 Combine remaining vinegar, sugar and salt until completely dissolved. Transfer mixture to a clean plastic bag and add lotus root. Seal and shake well. Refrigerate for at least 1 hour before use. Pickled lotus root can be kept refrigerated for up to 3 days.

3 Prepare dish at least 1 day ahead. Sprinkle fish fillets with salt and refrigerate for 30 minutes. Combine ingredients for marinade and set aside.

4 Remove fish from refrigerator and pat dry with absorbent paper. Wrap fish in a clean piece of cotton gauze or muslin cloth.

5 Put half the amount of marinade in a plastic container and place wrapped fish into container. Top with remaining marinade. Refrigerate overnight, or for up to 1 week.

6 To cook, unwrap fish and pat dry with absorbent paper. Grill over medium heat, skin side first, for 2–3 minutes. Turn fish over and grill other side for 2–3 minutes until brown.

7 Alternatively, grill fish fillets in a preheated oven at 200°C (400°F), skin side up, for 10 minutes. Turn fish over and grill other side for 5 minutes, or until brown.

8 Arrange fish on individual serving plates. Serve hot with pickled lotus root on the side.

Main Courses 123

KOREAN

Mushroom Stew with Vegetables
A rich casserole of beef, mushrooms, leek and carrot.

Beef	225 g (8 oz), cut into thin strips
Onion	1, peeled and sliced
Leek	1, sliced
Carrot	½, sliced
Red chillies	2, sliced
Shiitake mushrooms	5, stems discarded and sliced
Enokitake mushrooms	100 g (3½ oz), ends trimmed
Oyster mushrooms	100 g (3½ oz), torn into shreds
Honshimeji mushrooms	70 g (2½ oz), ends trimmed and sliced
Water or basic beef stock (page 19)	750 ml (24 fl oz / 3 cups)
Salt or light soy sauce	to taste

SEASONING
Light soy sauce	1 Tbsp
Minced garlic	2 tsp
Ground black pepper	2 tsp
Sugar	1 tsp
Sesame oil	1 Tbsp

1. Mix beef well with seasoning.
2. Arrange beef, onion, leek, carrot, chillies and mushrooms neatly in a 5-cm (2-in) deep, heavy-based pan or casserole dish.
3. Pour in water or beef stock, then sprinkle with salt or light soy sauce. Bring to the boil before serving. Garnish as desired.

KOREAN

Grilled Salmon

Seasoned grilled salmon with onion sauce.

Salmon	400 g (14⅓ oz), cut into 2-cm (1-in) thick slices
Coarse salt	1 Tbsp
Ground white pepper	to taste
Cooking oil	3 Tbsp

SAUCE
Light soy sauce	125 ml (4 fl oz / ½ cup)
Sugar	2 Tbsp
Cooking wine	2 Tbsp
Onion	½, peeled and chopped
Ginger	2–3 slices, chopped

1. Sprinkle salmon with salt and pepper. Leave for 2 hours.
2. Combine sauce ingredients and mix well with a blender. Strain sauce through a sieve. Discard residue.
3. Dry salmon using absorbent paper and place in sauce. Refrigerate for 6 hours.
4. Drain salmon. Heat oil and grill. Serve hot with lemon slices and wasabi if desired.

THAI

Duck with Curry

A unique dish of roast duck in a spicy red curry. This dish goes well with plain white rice.

Roast duck	1, medium
Coconut cream	750 ml (24 fl oz / 3 cups)
Water	125 ml (4 fl oz / ½ cup)
Red curry paste (page 18)	2–3 Tbsp
Kaffir lime leaves	10
Fish sauce	3 Tbsp
Frozen peas	85 g (3 oz)
Tomatoes	5, small, cut in half
Red or green chillies	4, cut into strips
Thai sweet basil	1 sprig

1. Debone duck and cut into bite-size pieces.
2. Bring half the coconut cream to the boil with water. Leave to simmer.
3. In a wok, bring to the boil a third of the remaining coconut cream, then stir in red curry paste. Cook for a few minutes before adding kaffir lime leaves and pieces of duck. Stir well.
4. Add simmering coconut cream and turn up the heat.
5. Add fish sauce, peas, tomatoes and chillies. Simmer until peas are cooked then add remaining coconut cream and bring to the boil.
6. Sprinkle with basil leaves and remove from heat. Serve with plain rice.

THAI

Crabs with Glass Noodles

This dish of crabs and glass noodles can be served as a complete meal on its own or with additional side dishes.

Crabs	500 g (1 lb 1½ oz), cleaned and cut into pieces
Cooking oil	3 Tbsp
Glass noodles	55 g (2 oz), soaked for 5 minutes and drained
Basic stock (page 19)	375 ml (12 fl oz / 1½ cups)
Coriander leaves (cilantro)	1 sprig, cut into 1-cm (½-in) lengths
Red chilli	1, seeded and cut into thin strips

SEASONING

Fish sauce	2 Tbsp
Sesame oil	2 Tbsp
Lea & Perrins sauce	1 Tbsp
Light soy sauce	1 Tbsp

PASTE

Black peppercorns	1 Tbsp
Ginger	1-cm (½-in) knob, peeled
Coriander (cilantro) roots	3, chopped
Garlic	3 cloves, peeled

1. Combine seasoning ingredients and blend. Marinate crabs in seasoning for 30 minutes.
2. Combine paste ingredients and grind into a fine paste.
3. Heat cooking oil in a claypot and fry finely ground paste for 5 minutes or until fragrant. Add marinated crabs, glass noodles and chicken stock. Stir well.
4. Cover claypot and simmer for 8 minutes. Garnish with coriander leaves and chilli strips. Serve hot.

Main Courses

RICE

BALINESE

130 Yellow Rice
131 Fried Rice with Chicken and Prawns
132 Rice Porridge with Chicken

CHINESE

133 Chinese-style Porridge
134 Chinese-style Fried Rice
135 Steamed Chicken Glutinous Rice

FILIPINO

136 Paella de Madrid
137 Filipino-style Chicken Porridge
138 Filipino-style Fried Rice

INDIAN

139 Indian-style Fried Rice
140 Fruit and Nut Pilaf
141 Prawn Pilaf
142 Savoury Rice Balls

INDONESIAN

143 Fried Rice with Noodles
144 Beef Soup with Rice Cakes
145 Indonesian-style Fried Rice
146 Bean Curd Omelette on Rice Cakes

JAPANESE

147 Chicken and Eggs on Rice
148 Mixed Rice
149 Red Rice
150 Deep-fried Bean Curd Stuffed with Vinegared Rice
151 Sukiyaki Beef Bowl
152 Thick-rolled Sushi

KOREAN

154 Pumpkin Porridge
155 Rice Mixed with Vegetables and Beef
156 Fried Rice Cake with Spicy Sauce
157 Sliced Rice Cake in Soup

THAI

158 Fried Rice with Dried Prawn Paste
159 Fried Rice with Chicken and Basil
160 Pork Fried Rice with Tomato Sauce
161 Pineapple Rice

VIETNAMESE

162 Saigon Fish Congee
163 Duck Cooked in Fermented Bean Curd

BALINESE

Yellow Rice

This rice dish looks and smells great and generally goes well with stewed dishes. For a lighter meal, replace the 125 ml (4 fl oz / ½ cup) coconut milk in this recipe with chicken stock.

Long-grain rice	250 g (9 oz), washed and drained
Vegetable oil	1 Tbsp
Shallots	55 g (2 oz), peeled and chopped
Garlic	25 g ($4/5$ oz), peeled and chopped
Lemongrass	1 stalk, bruised
Salam leaves	2
Screwpine leaf	1
Indonesian-style stock (page 20)	375 ml (12 fl oz / 1½ cups)
Turmeric	30 g (1 oz), peeled, finely chopped, ground until fine with 4 Tbsp water and strained
Coconut milk	125 ml (4 fl oz / ½ cup)
Salt	a pinch or to taste
Ground black pepper	a pinch or to taste

1. Soak cleaned rice in fresh water for 5 minutes. Drain and steam for 25 minutes.
2. Meanwhile, prepare dressing. Heat oil in a saucepan. Add shallots and garlic. Sauté for 1 minute.
3. Add lemongrass and salam and screwpine leaves. Sauté for 1 minute.
4. Pour in chicken stock and turmeric juice. Bring to the boil, reduce heat and simmer for 1 minute.
5. Add coconut milk, return to the boil and simmer for 2 minutes. Season to taste with salt and pepper.
6. Combine steamed rice and hot dressing in a large bowl. Mix well and set aside.
7. When rice has absorbed the yellow liquid, return rice to steamer and steam for another 25 minutes or until rice is done.
8. To prepare using a rice cooker, combine washed and drained rice with cooled dressing and cook until done.

BALINESE

Fried Rice with Chicken and Prawns

For a healthier version, use a non-stick pan and reduce the amount of oil used. A one-dish meal, fried rice can be prepared with any combination of meat and vegetables. Use leftover meat liberally.

Vegetable oil	90 ml (3 fl oz / ⅜ cup)
Shallots	70 g (2½ oz), peeled, halved lengthways and sliced
Garlic	55 g (2 oz), peeled and sliced
Red chillies	2, large, halved, seeded and finely sliced
Bird's eye chillies (optional)	2, finely sliced
Cabbage	100 g (3½ oz), sliced into strips
Spiced tomato sauce (page 16)	1 Tbsp
Chicken meat	150 g (5⅓ oz), diced, preferably dark meat
Prawns (shrimps)	150 g (5⅓ oz), medium, shelled and cleaned
Indonesian salty soy sauce	2 Tbsp
Eggs	2, beaten
Cooked rice	600 g (1 lb 5⅓ oz), chilled
Chinese celery leaves	25 g (⅘ oz), sliced
Leek	55 g (2 oz), small, sliced
Spring onions (scallions)	55 g (2 oz), sliced
Spinach	55 g (2 oz), sliced
Salt	a pinch or to taste
Crisp-fried shallots	2 Tbsp

1. Heat oil in a wok or heavy frying pan. Add shallots, garlic and chillies. Sauté over medium heat for 1 minute or until golden yellow.
2. Add cabbage, spiced tomato sauce, chicken and prawns. Fry again for 1 minute. Add soy sauce and eggs. Fry until eggs are scrambled and mixture of ingredients is dry.
3. Add rice and fry for 3 minutes, then add all remaining ingredients. Mix well.
4. Adjust to taste with more salt if necessary. Dish out and serve.

BALINESE

Rice Porridge with Chicken

This recipe can be prepared with short instead of long-grain rice for a risotto dish. Reduce chicken stock to 1 litre (32 fl oz / 4 cups) and top with more when necessary during cooking process.

Chicken	1, about 1.2 kg (2 lb 10 oz)
Vegetable oil	2 Tbsp
Shallots	50 g (1⅔ oz), peeled and sliced
Garlic	30 g (1 oz), peeled and sliced
Salam leaves	3, left whole
Lemongrass	1 stalk, bruised or shredded and knotted
Long-grain rice	300 g (11 oz), washed, rinsed for 1 minute and drained
Indonesian-style stock (page 20)	1.5 litres (48 fl oz / 6 cups)
Salt	to taste
Crushed black peppercorns	to taste
Crisp-fried shallots	2 Tbsp

TOPPING

Shredded chicken	800 g (1¾ lb)
Chicken spice paste	2 Tbsp
Vegetable oil	1 Tbsp
Spring onions (scallions)	55 g (2 oz), sliced
Chinese celery leaves	55 g (2 oz), sliced
Bird's eye chillies	2, chopped

1. Prepare chicken stock. When stock has simmered for 4 hours, add chicken and simmer for 1 hour or until chicken is very tender and meat almost falls off the bone.
2. Remove chicken from stock and place inside a deep container. Strain stock through a fine sieve over chicken. Leave chicken to cool in stock.
3. Remove chicken from cold stock, separate meat from bones and shred very finely. Set aside.
4. Prepare porridge. Heat oil in a heavy saucepan. Add shallots, garlic, salam leaves and lemongrass. Sauté for 2 minutes.
5. Add rice and sauté for 1 minute.
6. Add half the chicken stock, bring to the boil and simmer until rice is very soft but not overcooked. While simmering, top up with more stock as it evaporates.
7. Mix in half the shredded chicken. Season to taste with salt and black pepper.
8. Combine remaining shredded chicken with all topping ingredients. Mix well. Season to taste with salt and pepper.
9. Divide porridge into 4 serving bowls. Spoon topping over. Garnish with crisp-fried shallots and serve.

Chinese-style Porridge

Soft-boiled rice served with pork, liver and fish slices.

Fresh fish fillet (any kind)	450 g (1 lb), thinly sliced
Pork	85 g (3 oz), thinly sliced
Liver	55 g (2 oz), thinly sliced
Ginger juice	2 tsp
Rice wine	1 tsp
Light soy sauce	1 Tbsp
Long-grain rice	220 g (8 oz)
Minced pork	125 g (4½ oz)
Salt	to taste
Ground white pepper	
Parsley	2 sprigs, chopped
Crisp-fried shallots	1 Tbsp

1. Season fish fillet, sliced pork and liver with ginger juice, rice wine and soy sauce.
2. Wash rice and boil in 1.5 litres (48 fl oz / 6 cups) water over medium heat for 30 minutes. Add minced pork, stir to mix well and boil over low heat for another 1½ hours. Add salt.
3. When rice is still boiling, add seasoned ingredients. Turn off heat immediately.
4. Serve in individual bowls, garnished with pepper, chopped parsley and crisp-fried shallots. If desired, a raw egg may be broken into each bowl before boiling porridge is ladled in.

CHINESE

Chinese-style Fried Rice

Stir-fried rice with prawns, ham and peas garnished with egg strips.

Cooked rice	600 g (1 lb 5⅓ oz)
Prawns (shrimps)	220 g (8 oz), peeled and deveined
Cooking oil	8 Tbsp
Garlic	2 cloves, peeled and finely chopped
Chinese cooking wine sor medium-dry sherry	1 Tbsp
Salt	
Spring onions (scallions)	4
Eggs	2, large
Peas	220 g (8 oz)
Cooked ham	220 g (8 oz), diced
Dark soy sauce	1½ Tbsp
Basic stock (page 19)	2–3 Tbsp
Dark soy sauce	1 tsp (optional)

MARINADE
Salt	½ tsp
Corn flour (cornstarch)	2½ tsp
Egg white	1 Tbsp

1. Cut prawns into 2-cm (1-in) pieces. Mix marinade ingredients and stir in prawns. Coat evenly and refrigerate.
2. Heat a wok over high heat until it smokes. Add 2 Tbsp oil and swirl it around. Add in chopped garlic and when it browns, add prawns. When prawns turn pinkish, add wine or sherry along the rim of the wok. As soon as the sizzling dies down, remove prawns and reserve them. Wash and dry the wok.
3. Chop spring onions across into rounds, separating the greens from the whites.
4. Beat eggs lightly with 1 Tbsp of the oil and a little salt. Heat a large flat frying pan until moderately hot, add 1 Tbsp oil and swirl it around to cover the whole surface.
5. Pour in half the beaten egg and tip the pan to spread egg evenly to the edges. When firm, turn egg over and fry the other side for a few seconds. Put egg on a plate and slice into strips.
6. Stir cooked rice to loosen it. Blanch peas in boiling water for 3 minutes and drain.
7. Reheat the wok over high heat until it smokes. Add remaining oil and swirl it around. Add white rounds of spring onion and stir. Pour in remaining egg and tip in the rice. Toss rice, separating any lumps.
8. When rice is thoroughly hot, add ham, stir, peas, stir and prawns. Still stirring, add soy sauce and stock. Stir in the extra thick soy sauce for a more pronounced colour if desired. Finally, stir in half the egg strips and serve warm. Top with remaining egg strips and spring onions.

CHINESE

Steamed Chicken Glutinous Rice

Chicken that is richly flavoured in oyster sauce, ginger juice and sesame oil, then with steamed glutinous rice.

Chicken	1.5 kg (3 lb 4½ oz)
Glutinous rice	1 kg (2 lb 3 oz)
Cooking oil	125 ml (4 fl oz / ½ cup)
Dried Chinese mushrooms	55 g (2 oz), soaked and cut into strips
Shallots	8, peeled and sliced
Salt	2 tsp
Thick dark soy sauce	1 tsp
Five-spice powder	1 heaped tsp
Water	1 litre (32 fl oz / 4 cups)
Red chillies	2, seeded and sliced
Spring onions (scallions)	2, chopped
Coriander leaves (cilantro)	4 sprigs, cut into 2.5-cm (1-in) lengths
Chilli sauce	

SEASONING

Oyster sauce	4 Tbsp
Rice wine	2 tsp
Thick soy sauce	1 tsp
Light soy sauce	2 tsp
Ginger juice	2 tsp
Sesame oil	1 tsp
Sugar	1 tsp
Ground white pepper	½ tsp
Corn flour (cornstarch)	1 heaped tsp

1. Debone chicken and cut into 1.5-cm (¾-in) thick slices. Season with seasoning ingredients for at least 1 hour.
2. Wash and drain glutinous rice and steam for 45 minutes.
3. Heat oil in a wok and fry mushrooms for 1–2 minutes. Drain from oil and set aside.
4. Lightly brown shallots and put in glutinous rice, salt, thick soy sauce and five-spice powder and fry for 1 minute. Add water, mix well and simmer gently, covered, for 5–10 minutes. Remove from heat.
5. Grease 12 medium rice bowls and put in some fried mushrooms and seasoned chicken at the bottom of each bowl. Fill with glutinous rice and press with the back of a spoon to fill half of rice bowl.
6. Steam over rapidly boiling water for 45 minutes.
7. To serve, turn steamed glutinous rice onto a small dish. Garnish with chillies, spring onions and coriander leaves and serve hot with chilli sauce.

Rice 135

FILIPINO

Paella de Madrid

A Spanish dish that was supposedly the food of peasants, paella consists of a mixture of meat, seafood, rice, herbs and vegetables cooked in a *paellera*, a heavy pan designed for cooking paella. Paella de Madrid is one of the many variations of the dishes. Serve on its own, or as a savoury stuffing for roast chicken or spit-roasted pig.

Olive oil	150 ml (5 fl oz / ⅔ cup)
Garlic	2 heads, peeled and chopped
Turmeric powder	1 tsp
Jasmine rice	300 g (11 oz), washed
Glutinous (sticky) rice	55 g (2 oz), washed
Thin coconut milk	875 ml (28 fl oz / 3½ cups)
Screwpine leaves	3, knotted
Chicken	500 g (1 lb 1½ oz) cut into bite-size pieces
Onion	1, medium, peeled and chopped
Chorizo or any kind of spicy sausage	250 g (9 oz), sliced diagonally into 1-cm (½-in) thickness
Tomato paste	45 g (1½ oz)
Paprika	1 tsp
Salt	2 tsp
Sugar	½ Tbsp
Ground black pepper	1 tsp
Chicken stock	375 ml (12 fl oz / 1½ cups)
Prawns (shrimps)	300 g (11 oz), medium, trimmed
Clams	300 g (11 oz), rinsed and scrubbed
Red capsicum (bell pepper)	1, small, cored, seeded and sliced into strips
Limes	2, cut into quarters

1. In a *paellera* or large frying pan, heat 90 ml (3 fl oz / ⅜ cup) oil over medium heat. Fry half the garlic until fragrant, then add turmeric powder and mix well.

2. Add jasmine and glutinous rice and stir-fry until rice turns translucent. Add coconut milk and screwpine leaves. Increase heat to high and bring mixture to the boil while stirring constantly.

3. Reduce heat to medium, cover pan and cook until rice is tender. Reduce heat further and continue cooking for another 3 minutes, until rice has absorbed all the liquid, stirring occasionally to prevent burning. Remove from heat, set aside and keep warm.

4. In a clean frying pan, heat remaining oil over medium heat. Fry chicken pieces until light brown. Remove from heat, and place on absorbent paper to drain.

5. Using same oil, fry remaining garlic until fragrant, then add onion and fry until soft and translucent.

6. Add chorizo, tomato paste and paprika. Mix well. Season with salt, sugar and pepper. Add chicken stock and bring mixture to the boil. Reduce heat and leave mixture to simmer for 10 minutes or until thickened.

7. Add prawns, clams and capsicum and cook for another 10 minutes or until prawns turn pink and are cooked. Discard any clams that do not open. Return fried chicken to mixture and stir to mix well. Taste and adjust seasoning, then remove from heat.

8. Divide chicken and seafood mixture into 2 equal portions. Return paella rice to stove and add 1 portion of chicken and seafood mixture. Stir and cook for 3 minutes over medium heat, tossing gently to mix well. Transfer to a serving dish. Scoop remaining chicken and seafood mixture on top of paella and decorate with lime quarters. Serve immediately.

Filipino-style Chicken Porridge

This simple, tasty dish of rice boiled in stock makes a nourishing meal.

Cooking oil	3 Tbsp
Garlic	5 cloves, peeled and chopped
Onion	1, medium, peeled and chopped
Ginger	30 g (1 oz), peeled and finely sliced
Fish sauce	3 Tbsp
Chicken	1 kg (2 lb 3 oz), cut into pieces
Long-grain rice	375 g (13$^{2}/_{5}$ oz), washed
Glutinous (sticky) rice	175 g (6¼ oz), washed
Rice-rinsing water or basic chicken stock (page 19)	2 litres (64 fl oz / 8 cups)
Chicken stock cubes	2
Salt	to taste
Ground white pepper	to taste

CONDIMENTS

Chicken crackling	as desired
Spring onions (scallions)	2, chopped
Garlic	1 head, peeled, finely sliced and deep-fried until golden brown and crisp
Calamansi limes	2, halved
Fish sauce	
Hard-boiled eggs	2, peeled and halved

1. In a medium pot, heat oil over high heat. Fry garlic until light brown, then add onion and ginger and fry for 2 minutes or until fragrant and onion is soft.

2. Add fish sauce and chicken pieces and stir to mix well. Stir-fry for 5 minutes.

3. Add both types of rice, rice-rinsing water or chicken stock and stock cubes. Bring mixture to the boil, then reduce heat to medium, cover pot and leave to cook for 1 hour or until rice is tender. Stir occasionally to prevent burning. If a smoother consistency is desired, leave to cook for 2–4 hours.

4. Season with salt and pepper and simmer for another 3 minutes before removing from heat. Dish out and serve immediately, with condiments on the side.

FILIPINO

Filipino-style Fried Rice

This simple dish of garlic fried rice is typically consumed on its own as a breakfast dish. However, it can be served up as a staple during a main meal, with other dishes.

Cooking oil	4 Tbsp
Garlic	1 head, peeled and minced
Cooked rice	1 kg (2 lb 3 oz) preferably refrigerated and chilled overnight
Salt	1 tsp
Tomatoes	2, chopped
Red onion	1, peeled and finely sliced

1 In a wok, heat oil over medium heat. Fry garlic until golden brown, then gradually add rice and salt. Toss rice to mix evenly and use your spatula to break up any lumps.

2 Cook for 5 minutes or until heated through before removing from heat.

3 Transfer rice to prepared serving plates and garnish with tomatoes and onion.

4 Serve as part of a main meal with other dishes, or on its own.

Indian-style Fried Rice

This is a quick and easy-to-prepare dish. You can add any leftover meats to it for a variation to this recipe.

Eggs	2, lightly beaten with a dash of pepper
Cooking oil	2 Tbsp
Curry leaves	2 stalks
Onion	1, peeled and sliced
Green chillies	2, sliced
Garlic	5 cloves, peeled and minced
Prawns (shrimps)	200 g (7 oz), peeled and deveined
Carrot	110 g (4 oz), peeled and grated
Cabbage	100 g (3½ oz), shredded
Chilli paste	1 Tbsp
Salt	to taste
Freshly ground black pepper	1 tsp
Chilli sauce	1 Tbsp
Dark soy sauce	1 Tbsp
Light soy sauce	1 tsp
Cooked rice	400 g (14⅓ oz)
Green peas	100 g (3½ oz)

1. Prepare eggs for garnish. Heat some oil in a wok and pour in egg to coat wok. When egg is cooked, remove and leave to cool. Roll cooled egg up and slice into strips. Set aside.
2. Heat oil in a wok. Add curry leaves, onion, green chillies and garlic and sauté until fragrant.
3. Add prawns, carrot and cabbage and stir well. Add chilli paste and salt, pepper, and chilli sauce. Stir in dark and light soy sauces.
4. Fluff up cooked rice with a wooden spoon and add to ingredients in wok. Turn up heat to high and very quickly mix ingredients well.
5. Sprinkle in peas and heat through. Serve hot with fried egg strips and garnish as desired.

Fruit and Nut Pilaf

This basic rice dish is a perfect accompaniment to any spicy curry.

Ghee (clarified butter)	4 Tbsp
Cinnamon stick	1
Cardamom	5 pods
Cloves	5
Screwpine leaves	2, tied into a knot
Onions	2, peeled and sliced
Basmati rice	400 g (14⅓ oz), washed and drained
Water	750 ml (24 fl oz / 3 cups)
Salt	to taste
Saffron strands	10, crushed with the back of a spoon
Yellow food colouring	¼ tsp, mixed 1 Tbsp water

GINGER AND GARLIC PASTE
| Ginger | 1-cm (½-in) knob, peeled and chopped |
| Garlic | 5 cloves, peeled and chopped |

GARNISH
Raisins or sultanas	10, fried
Cashew nuts	10, fried
Shallots	5, peeled, sliced and crisp-fried

1. Blend ginger and garlic paste ingredients. Set aside.
2. Heat ghee in a wok. When melted, add cinnamon, cardamom, cloves and screwpine leaves. Stir to infuse.
3. After 2–3 minutes, add onions and stir-fry until golden brown.
4. Add rice and stir to coat with spice-infused ghee. Add garlic and ginger paste. Stir well to combine.
5. Transfer ingredients to a rice cooker. Add water, salt and saffron. Give it a quick stir and switch on rice cooker.
6. When rice is cooked, add yellow colouring.
7. Use a fork to fluff up rice then stir in half the garnish, and top with remaining half. Serve hot with a spicy curry.

Prawn Pilaf

This is a very fragrant rice dish.

Medium-size prawns (shrimps)	1 kg (2 lb 3 oz), cleaned
Old ginger	5 slices
Water	1 litre (32 fl oz / 4 cups)
Cooking oil or ghee (clarified butter)	3 Tbsp
Cinnamon sticks	2
Cardamom	4 pods
Cloves	4
Onions	2, peeled and sliced
Ginger	2.5-cm knob (1-in), peeled and minced
Garlic	4 cloves, peeled and minced
Basmati rice	300 g (11 oz), washed and drained
Salt	to taste

PRAWN MASALA

Cooking oil	2 Tbsp
Onions	2, peeled and sliced
Celery seeds	¼ tsp
Green chillies	3, sliced
Garlic	5 cloves, peeled and minced
Tomatoes	2, finely chopped
Chilli paste	2 Tbsp
Tomato paste	2 tsp
Yoghurt	110 g (4 oz)
Salt	to taste
Sugar	1 tsp

PASTE

Grated coconut	100 g (3½ oz)
Garlic	4 cloves, peeled
Tomatoes	2, chopped
Coriander leaves (cilantro)	1 sprig

GARNISH

Fried cashew nuts and raisins

1. Place prawns in a saucepan with slices of ginger. Add water and simmer for 30 minutes. Peel prawns and reserve meat for masala. Set stock aside. Heat oil/ghee in a pan. Add cinnamon, cardamom, cloves, onions, ginger and garlic. Fry until onions brown.

2. Add rice and fry for 2–3 minutes. Pour in 750 ml (24 fl oz / 3 cups) prawn stock and add salt. Stir and bring to the boil. Reduce heat. Cover and cook until water has evaporated and rice is fluffy. Loosen rice with a wooden spoon. Set aside. Combine paste ingredients and grind. Prepare prawn masala. Heat oil in a wok and add onions, then celery seeds, green chillies and garlic. Stir-fry until fragrant.

3. Add tomatoes and when softened, add chilli and tomato pastes. Stir-fry for 2 minutes then add ground paste. Cook for at least 5 minutes over medium heat.

4. Add prawns, yoghurt, salt and sugar and cook until gravy is slightly thick.

5. To serve, line a bowl with pilaf rice then add some prawn masala. Continue to layer to fill bowl. Garnish with fried cashew nuts and raisins to serve. Add a few unpeeled prawns as garnish, if desired.

INDIAN

Savoury Rice Balls

This is an age-old recipe from Kerala in southern India. These rice balls can be eaten as a sweet snack or as part of a main meal with curry.

Rice	190 g (6¾ oz), soaked for at least 2 hours and drained
Water	125 ml (4 fl oz / ½ cup)
Grated coconut	100 g (3½ oz)
Salt	1½ tsp
Cooking oil	½ Tbsp
Mustard seeds	1 tsp
Curry leaves	2 stalks

1. Blend soaked rice and water into a grainy paste.
2. Add grated coconut and pulse to blend. Remove from blender and stir in salt.
3. Heat oil in a wok. Add mustard seeds and curry leaves. When seeds begin to pop, pour in blended ingredients.
4. Add salt and stir until mixture changes to a translucent white and comes away from sides of wok. Turn off heat and allow to cool slightly.
5. Meanwhile, get the steamer going. Divide rice dough into 24 equal portions. Oil your hands before handling dough to prevent sticking. Shape each portion into a ball with your hands.
6. Line a tray with a piece of banana leaf and place dough balls on it. Steam for about 10 minutes.
7. Serve hot with grated coconut and brown sugar or a good curry.

Fried Rice with Noodles

This unusual recipe combines both rice and noodles in a single dish, but the result is simply delicious. This is a popular dish in East Java.

Vegetable oil	3 Tbsp
Chicken thighs	100 g (3½ oz), boned and cut into 1-cm (½-in) cubes
Peeled prawns (shrimps)	100 g (3½ oz), deveined and cut into 1-cm (½-in) pieces
Red chillies	20 g (⅔ oz), halved, seeded and sliced
White cabbage	55 g (2 oz), sliced
Nasi goreng sauce (page 19)	3 Tbsp
Indonesian salty soy sauce	2 Tbsp
Eggs	2
Cooked rice	300 g (11 oz), thoroughly cooled
Egg noodles	300 g (11 oz), cooked and cooled
Spinach	30 g (1 oz), cleaned and roughly sliced
Leek or spring onions (scallions)	30 g (1 oz), sliced
Celery leaves	20 g (⅔ oz), sliced
Salt	to taste
Freshly crushed black pepper	to taste
Crisp-fried shallots	2 Tbsp

1. Heat oil in a heavy saucepan or wok. Add chicken and prawns and stir-fry for 1 minute or until both ingredients have changed colour.
2. Add chillies and cabbage and sauté for 1 minute more.
3. Add *nasi goreng* and salty soy sauces. Stir-fry until all ingredients are evenly coated, then add eggs and scramble over high heat.
4. Add rice and noodles and continue to stir-fry until all ingredients are well mixed and hot, after about 3 minutes.
5. Add spinach, leek or spring onions and celery. Stir-fry for 1 minute and season to taste with salt and pepper.
6. Dish out and garnish with crisp-fried shallots before serving.

INDONESIAN

Beef Soup with Rice Cakes

The rich, creamy taste of this beef soup goes well with the plain-tasting sticky rice cakes, which make a great alternative to steamed rice.

Beef legs	1 kg (2 lb 3 oz), deboned
Water	5 litres (160 fl oz / 20 cups)
Ginger	85 g (3 oz), peeled, sliced and bruised
Salt	1 Tbsp
Lemongrass	6 stalks, bruised
Vegetable oil	3 Tbsp
East Javanese yellow spice paste (page 16)	250 g (9 oz)
Kaffir lime leaves	5
Indonesian-style stock (page 20)	1 litre (32 fl oz / 4 cups)
Coconut cream	250 ml (8 fl oz / 1 cup)
Salt	to taste
Freshly crushed black pepper	to taste
Compressed rice cake (*lontong*) (page 21)	300 g (11 oz)
Chinese celery leaves	30 g (1 oz), sliced
Crisp-fried shallots	2 Tbsp

1. Wash beef legs thoroughly under running water, drain and set aside.
2. Combine water, ginger, salt and 3 stalks of lemongrass and bring to the boil.
3. Add beef, reduce heat and simmer for several hours or until meat is very soft.
4. When meat is soft, drain and leave to cool. Discard boiling liquid. Slice cooled leg meat into small, even strips and set aside until needed.
5. Heat oil in a heavy saucepan. Add spice paste, kaffir lime leaves and remaining lemongrass. Sauté until fragrant. Add beef stock, bring to the boil and simmer for 5 minutes over medium heat.
6. Add coconut cream, return to the boil and season to taste with salt and pepper. Keep soup warm. Meanwhile, steam rice cake until hot, then cut into even slices and divide among individual serving bowls.
7. Ladle beef soup over rice cakes and garnish as desired with celery and crisp-fried shallots. Serve hot.

Indonesian Fried Rice

Using cooked rice that has been left overnight will yield better results when preparing this fried rice dish.

Cooking oil	5 Tbsp
Cooked rice	600 g (1 lb 5⅓ oz), chilled or thoroughly cooled
Indonesian sweet soy sauce	1–2 Tbsp
Eggs	2–3, fried sunny-side up style
Cucumber	finely sliced
Crisp-fried shallots	for garnishing

SPICES (GROUND)

Shallots	5, peeled
Garlic	3 cloves, peeled
Red chillies	3–5
Dried prawn (shrimp) paste	½ tsp

1. Heat oil in a frying pan or wok over medium heat. Sauté ground spices until fragrant and thoroughly cooked. Add rice and sweet soy sauce.
2. Mix ingredients well until rice is thoroughly warmed through. Remove from heat.
3. Serve fried rice with fried eggs, finely sliced cucumber and crisp-fried shallots.

INDONESIAN

Bean Curd Omelette on Rice Cakes

The black dried prawn (shrimp) paste is a common ingredient in Indonesian cooking. It has a strong, distinctive flavour and may take some getting used to.

Compressed rice cakes (*lontong*) (page 21)	300 g (11 oz)
Firm bean curd	300 g (11 oz), sliced into rectangles
Rice flour	2 Tbsp
Vegetable oil	2 Tbsp + enough for shallow-frying
Eggs	4, well beaten
Salt	to taste
Ground white pepper	to taste
Bean sprouts	100 g (3½ oz)
Celery leaves	10 g (⅓ oz), sliced
Ready-fried prawn (shrimp) crackers	20 g (⅔ oz)

SAUCE

Raw peanuts	250 g (9 oz), with skins intact and deep-fried or toasted until golden
Bird's eye chillies	3–5, sliced
Garlic	2 cloves, peeled and sliced
Indonesian sweet soy sauce	2 Tbsp
Indonesian salty soy sauce	¾ Tbsp
Black prawn (shrimp) paste	1 tsp
Lime juice	1 tsp
Salt	to taste

1. Steam rice cake until hot, then slice into rounds of similar thickness and arrange on a plate. Dust sliced bean curd with flour and shallow-fry in medium-hot oil until golden. Remove and drain on absorbent paper towels.
2. Season beaten eggs with salt and pepper to taste before adding cooled bean curd. Mix well.
3. Heat 2 Tbsp oil in a non-stick pan and add egg and bean curd mix. Mixture should begin to cook immediately at the outer edges.
4. Lift cooked portion at the outer edges so the uncooked portions flow underneath. Slide pan rapidly back and forth over heat to keep mixture moving and avoid sticking. After 1 minute, turn omelette over and repeat the process on the other side. Colour both sides lightly but avoid overcooking.
5. Slice omelette into even strips and sprinkle over sliced rice cakes. Sprinkle bean sprouts and celery leaves over omelette.
6. Prepare sauce. Combine all ingredients, except salt, in a stone mortar or blender and grind into a fine paste. Gradually add warm water until a lightly runny consistency is reached. Season to taste with salt.
7. Either drizzle sauce over ingredients on the plate or serve it on the side. Garnish, if desired, with sliced red chillies and serve with prawn crackers.

JAPANESE

Chicken and Eggs on Rice

The Japanese name of this dish, *oyako*, refers to "parent and child", making reference to the use of chicken and eggs in this dish. This is popularly eaten for family lunches in Japan.

Boneless chicken thighs	400 g (14⅓ oz), cut into bite-size pieces
White onions	2, medium, peeled
Eggs	6, lightly beaten and divided into 4 equal portions
Mirin	90 ml (3 fl oz / ⅜ cup)
Japanese dark soy sauce	4 Tbsp
Cooked Japanese short-grain rice	4 servings, kept warm
Trefoil (*mitsuba*)	1 small bunch, cut into 2.5-cm (1-in) lengths
Japanese seven-spice seasoning (optional) or ground Japanese pepper	

DASHI
Water	200 ml (7 fl oz / ¾ cup)
Dried kelp (*konbu*)	5-cm (2-in) piece
Bonito flakes	10 g (⅓ oz)

1. Prepare dashi (page 19). Put 150 ml (5 fl oz / ⅗ cup) dashi, mirin and soy sauce into a medium saucepan. Bring to the boil, then add chicken and onions. Reduce heat to medium and simmer for 3–5 minutes, covered.

2. Remove from heat and divide into 4 equal portions. Prepare a single serving of Chicken and Eggs on Rice. Pour 1 portion of chicken and onion mixture into a non-stick saucepan. Bring to the boil and pour in three-quarters of a portion of eggs.

3. Cover and simmer for about 30 seconds over medium-low heat, then uncover and pour in remaining egg mixture. Cover and simmer for a few more seconds until mixture is almost set. Remove from heat.

4. Gently slide chicken and egg mixture onto a serving bowl of rice. Garnish with trefoil and serve hot, sprinkled with seven-spice seasoning or Japanese pepper, if desired.

5. Repeat cooking procedure with balance portions of chicken and onion mixture, and eggs to prepare remaining 3 servings. Serve as you cook, as the dish should be eaten hot.

Rice 147

JAPANESE

Mixed Rice

A wide variety of mixed rice dishes are available in Japanese cuisine. This dish is commonly packed into lunch boxes, or served for simple home meals and elaborate parties.

Japanese short-grain rice	320 g (11½ oz)
Short-grain glutinous rice	160 g (5¾ oz)
Chicken thighs	150 g (5⅓ oz), boned and cubed
Sake	3 Tbsp
Japanese dark soy sauce	2 Tbsp
Salt	½ tsp
Carrot	80 g (2⅘ oz), peeled and julienned
Honshimeji mushrooms	130 g (4⅔ oz), ends trimmed
Deep-fried bean curd	1, blanched, halved lengthways and cut crossways into long strips

CHICKEN MARINADE

Sake	½ Tbsp
Japanese dark soy sauce	1 tsp

DASHI

Water	500 ml (16 fl oz / 2 cups)
Dried kelp (*konbu*)	6-cm (2½-in) piece
Bonito flakes	15 g (½ oz)

1. Prepare dashi (page 19). Combine chicken with ingredients for marinade. Set aside.
2. Put both types of rice into a mixing bowl and fill with cold water. Stir quickly with fingers and drain. Press rice down repeatedly using your palm for 20–30 times to rub rice grains against one other.
3. Refill bowl with tap water, then repeat the rubbing and rinsing process another 2–3 times until water almost runs clear.
4. Soak washed rice in water for 30 minutes. Drain well. Transfer drained rice to a rice cooker. Add 450 ml (15 fl oz / 1⅘ cups) dashi, sake, soy sauce and salt. Mix well.
5. Layer chicken, carrot, mushrooms and bean curd on top of rice. Cook rice.
6. When rice is cooked, fold mixture gently with a wet spatula. Mix well.
7. Transfer to individual serving bowls. Garnish as desired and serve hot.

JAPANESE

Red Rice

This is a traditional Japanese festive dish. It is often prepared and presented as a gift to relatives, neighbours and friends during special occasions such as birthdays and weddings.

Japanese short-grain glutinous rice	480 g (1 lb 1 oz)
Dried Japanese red beans	60 g (2¼ oz), washed and drained
Water	600 ml (20 fl oz / 2½ cups)
Toasted black sesame seeds	1 Tbsp
Salt	½ tsp

1. Prepare rice for cooking. Soak washed rice in water for 30–60 minutes. Drain well.
2. Cover red beans with water in a pot. Bring to the boil for 1–2 minutes. Drain well. Return drained beans to pot and add water. Heat and simmer for about 30 minutes, until beans are soft.
3. Strain mixture to separate red beans and cooking liquid. Measure 330 ml (11 fl oz / 1⅓ cups) liquid ßto reserve for cooking rice. Discard excess liquid, or top up with water, if amount is insufficient.
4. Transfer drained rice, red beans and cooking liquid to rice cooker. When rice is cooked, fold mixture gently with a wet spatula. Mix well.
5. Transfer to serving bowls, or a traditional Japanese lacquer box. Sprinkle black sesame seeds and salt on top before serving.

Rice 149

JAPANESE

Deep-fried Bean Curd Stuffed with Vinegared Rice

Named after Inari, one of the Shinto gods of grain and agriculture, this sushi is traditionally presented as an offering to the god. According to legend, the pair of foxes that serve as the messengers of Inari have a fondness for deep-fried bean curd, hence the use of the ingredient in this dish.

Japanese short-grain rice	320 g (11½ oz)
Water	430 ml (14 fl oz / 1¾ cups)
Rice vinegar	4 Tbsp
Sugar	1 Tbsp
Salt	⅔ tsp
Toasted white sesame seeds	2 Tbsp
Toasted black sesame seeds	1 Tbsp
Thinly sliced pickled ginger	to taste

BEAN CURD POCKETS
Deep-fried bean curd (*abura age*)	10, thawed before use if frozen
Japanese dark soy sauce	4 Tbsp
Sugar	5 Tbsp
Sake	3 Tbsp
Mirin	3 Tbsp

DASHI
Water	500 ml (16 fl oz / 2 cups)
Dried kelp (*konbu*)	10-cm (4-in) piece
Bonito flakes	20 g (⅔ oz)

1. Prepare dashi (page 19).

2. Prepare bean curd pockets. Roll a chopstick over each bean curd and halve crossways. Carefully pull open cut ends to form pockets. Blanch with boiling water to remove excess oil.

3. Put 400 ml (13 fl oz) dashi, soy sauce, sugar, sake and mirin into a medium saucepan. Heat and bring to boil. Add bean curd, reduce heat to medium and simmer, covered, with a drop-in lid or baking paper trimmed to fit pan. Cook until liquid has reduced by three-quarters.

4. Add mirin and simmer for 2–3 minutes. Remove from heat and set aside until cool. This allows the bean curd to fully absorb the flavours of the seasoning. Transfer to a flat sieve and drain well before use.

5. Prepare rice for cooking. Put rice into a mixing bowl and fill with cold tap water. Stir quickly with fingers and drain. Press rice down repeatedly using your palm for 20–30 times to rub rice grains against one other. Refill bowl with tap water, then repeat to rub and rinse 2–3 times until water almost runs clear.

6. Leave rice to drain in a sieve for about 30 minutes. Transfer to a rice cooker. Add 430 ml (14 fl oz / 1¾ cups) water and turn on rice cooker. When cooked, fluff rice gently, using a wet spatula. Set aside.

7. Prepare sushi rice. Mix vinegar, sugar and salt in a small pot. Cook over low heat until fully dissolved. Transfer cooked rice to a damp wooden sushi tub or mixing bowl. Sprinkle vinegar dressing over while rice is still hot to give rice a glossy sheen.

8. Fold rice with cutting strokes, and fan to cool at the same time. This prevents rice from clumping together. Do not mash. Mix in white and black sesame seeds. Cover tub or bowl with a clean wet cloth. Set aside.

9. Assemble stuffed bean curd. Carefully open a bean curd pocket. Using wet fingers, stuff vinegared rice into pocket, leaving a 1-cm (½-in) margin from the edges. Press edges together and fold over to one side to seal pocket. Sit stuffed bean curd on folded edges to prevent it from opening up. Repeat until ingredients are used up.

10. Arrange stuffed bean curd on a serving plate. Serve, accompanied with thinly sliced pickled ginger to taste.

JAPANESE

Sukiyaki Beef Bowl

Sukiyaki is a popular seasoning sauce that usually comprises soy sauce, dashi, sake, sugar and mirin. Use beef belly for this dish, as its fat will melt during cooking and impart a wonderful flavour to the rice.

Cooking oil	2 tsp
Thinly sliced beef belly	400 g (14⅓ oz)
Japanese dark soy sauce	4 Tbsp
Sugar	3 Tbsp
White onion	1, large, peeled and cut into 12 wedges along the grain
Sake	4 Tbsp
Mirin	2 Tbsp
Cooked Japanese short-grain rice	4 servings, kept warm
Egg yolks	4
Pickled red ginger	4 tsp
Chopped spring onions (scallions), green portion only	4 tsp
Japanese seven-spice seasoning	(optional)

DASHI

Water	200 ml (7 fl oz / ¾ cup)
Dried kelp (*konbu*)	5-cm (2-in) piece
Bonito flakes	10 g (⅓ oz)

1. Prepare dashi (page 19).
2. Cut beef belly crossways into 5-cm (2-in) wide pieces. Heat oil in a frying pan. Stir-fry beef for 1 minute.
3. Combine soy sauce and sugar in a small bowl and stir until sugar is dissolved. Add seasoning mixture to pan. Mix well. Cook for 1–2 minutes, then transfer to a plate and set aside.
4. In the same pan, add 150 ml (5 fl oz / ⅗ cup) dashi, sake and mirin. Heat and bring to the boil. Add onion and cook for 3–5 minutes until soft. Return beef to pan and heat through for 1–2 minutes. Remove from heat.
5. Divide beef and onion mixture equally among 4 serving bowls of rice. Top the centre of each bowl with an egg yolk. Garnish each bowl with 1 tsp pickled red ginger and 1 tsp chopped spring onions.
6. Sprinkle with Japanese seven-spice seasoning, if desired. Serve immediately.

Rice

JAPANESE

Thick-rolled Sushi

Sushi can be described as the most popular Japanese food in the world. This recipe features thick-rolled sushi that is commonly served in Japanese homes.

Nori seaweed sheets	5
Wasabi	to taste
Japanese light soy sauce	to taste

SUSHI RICE (VINEGARED RICE)

Japanese short-grain rice	480 g (1 lb 1 oz)
Water	650 ml (21²⁄₃ fl oz / 2²⁄₃ cups)
Rice vinegar	90 ml (3 fl oz / ³⁄₈ cup)
Sugar	1½ Tbsp
Salt	1 tsp

JAPANESE-STYLE FILLING

Broiled eel	1, cut lengthways into long strips
Spinach	200 g (7 oz), trimmed to length of laver sheet and blanched in salted boiling water; refreshed with ice or tap water; then squeezed dry
Thinly sliced pickled ginger	to taste

*ROLLED OMELETTE

Eggs	3, lightly beaten
Sugar	3 Tbsp
Salt	⅓ tsp
Sake	½ Tbsp
Cooking oil	

DASHI

	2 Tbsp
Water	500 ml (16 fl oz / 2 cups)
Dried kelp (*konbu*)	6-cm (2½-in) piece
Bonito flakes	15 g (½ oz)

WESTERN-STYLE FILLING

Toasted white sesame seeds	
Avocado	1, skinned, stoned and cut lengthways into long, thick strips
Cucumber	1, quartered lengthways and cored
Smoked salmon	200 g (7 oz), cut into long strips and trimmed to length of laver sheet
Crabsticks	4–6, halved and mixed with 2 Tbsp mayonnaise, salt and ground black pepper to taste

1. Prepare rolled omelette and dashi (page 19). Combine eggs, dashi, sugar, salt and sake in a bowl.

2. Heat a greased rectangular omelette or non-stick pan. Pour one-fifth of the egg mixture into pan to thinly cover base. When omelette sets, fold in half towards you.

3. Grease empty half of pan and push omelette to oiled part of pan. Pour another one-fifth of the egg mixture into empty part of pan, then lift the edges of the first omelette to allow egg mixture to run underneath, and replace.

4. When second omelette is lightly set, fold it over the first. Repeat greasing, frying and folding procedure another 3 times to form a single multi-layered omelette at the end.

5. Remove from pan and cool completely. Cut into 1.5-cm (¾-in) wide strips.

6. Assemble sushi with Japanese-style filling. Place a laver sheet on a sushi-rolling mat.

JAPANESE

7 Spread about 220 g (8 oz) cooled rice onto it lightly and evenly, leaving a 1-cm (½-in) margin along top and bottom edges.

8 Make a shallow depression across the centre of rice. Wet fingers to prevent rice from sticking. Fill with some strips of omelette, eel, spinach and pickled ginger.

9 Use a damp tea towel to lift and roll laver and rice over filling firmly. Unwrap sushi roll, set aside and repeat to make 2 more rolls.

10 Assemble sushi with western-style filling. Put sushi-rolling mat into a resealable bag which fits nicely. Place a laver sheet on it. Spread about 220 g (8 oz) cooled rice onto it lightly and evenly to cover whole sheet.

11 Sprinkle white sesame seeds all over. Press lightly but firmly to help sesame seeds adhere to rice.

12 Turn laver sheet over on mat so that the surface with laver is now facing you.

13 Line the centre of laver sheet with some strips of avocado, cucumber, smoked salmon and crabsticks.

14 Use mat to lift and roll rice and laver over filling firmly. Unwrap sushi roll, set aside and repeat to make 1 more roll.

15 When all sushi rolls are ready, slice each roll crossways into 2-cm (1-in) pieces. Wet knife with rice vinegar or water after each cut; this ensures clean, neat slices.

16 Serve with soy sauce and *wasabi* on the side for dipping, if desired.

KOREAN

Pumpkin Porridge

This is a classic Korean pumpkin porridge. Kidney beans or sweet pear are often added for extra texture and flavour.

Glutinous rice	2 Tbsp, soaked for 1 hour, then drained
Pumpkin	400 g (14⅓ oz), peeled, washed and steamed
Water	250 ml (8 fl oz / 1 cup)
Salt	½ Tbsp
Sugar	2 Tbsp

1 Grind glutinous rice in a blender with 125 ml (4 fl oz / ½ cup) water. Remove and set aside.

2 Puree steamed pumpkin in a blender with remaining water. Remove and set aside.

3 Place ground glutinous rice mixture in a heavy pot and bring to the boil, stirring occasionally. Add puréed pumpkin and simmer for 15 minutes.

4 Add salt and sugar then return to the boil before serving.

KOREAN

Rice Mixed with Vegetables and Beef

Rice topped with beef and vegetables and served with a chilli paste.

Japanese rice	450 g (1 lb)
Light soy sauce	2 tsp
Ground black pepper	1 pinch
Sugar	1 tsp
Minced garlic	1 tsp
Sesame oil	2 tsp
Ground or chopped beef	100 g (3½ oz)
Cooking oil	1 tsp
Courgette (zucchini)	½, peeled and cut into thin strips
Carrots	½, peeled and cut into thin strips
Fresh shiitake mushrooms	2, cut into thin strips, stems discarded
Bean sprouts	30 g (1 oz), parboiled in lightly salted water and squeezed dry
Egg	1, cooked, sunny-side up

BEAN SPROUTS SEASONING
Salt	½ tsp
Scallion (spring onion)	1
Garlic	2 cloves, peeled and minced
Sesame oil	1 tsp
White sesame seeds	1 tsp, roasted

CHILLI PASTE WITH SESAME
Hot chilli paste	4 Tbsp
White sesame seeds	1 Tbsp, roasted
Sesame oil	2 tsp

CHILLI PASTE WITH SESAME
Cooking oil	2 Tbsp
Minced beef	700 g (1½ lb)
Light soy sauce	2 tsp
Ground white pepper	2 Tbsp
Sugar	180 g (6½ oz)
Hot chilli paste	1 kg (2 lb 3 oz)
Mirin	375 ml (12 fl oz / 1½ oz)
Glucose	150 ml (5 fl oz / ⅗ cup)
Pine nuts	

1. Wash rice then soak for 30 minutes and drain. Cook rice in a rice cooker with 500 ml (16 fl oz / 2 cups) water.
2. Combine soy sauce, pepper, sugar, garlic and sesame oil. Marinate beef, then stir-fry lightly until cooked.
3. Heat oil in a frying pan and stir-fry zucchini quickly so the colour stays vivid. Remove. Stir-fry carrots and mushrooms in the same way.
4. Sprinkle bean sprouts seasoning over parboiled bean sprouts.
5. Prepare chilli paste with sesame. Combine ingredients and use as needed, or prepare pan-broiled chilli paste.
6. Arrange beef, vegetables and egg in a bowl. Serve accompanied with rice, chilli paste with sesame or pan-broiled chilli paste.

Rice 155

KOREAN

Fried Rice Cake with Spicy Sauce

Rice cakes cooked in a spicy-sweet sauce with mixed vegetables.

Cooking oil	2 Tbsp
Hot chilli paste	2 Tbsp
Chilli powder	½ Tbsp
Beef seasoning powder	1½ tsp (optional)
Sugar	1½ Tbsp
Frozen rice cake rolls	200 g (7 oz), cut in half
Water	180 ml (6 fl oz / ¾ cup)
Fish cakes	70 g (2½ oz), sliced
Cabbage leaves	3, sliced
White sesame seeds	1 tsp, toasted
Spring onion (scallion) or leek	1, sliced

1. Heat a wok for 5 minutes then pour in cooking oil. Add hot chilli paste, chilli and beef powder, sugar and rice cake rolls. Stir-fry for 5 minutes over medium heat.
2. Add water and simmer with fish cakes and cabbage for 10 minutes.
3. Garnish with sesame seeds and spring onion or leek before serving.

Sliced Rice Cake in Soup

Korean rice cake in a light beef stock. This festive dish is eaten during the Korean new year.

Beef	300 g (11 oz)
Garlic	2 cloves
Water	2.5 litres (80 fl oz / 10 cups)
Ground black pepper	1 tsp
Light soy sauce	1 Tbsp
Salt	2 tsp
Sesame oil	1 tsp
Frozen rice cake slices	125 g (4½ oz)
Spring onion (scallion)	1, sliced
Egg	1, separated and fried into thin omelettes and thinly sliced

1. Place beef, garlic and water in a pot and bring to the boil. Reduce heat to a simmer and cook for 30–40 minutes.
2. Drain beef and slice thinly. Season with pepper, soy sauce, 1 tsp salt and sesame oil and set aside.
3. Season beef stock to taste with remaining salt then bring to the boil. When stock starts to boil, add rice cakes and cook for 20 minutes.
4. Return beef to the stock and bring stock back to the boil. Add spring onion.
5. Ladle rice cakes, beef and stock into individual bowls. Top with sliced omelette and serve hot.

THAI

Fried Rice with Dried Prawn Paste

A simple rice dish made fragrant with prawn paste.

Dried prawn (shrimp) paste	2 Tbsp
Water	2 Tbsp
Cooked rice	750 g (1 lb 11 oz)
Cooking oil	3 Tbsp
Garlic	2 cloves, peeled and crushed
Salt	to taste
Dried prawns (shrimps)	2 Tbsp, finely ground

GARNISH

Shallots	4, peeled and finely sliced
Red capsicum (bell pepper)	¼, cut into strips
Omelette	cooked using 2 eggs, thinly sliced
Lemon	1, cut into quarters

1. Dilute prawn paste in water and mix well with cooked rice.
2. Heat oil and brown garlic. Add rice and sauté over medium heat for 5 minutes, adding salt to taste. Sprinkle finely ground dried prawns over rice. Remove from heat.
3. Serve garnished with shallots, red capsicum, slices of omelette and lemon quarters.

Fried Rice with Chicken and Basil

A quick and tasty dish made using some of Thailand's favourite ingredients—fish sauce and Thai sweet basil.

Cooking oil	4 Tbsp
Garlic	2 cloves, peeled and crushed
Red bird's eye chillies	2, crushed
Chicken breast	300 g (11 oz), finely sliced
Fish sauce	2 Tbsp
Thai sweet basil	20 leaves
Cooked rice	750 g (1 lb 11 oz)

GARNISH
Crisp-fried shallots   1 Tbsp

1. Heat oil and lightly brown garlic and chilli. Add chicken and sauté for 2–3 minutes before mixing in fish sauce and basil leaves.
2. Take out a few basil leaves and reserve for garnish then add rice. Sauté over strong heat for 3 minutes, stirring briskly. Remove from heat.
3. Transfer to a large serving dish or individual bowls. Garnish with reserved basil leaves and fried shallot.
4. Serve with fish sauce with chopped bird's eye chillies.

THAI

Pork Fried Rice with Tomato Sauce

A unique combination of rice stir-fried with meat and tomato sauce.

Cooking oil	2 Tbsp
Garlic	3 cloves, crushed
Pork or chicken	300 g (11 oz), finely sliced
Onion	1, peeled and diced
Fish sauce	2 Tbsp
Canned tomato purée	3 Tbsp
Cooked rice	750 g (1 lb 11 oz)
Ground white pepper	to taste

GARNISH

Cucumber	1, sliced into rounds
Spring onions (scallions)	4
Coriander leaves (cilantro)	1 sprig
Lemon (optional)	1

1 Heat oil and brown garlic. Add pork or chicken and sauté for about 3 minutes.

2 Add onion, fish sauce and tomato purée. Stir well, adding a little water and oil if the mixture becomes too dry.

3 Turn up heat. When mixture is cooked after about 3 minutes more, add rice and sauté for a further 3 minutes. Season to taste with pepper.

4 Serve in a large dish, garnished with cucumber rounds, spring onions and coriander leaves. Squeeze lemon juice over the rice if you like it sour.

THAI

Pineapple Rice

A dish of stir-fried rice sweetened with pineapple cubes and made complete with chicken and chicken sausage.

Thai fragrant rice	375 g (13$^{2}/_{5}$ oz), washed and drained
Water	625 ml (20 fl oz / 2½ cups)
Ripe pineapple	1, about 1.5 kg (3 lb / 4½ oz)
Cooking oil	3 Tbsp
Shallots	10, peeled and sliced
Dried prawns (shrimps)	85 g (3 oz), soaked in hot water for 5 minutes, drained and chopped
Chicken breast	280 g (10 oz), cut into small cubes
Chicken sausages	4, cut into small cubes
Fish sauce	3 Tbsp
Meat curry powder (optional)	2 Tbsp
Light soy sauce	4 Tbsp
Sugar	1½ Tbsp

GARNISH
Lettuce leaves	
Coriander leaves (cilantro)	55 g (2 oz), chopped
Red chilli	1, cut into small strips and soaked in cold water

1. Combine rice and water and cook. Fluff rice and set aside to cool.
2. Cut pineapple in half lengthways. Run a knife around the edge of pineapple, cut and scoop out flesh. Cut flesh into 1-cm (½-in) cubes to get 200 g (7 oz). Keep shell aside.
3. Heat cooking oil and fry shallots until brown and crisp. Set aside. In the same oil sauté dried prawns until fragrant. Add chicken and sausage cubes and fry until chicken is cooked.
4. Add fish sauce, meat curry powder, if desired, soy sauce, sugar and cooked rice. Mix well. Add pineapple cubes and fry for 2–3 minutes. Set aside.
5. Heat pineapple shell in a 180°C (350°F) preheated oven for 10 minutes. Remove from oven and fill with pineapple fried rice.
6. Garnish rice with lettuce, crisp-fried shallots, coriander leaves and chilli strips.

VIETNAMESE

Saigon Fish Congee

The Vietnamese touch of adding yam cubes and green beans to Chinese fish congee provides for a nutty aroma and more complex texture.

Mud fish, red snapper or sea bass	1, about 1.3 kg (2 lb 14 oz)
Water	2.5 litres (80 fl oz / 10 cups)
Jasmine rice	250 g (9 oz), washed and lightly roasted
Green (mung) beans	150 g (5⅓ oz), soaked in water for 1 hour or until softened and skins discarded
Yam	300 g (11 oz), washed, peeled and cut into large cubes
Straw mushrooms	200 g (7 oz)
Bean sprouts	200 g (7 oz), washed and drained well
Chopped spring onions (scallions)	3 Tbsp
Ginger	2-cm (1-in) knob, peeled and shredded
Ground black pepper	½ tsp

SEASONING

Crisp-fried shallots	4 tsp
Sesame oil	2 tsp
Salt	2 tsp
Chicken seasoning powder	3 tsp

1. Skin, bone and fillet fish. Reserve skin and bones for stock. Slice fillets.
2. Put fish slices in a bowl. Add seasoning ingredients, mix and set aside for 15 minutes.
3. In a pot, combine fish skin and bones and water. Bring to the boil, then lower heat and simmer for 30 minutes.
4. Strain stock and discard solid ingredients. Add rice to stock and cook for 1 hour until rice softens. Add green beans and yam. Simmer for 15 minutes. Then, add fish slices and mushrooms. Simmer for 5 minutes more or until the fish is cooked through.
5. Put some bean sprouts into individual serving bowls. Ladle hot porridge over.
6. Top with desired amounts of chopped spring onions, shredded ginger and ground black pepper before serving.

VIETNAMESE

Duck Cooked in Fermented Bean Curd

Duck, red fermented bean curd and coconut milk come together to spike the tongue with a series of forward flavours.

Duck	1, whole, 1.5–2 kg (3 lb 4½ oz–4 lb 6 oz)
Rice wine	2 Tbsp
Ginger	1 large knob, about 55 g (2 oz), peeled and pounded until fine
Coconut milk	about 400 ml (13½ fl oz)
Water	500 ml (16 fl oz / 2 cups)
Yam (taro)	500 g (1 lb 1½ oz), peeled and cut to bite-sized pieces
Salt	1 pinch or to taste
Chicken seasoning powder	½ tsp or to taste
Cooked rice	1 kg (2 lb 3 oz), or fresh rice vermicelli
Water convolvulus (kang kong)	500 g (1 lb 1½ oz), leaves separated and stems cut into 4-cm (1¾-in) lengths

MARINADE (COMBINED)

Ground black pepper	½ tsp
Salt	1 tsp
Oyster sauce	1 tsp
Red fermented bean curd	55 g (2 oz)
Sugar	1 Tbsp
Chopped garlic	1 Tbsp, fried until golden brown

DIPPING SAUCE

Red fermented bean curd	55 g (2 oz)
Sugar	3 tsp
Coarsely chopped garlic	1 Tbsp, fried until golden brown

1. Rub duck all over with rice wine and ginger combined. Set aside for 15 minutes, then rinse and drain. Chop duck into bite-sized pieces and marinate them for 15 minutes.
2. Bring coconut milk and water to boil. Add duck pieces and cook over low heat for 15 minutes. Add yam and simmer until soft.
3. Meanwhile, prepare dipping sauce. Blend red fermented bean curd and sugar together until well combined. Then, stir in fried chopped garlic. Set aside.
4. Adjust soup to taste with salt and seasoning powder. Sustain soup at a slow boil.
5. To serve, spoon steamed rice into individual serving bowls. Blanch some greens in hot soup to add on top. Drain and add some duck and yam pieces, then ladle on soup. Eat with dipping sauce.

Rice

NOODLES

BALINESE
166 Fried Noodles with Vegetables

CHINESE
167 Fried Yellow Noodles with Meat and Prawns
168 Glass Noodles and Fish Ball Soup
169 Pork Chow Mein
170 Fried Flat Rice Noodles with Beef

FILIPINO
171 Stir-fried Noodles with Sponge Gourd and Prawns
172 Stir-fried Egg Noodles
173 Stir-fried Glass Noodles
174 Filpino-style Spaghetti

INDIAN
175 Indian Mee Goreng

INDONESIAN
176 Meat Dumpling Noodle Soup
177 Prawn and Chicken Noodle Soup

JAPANESE
178 Cold Buckwheat Noodles

KOREAN
179 Sweet Potato Noodles
180 Cold Noodles
181 Noodle Salad

STRAITS CHINESE
182 Spicy Fried Vermicelli in Tangy Sauce

THAI
183 Spicy Fried Noodles with Seafood
184 Beef Noodle Soup
185 Rice Vermicelli in Coconut Milk
186 Noodles with Meat Sauce

VIETNAMESE
187 Traditional Chicken Noodle Soup
188 Quang Noodles
189 Crabmeat Noodle Soup
190 Duck Noodle Soup
191 Beef Noodles

BALINESE

Fried Noodles with Vegetables

Although egg noodles are used here, the dish can also be prepared with pasta of choice.

Cooked egg noodles	600 g (1 lb 5⅓ oz), chilled
Vegetable oil	90 ml (3 fl oz / ⅜ cup)
Shallots	70 g (2½ oz), peeled, halved lengthways and sliced
Garlic	55 g (2 oz), peeled and sliced
Red chillies	2, large, halved, seeded and finely sliced
Bird's eye chillies (optional)	2, finely sliced
Cabbage	100 g (3½ oz), sliced into strips
Spiced tomato sauce (page 16)	1 Tbsp
Indonesian salty soy sauce	2 Tbsp
Eggs	2, beaten
Chinese celery leaves	40 g (1⅓ oz), sliced
Leek	55 g (2 oz), small, sliced
Spring onions (scallions)	80 g (2⅘ oz), sliced
Spinach	80 g (2⅘ oz), sliced
Crisp-fried shallots	2 Tbsp
Salt	a pinch or to taste

1. Cook noodles or pasta in rapidly boiling water at a ratio of 500 g (1 lb 1½ oz) noodles to 5 litres (160 fl oz / 20 cups) water. Add 1 Tbsp oil and 2 Tbsp salt to boiling water.
2. Cook until noodles or paste are not too soft, but firm to the bite. Drain noodles just before the al dente stage is reached and leave to cool. If not using immediately, rinse with cold water and drain again, then toss with 2 Tbsp vegetable oil, which will prevent sticking.
3. Heat vegetable oil in wok or heavy frying pan. Add shallots, garlic and chillies. Sauté over medium heat for 1 minute or until golden yellow.
4. Add cabbage and spiced tomato sauce. Fry again for 1 minute, then add soy sauce and fry until dry.
5. Add eggs and continue frying until eggs are scrambled. Add noodles and fry for 3 minutes, then add remaining ingredients, mix well and season to taste. Dish out and serve garnished with vegetable crackers if desired.

Fried Yellow Noodles with Meat and Prawns

A complete meal of yellow noodles, meat and prawns in a light gravy.

Small prawns (shrimps)	120 g (4⅓ oz), peeled, deveined and washed
Salt	¼ tsp
Sugar	¼ tsp
Ground white pepper	to taste
Sesame oil	a dash
Cooked chicken or pork	120 g (4⅓ oz), shredded
Light soy sauce	¼ tsp
Sugar	¼ tsp
Corn flour (cornstarch)	½ tsp
Cooking oil	3 Tbsp
Garlic	2 cloves, peeled and minced
Mustard greens	2 stalks, washed and cut into 5-cm (2-in) lengths
Shallots	4, peeled and sliced
Fresh yellow noodles	300 g (11 oz)
Corn flour (cornstarch)	1 tsp, mixed with 1 Tbsp water
Crisp-fried shallots	1 Tbsp
Spring onion (scallion)	1, chopped

SAUCE (COMBINED)

Basic stock (page 19) or water	125 ml (4 fl oz / ½ cup)
Light soy sauce	1 Tbsp
Dark soy sauce	½ tsp
Sugar	½ tsp
Salt	¼ tsp
Ground white pepper	¼ tsp

1. Marinate prawns with salt, sugar, pepper and sesame oil and meat with light soy sauce, sugar and corn flour and leave for 15 minutes.
2. Heat 1 Tbsp oil in a wok until hot and lightly brown garlic. Put in meat, then prawns and toss until meat changes colour. Add mustard green and stir-fry for 1 minute. Remove and leave aside.
3. Reheat wok with 2 Tbsp oil and lightly brown shallots. Put in noodles and stir-fry briskly for 1–2 minutes.
4. Stir in combined sauce ingredients and return fried meat mixture to the wok. Stir well and thicken with corn flour mixture. Garnish with crisp-fried shallots and spring onion.

Glass Noodles and Fish Ball Soup

Glass noodles add a different twist to this popular fish ball soup.

Glass noodles	45 g (1½ oz), cut into 10-cm (4-in) lengths and soaked for 10 minutes
Cooking oil	2 Tbsp
Shallots	2, peeled and sliced
Garlic	2 cloves, peeled and minced
Basic chicken stock (page 19)	1 litre (32 fl oz / 4 cups)
Salted cabbage	1 small piece, rinsed and chopped
Fishballs	15, medium, rinsed
Salt	to taste
Ground white pepper	to taste
Spring onions (scallions)	2, chopped

1 Drain softened glass noodles and set aside.

2 Heat oil in a pot until hot and stir-fry shallots and garlic until lightly browned. Remove shallots and garlic crisps from oil and set aside.

3 Pour in strained stock and bring to the boil. Add glass noodles and preserved dried Chinese white cabbage and boil for 5 minutes. Put in the fishballs and boil for 2–3 minutes longer. Add salt and pepper to taste.

4 Serve hot soup garnished with a sprinkling of shallot and garlic crisps and spring onions.

CHINESE

Pork Chow Mein

Chinese noodles fried with pork, mushrooms and prawns served with shredded lettuce.

Chinese noodles or spaghetti	220 g (8 oz)
Prawns (shrimps)	100 g (3½ oz), large, boiled and peeled
Salt	to taste
Ground black pepper	to taste
Vegetable oil	4 Tbsp
Onions	2 medium, peeled, halved and thinly sliced
Streaky pork	100 g (3½ oz), or leftover roast pork or lamb, cut into thin strips
Button mushrooms	3–4 large, cut into medium-fine strips
Light soy sauce	3½ Tbsp
Dry sherry	3 Tbsp
Butter or lard	2 Tbsp
Large lettuce leaves	3, shredded

1. Boil noodles or spaghetti in salted water for 6–12 minutes or until just tender, then drain and rinse under cold water to separate strands. Sprinkle prawns with salt and pepper to taste. Rub seasoning in.

2. Heat oil in a wok or large saucepan over high heat. Add onions and stir-fry for 1 minute. Add pork and mushrooms and stir-fry with onions for 1½ minutes. Sprinkle over two-thirds of the soy sauce and stir-fry for another 1½ minutes. Turn heat to medium.

3. Add noodles or spaghetti to pan and stir until all ingredients are well mixed. Sprinkle in the rest of the soy sauce and half the sherry, reduce heat and simmer for 2–3 minutes.

4. Heat butter or lard in small frying-pan over medium heat. When it starts melting, add prawns and stir-fry them for 1½ minutes. Add lettuce and stir-fry for 30 seconds. Place mixture from the wok in large, deep and well heated serving dish. Put prawns and lettuce on top. Sprinkle with remaining sherry to serve.

Noodles

CHINESE

Fried Flat Rice Noodles with Beef

Beef marinated in ginger juice and corn flour add colour and taste to fried flat rice noodles.

Beef	120 g (4⅓ oz), cut into thin slices
Cooking oil	6 Tbsp
Salt	½ tsp
Mustard greens	5 small stalks, both ends trimmed
Fresh flat rice noodles	300 g (11 oz), strands separated
Light soy sauce	1 Tbsp, mixed with 1 Tbsp chicken stock or water
Bean sprouts	100 g, tailed
Spring onion (scallion)	1, cut into 2.5-cm (1-in) lengths
Coriander (cilantro) leaves	1 sprig, cut into 2.5-cm (1-in) lengths

SEASONING

Sodium bicarbonate	⅓ tsp
Ginger juice	2 tsp
Salt	½ tsp
Sugar	¼ tsp
Corn flour (cornstarch)	2 tsp
Cooking oil	1 Tbsp, added after all the above ingredients are well mixed with the meat

SAUCE (COMBINED)

Fresh chicken stock	5 Tbsp
Light soy sauce	½ tsp
Dark soy sauce	2 tsp
Corn flour (cornstarch)	3 tsp

1 Marinate beef with seasoning ingredients for at least 20 minutes. Bring half a saucepan of water to the boil. Add 1 Tbsp oil and ½ tsp salt. Scald mustard green until just cooked. Drain well and arrange on an oval dish. Turn off heat and scald beef. Allow to soak for 1 minute. Remove scum from surface, drain meat and leave aside.

2 Heat wok with 1 Tbsp of oil. Ensure that the whole wok is well greased, then pour off excess oil. Put in rice noodles and toss in hot wok for 2 minutes.

3 Add light soy sauce mixed with chicken stock, and stir-fry until well mixed. Remove and place noodles on mustard green.

4 Reheat wok with 1 Tbsp of oil and stir-fry bean sprouts for 30 seconds. Remove. Place over fried rice noodles.

5 Wash wok and reheat with 1 Tbsp of oil. Put in combined sauce ingredients. Add meat, spring onion and coriander leaves. Toss quickly then add 2 Tbsp of cooking oil and mix.

6 Pour meat mixture over noodles. Serve with cut red chillies and light soy sauce.

FILIPINO

Stir-fried Noodles with Sponge Gourd and Prawns

This is a popular noodle dish that is both delicious and easy to prepare. If sponge gourd is unavailable, substitute with other vegetables such as spinach, carrot, burdock, lotus root, broccoli or aubergine (brinjal/eggplant).

Cooking oil	4 Tbsp
Garlic	5 cloves, peeled and crushed
Onion	1, medium, peeled and sliced
Fish sauce	2 Tbsp
Prawns (shrimps)	200 g (7 oz), peeled
Sponge gourd	500 g (1 lb 1½ oz), ridges trimmed and sliced
Chicken stock or water	500 ml (16 fl oz / 2 cups)
Thin wheat noodles	200 g (7 oz)
Salt	to taste
Ground white pepper	to taste

1. In a frying pan, heat oil over medium heat. Fry garlic until light brown, then add onion and cook until soft and translucent.

2. Add fish sauce and stir to mix well. Add prawns and cook until prawns turn pink and are cooked. Add sponge gourd and stock or water and bring mixture to the boil. Sponge gourd is cooked when soft.

3. Add noodles and cook until noodles are tender. Season with salt and pepper.

4. Dish out and serve immediately.

FILIPINO

Stir-fried Egg Noodles

This is a popular Filipino-Chinese dish that is both tasty and filling.

Cooking oil	85 ml (2½ fl oz / ⅓ cup)
Garlic	3 cloves, peeled and finely minced
Onion	1, medium, peeled and chopped
Chicken breasts or fillets	500 g (1 lb 1½ oz), cut into strips
Prawns (shrimps)	400 g (14⅓ oz), medium, peeled
Dried Chinese mushrooms	12, soaked to soften, stems discarded and sliced
Carrots	2, medium, cut into thin strips
Leeks	85 g (3 oz), thinly sliced
Snow peas	200 g (7 oz)
Cabbage	200 g (7 oz), sliced
Oyster sauce	4 Tbsp
Light soy sauce	4 Tbsp
Chicken stock	1 litre (32 fl oz / 4 cups)
Corn flour (cornstarch) (optional)	55 g (2 oz), mixed with 3 Tbsp water
Ground white pepper	1 tsp
Salt	to taste
Dried egg noodles	500 g (1 lb 1½ oz), soaked to soften for 2 minutes and drained
Calamansi limes	2, halved

1. In a wok, heat oil over medium heat. Fry garlic until light brown, then add onion and fry until soft and translucent. Increase heat, add chicken pieces and fry until lightly browned.

2. Add prawns, mushrooms, carrots and leeks. Stir-fry for 3–5 minutes. Add snow peas and cabbage and stir to mix well. Add soy sauce, oyster sauce and chicken stock. Bring mixture to the boil, then reduce heat to low and leave to simmer for 3 minutes. Season with pepper and salt.

3. If a thicker gravy is desired, stir in corn flour mixture and cook for 1 minute, stirring constantly. Gradually add noodles and gently toss to mix well. Stir-fry until noodles are tender. Dish out and serve, with lime halves on the side.

Stir-fried Glass Noodles

Noodles, or *pancit* is the most obvious influence the Chinese have had on Filipino cuisine. As an all-time Filipino favourite, this stir-fried noodle dish known as *sotanghon guisado* is the perfect meal to serve on occasions like birthdays.

Cooking oil	90 ml (3 fl oz / ⅜ cup)
Garlic	1 head, peeled and minced
Spanish onion	1, large, peeled and sliced
Fish sauce	3 Tbsp
Chicken breasts or fillets	500 g (1 lb 1½ oz), sliced into 2.5-cm (1-in) strips
Chicken liver (optional)	150 g (5⅓ oz), sliced
Fish cake	2, sliced into 2.5-cm (1-in) strips
Carrot	1, peeled and sliced into strips
Dried Chinese mushrooms	5, soaked to soften, stems discarded and sliced, reserve soaking liquid
Sweet or light soy sauce	4 Tbsp
Dark soy sauce	4 Tbsp
Chicken stock or water	3 litres (96 fl oz / 12 cups)
Glass noodles	1 kg (2 lb 3 oz), cut in half, soaked to soften and drained
Salt	1–2 tsp, or to taste
Ground white pepper	2 tsp
Cabbage	500 g (1 lb 1½ oz), sliced into strips
Spring onions (scallions)	2, finely chopped
Calamansi limes	4, halved

DIPPING SAUCE

Fish sauce	4 Tbsp
Red and green bird's eye chillies	2–3, chopped

1. In a wok, heat oil over medium heat. Fry garlic until golden brown and reserve 3 Tbsp. Add onion and fry until soft, then add fish sauce. Stir to mix well.
2. Add chicken pieces and liver, if desired. Fry for 5 minutes, then add fish cake, carrot, mushrooms and reserved soaking liquid. Stir to mix well and bring mixture to the boil.
3. Pour in soy sauces and chicken stock or water. Return mixture to the boil and add noodles, salt and pepper. Stir-fry noodles until most of the liquid has been absorbed.
4. Add cabbage and stir-fry until cooked. Toss to mix well and transfer to a serving platter.
5. Garnish with reserved fried garlic and spring onions.
6. Prepare dipping sauce. In a small saucer, combine fish sauce and bird's eye chillies. Serve hot, with dipping sauce and limes on the side.

FILIPINO

Filipino-style Spaghetti

This Filipino version is slightly sweeter than spaghetti Bolognese and is popularly served at children's parties.

Olive oil	3 Tbsp
Garlic	5 cloves, peeled and chopped
Minced beef or chicken	500 g (1 lb 1½ oz)
Ground black pepper	1 tsp
Frankfurter sausages	400 g (14⅓ oz), diagonally sliced
Canned button mushrooms	255 g (9 oz), drained and sliced
Dried Italian herb mix	2 tsp
Tomato paste	140 g (5 oz)
Tomato purée or canned tomato sauce	900 g (2 lb)
Water	1.5 litres (48 fl oz / 6 cups)
Salt	3 Tbsp
Sugar	100 g (3½ oz)
Spaghetti	500 g (1 lb 1½ oz), cooked until al dente and kept warm
Grated Parmesan or Cheddar cheese	3 heaped Tbsp, or any desired amount for sprinkling

1. In a large saucepan, heat oil over medium heat. Fry garlic until fragrant, then add minced beef or chicken and pepper. Cook until meat is evenly browned, stirring constantly and using the spatula to break up any lumps.

2. Add sliced sausages, mushrooms and dried herbs and fry for 3 minutes.

3. Stir in tomato paste, tomato purée or sauce and water. Bring to the boil, then reduce heat to low and leave to simmer for 10 minutes. Stir occasionally to prevent burning. Season with salt and sugar. Taste and adjust seasoning, if necessary.

4. Divide spaghetti among 3–4 individual serving plates. Remove sauce from heat and ladle over spaghetti. Sprinkle cheese over before serving.

INDIAN

Indian Mee Goreng

Mee goreng simply means fried noodles. The tomato ketchup gives these noodles an appetising red colour.

Mutton	200 g (7 oz), diced
Cooking oil	2 Tbsp
Onions	2, peeled and sliced
Garlic	4 cloves, peeled and chopped
Potato	1, peeled and cubed
Bean sprouts	50 g (1⅔ oz)
Bean curd squares	2, diced
Chinese flowering cabbage (*choy sum*)	5 stalks or any other green vegetable, cut into 5-cm (2½-in) lengths
Eggs	2, lightly beaten
Tomato ketchup	2 Tbsp
Dark soy sauce	1 Tbsp
Salt	to taste
Yellow egg noodles	300 g (11 oz)
Flat rice noodles	100 g (3½ oz)
Chinese chives	1–2 stalks, cut into 2.5-cm (1-in) lengths
Lime halves	

GINGER AND GARLIC PASTE
Garlic	5 cloves, peeled
Ginger	1-cm (½-in) knob, peeled

CHILLI PASTE
Dried red chillies	10, soaked in hot water to soften
Garlic	2 cloves, peeled

1. Prepare ginger and garlic paste. Blend ginger and garlic together into a paste. Set 1 tsp aside for boiling with mutton. Store the rest of paste refrigerated for use when stir-frying vegetables or meats.
2. Blend chilli paste ingredients until fine.
3. Boil mutton pieces with 1 tsp ginger and garlic paste until tender. Drain and reserve stock for use later.
4. Heat oil in a wok and stir-fry onions and garlic until fragrant. Add chilli paste and fry until oil separates.
5. Now start working really fast. Add mutton, potato cubes, bean sprouts, bean curd and flowering cabbage. Stir quickly.
6. Add eggs and allow to set slightly. Add tomato ketchup, soy sauce and salt. Finally, add noodles and mix well over high heat. Keep mixing and breaking noodles up into shorter lengths.
7. Taste for seasoning and adjust as necessary.
8. Drizzle some reserved stock over noodles if you find it too dry.
9. Sprinkle with Chinese chives and serve hot with lime halves.

INDONESIAN

Meat Dumpling Noodle Soup

This hearty noodle soup combines chicken wantons with two types of dumplings, making it an extravagant and a truly satisfying dish.

Cooking oil	for deep-frying
Indonesian-style stock (page 20)	1.5 litres (48 fl oz / 6 cups)
Yellow egg noodles	125 g (4½ oz), cooked
Firm bean curd	125 g (4½ oz), sliced

CHICKEN WANTONS

Chicken meat	150 g (5⅓ oz), minced
Spring onions (scallions)	10 g (⅓ oz), sliced
Potato flour	1 Tbsp
Wanton wrappers	8
Egg white	1, beaten

BEEF DUMPLINGS

Beef topside (round)	150 g (5⅓ oz), minced
Spring onions (scallions)	10 g (⅓ oz), sliced
Potato flour	1 Tbsp
Ground nutmeg	a pinch

SEAFOOD DUMPLINGS

Fish fillets	150 g (5⅓ oz), minced
Coriander leaves (cilantro)	10 g (⅓ oz), chopped
Sugar	a pinch

SEASONING (3 SETS)

Oyster sauce	1 Tbsp
Indonesian salty soy sauce	1 tsp
Indonesian sweet soy sauce	1 tsp
Ground white pepper	a pinch
Salt	a pinch

1. Prepare chicken wantons. Place all ingredients, except wrappers and egg white, in a bowl. Add 1 set of seasoning ingredients and mix well. Place 1 tsp filling onto the centre of each wrapper. Lift corners and bring together over filling. Secure with egg white. Deep-fry half the chicken wantons in medium–hot oil until golden and crispy. Remove and drain well. Prepare beef dumplings. Combine all ingredients with another set of seasoning ingredients and mix into a smooth paste. Use 2 tablespoons to shape mixture into round dumplings. Repeat with seafood mixture.

2. Bring stock to a simmer in a saucepan. Poach remaining chicken wantons for 3 minutes, then beef and seafood dumplings separately for 2 minutes each. Once last dumpling is removed, increase heat to bring stock to the boil.

3. Meanwhile, divide noodles, bean curd, wantons and dumplings among 4 individual bowls, then ladle boiling stock over. Garnish, if desired, with Chinese celery leaves and fried shallots. Serve with nasi goreng sauce (page 19) or sweet soy sauce on the side.

INDONESIAN

Prawn and Chicken Noodle Soup

This spicy noodle soup is rich with the flavours of coconut milk and fresh spices such as turmeric and coriander.

Vegetable oil	2 Tbsp
Lemongrass	2 stalks, bruised
Kaffir lime leaves	3, bruised
Chicken thigh meat	150 g (5⅓ oz), cut into 1-cm (½-in) cubes
Indonesian-style stock (page 20)	500 ml (16 fl oz / 2 cups)
Coconut milk	500 ml (16 fl oz / 2 cups)
Peeled prawns (shrimps)	150 g (5⅓ oz), deveined
Snapper fillet	150 g (5⅓ oz), cut into 1-cm (½-in) slices
Lemon basil	8 sprigs, roughly sliced
Salt	to taste
Freshly ground white pepper	to taste
Glass noodles	150 g (5⅓ oz), soaked in warm water for 5 minutes

SPICE PASTE

Garlic	40 g (1⅓ oz), peeled and sliced
Shallots	85 g (3 oz), peeled and sliced
Candlenuts	40 g (1⅓ oz), roasted
Turmeric	55 g (2 oz), peeled and sliced
Bird's eye chillies	3, sliced
Coriander seeds	1 tsp, toasted and finely crushed
Dried prawn (shrimp) paste	1 tsp, toasted and finely crumbed

GARNISHING
Crisp-fried shallots
Chopped celery leaves

1 Prepare spice paste. Place all ingredients in a stone mortar or blender and grind coarsely.

2 Heat oil in a heavy saucepan. Add spice paste, lemongrass and kaffir lime leaves. Sauté over medium heat until fragrant.

3 Add chicken and continue to sauté for 2 minutes more. Add stock and coconut milk. Bring to the boil and simmer for 1 minute. Add prawns and fish slices. Return to the boil and simmer over very low heat for 1 minute.

4 Add lemon basil and season to taste with salt and pepper. Separately blanch glass noodles briefly and divide among serving bowls.

5 Ladle soup over and top with chicken, prawns and fish. Garnish as desired and serve.

Noodles 177

JAPANESE

Cold Buckwheat Noodles

Soba noodles make a very healthy dish as they have a high content of vitamin B and protein. Substitute with dried or frozen wheat (*udon*) noodles for a variation to this recipe.

Dried buckwheat noodles (*soba*)	400 g (14⅓ oz)
Japanese spring onion (scallion)	¼, finely sliced
Shredded dried *nori* seaweed	4 Tbsp
Japanese seven-spice seasoning	to taste (optional)
Wasabi	to taste (optional)

DIPPING SAUCE
Japanese dark soy sauce	3 Tbsp
Mirin	3 Tbsp

DASHI
Water	250 ml (8 fl oz / 1 cup)
Dried kelp (*konbu*)	5-cm (2-in) piece
Bonito flakes	10 g (⅓ oz)

1. Prepare dashi (page 19). Prepare dipping sauce. Combine 200 ml (7 fl oz / ¾ cup) dashi, soy sauce and mirin in a small saucepan. Bring to the boil, then remove from heat immediately. Set aside to cool completely.

2. Bring a large pot of water to the boil. Add noodles and cook for 5 minutes, or until just tender (refer to cooking instructions on packet of noodles, if unsure). Drain noodles in a colander.

3. Rinse and rub drained noodles for 1–2 minutes under cold running water. Drain well.

4. Divide noodles among 4 individual serving plates. Sprinkle each plate with 1 Tbsp seaweed, spring onion and seven-spice seasoning, if desired. Divide dipping sauce among 4 bowls.

5. Serve noodles with dipping sauce on the side, adding a dollop of wasabi to sauce, if desired.

KOREAN

Sweet Potato Noodles

This is a festive dish which is usually prepared for special occasions. These noodles do not keep well, so cook just enough for serving.

Fresh or dried shiitake mushrooms	
Beef	30 g (1 oz), thinly sliced
Onion	30 g (1 oz), peeled and cut into thin strips
Carrot	20 g (⅔ oz), cut into thin strips
Green capsicum (bell pepper)	1, small, cored and cut into thin strips
Salt	to taste
Dried sweet potato noodles	55 g (2 oz)
White sesame seeds	1 tsp, toasted

SAUCE A

Light soy sauce	2 Tbsp
Sugar	1 Tbsp
Minced garlic	2 tsp
Sesame oil	2 tsp
White sesame seeds	2 tsp, toasted

SAUCE B

Light soy sauce	2 Tbsp
Sugar	2 Tbsp
Sesame oil	2 Tbsp

1. If using dried mushrooms, soak in warm water for 10 minutes to soften, then squeeze dry and cut into thin strips. If using fresh mushrooms, cut into thin strips.
2. Season beef and mushrooms with sauce A. Separately stir-fry onion, carrot and capsicum in lightly oiled pan. Sprinkle with salt to taste each time. Spread on large plate to cool.
3. In the same pan, stir-fry seasoned beef and mushrooms. Boil noodles until soft then drain and cut into shorter lengths. Mix in sauce B.
4. Stir-fry noodles, add beef and vegetables. Continue to stir-fry a while longer. Dish out and garnish with sesame seeds.

KOREAN

Cold Noodles

This cold noodle dish is often served during summer in Korea.

White wheat noodles	400 g (14⅓ oz)
Kimchi	200 g (7 oz), chopped
Sugar	1 Tbsp
Salt	1 Tbsp
Sesame oil	1 tsp, optional
Anchovy stock	750 ml (24 fl oz / 3 cups), chilled
Kimchi brine	125 ml (4 fl oz / ½ cup)
Vinegar	1 Tbsp
Mustard	1 Tbsp
Cucumber	1, sliced
Hardboiled eggs	2, peeled and sliced
Lettuce	½ head, finely sliced
Pine nuts	3 Tbsp

SAUTÉED DRIED ANCHOVIES

Dried anchovies	50 g (1⅔ oz)
Cooking wine	1 Tbsp
Light soy sauce	1 Tbsp
Sugar	1 Tbsp
Cooking oil	1 Tbsp
Sesame oil	1 Tbsp
Maltose	1 Tbsp

1 Prepare sautéed dried anchovies. Dry-fry anchovies over low heat until dry. Add cooking wine and continue frying until anchovies are dry again. Remove from heat. Combine remaining ingredients and bring to the boil. Once mixture boils, remove from heat and mix with anchovies.

2 Bring noodles to the boil in some water. Drain, then rinse noodles under running water before plunging into ice-cold water. Drain noodles in a sieve.

3 Mix kimchi with sugar, salt and sesame oil. Set aside. Place noodles in a pot with cold anchovy stock and kimchi brine. Stir in vinegar and mustard. Mix well.

4 Dish noodles out into individual bowls and top with cucumber, eggs, lettuce and kimchi. Sprinkle with pine nuts and serve with sautéed dried anchovies in a separate saucer.

KOREAN

Noodle Salad

Cold noodles mixed with vegetables in a spicy sauce.

Buckwheat noodles (*soba*)	2 bundles
Cabbage or lettuce	5 leaves, cut into thin 4-cm (2-in) lengths
Cucumber	1, medium, cut into thin 4-cm (2-in) lengths
Carrot	½, cut into thin 4-cm (2-in) lengths
Cherry tomatoes	10, each cut in half
Crabsticks	4, shredded

SAUCE
Light soy sauce	3 Tbsp
Vinegar	3 Tbsp
Lemon juice	3 Tbsp
Sugar	4 Tbsp
Oyster sauce	½ Tbsp
Crushed garlic	1 Tbsp
Wasabi	1½ tsp
Chilli powder	1 Tbsp
Sesame oil	1 Tbsp

1. Combine ingredients for sauce and blend well. Refrigerate.
2. Blanch noodles in boiling water then wash under cold running water. Drain well.
3. Mix noodles with chilled sauce and some vegetables and crabsticks.
4. Garnish with remaining vegetables and crabsticks and serve.

Spicy Fried Vermicelli in Tangy Sauce

This is a popular Malay dish. The gravy is poured over just before serving.

Cooking oil	200 ml (7 fl oz / ¾ cup)
Coconut cream	90 ml (3 fl oz / ⅜ cup)
Prawns (shrimps)	400 g (14⅓ oz), medium, shelled and deveined
Firm bean curd	3 pieces, cut into strips and fried
Water	125 ml (4 fl oz / ½ cup)
Light soy sauce	4 Tbsp
Anchovy stock granules	4 tsp
Salt	1½ tsp
Sugar	4 tsp
Rice vermicelli	400 g (14⅓ oz), soaked in water until soft, and drained
Chinese chives	30 g (1 oz), cut into short lengths
Bean sprouts	400 g (14⅓ oz), tailed

SPICE PASTE

Dried chillies	25, soaked in water and drained
Shallots	16, peeled
Dried prawn (shrimp) paste	1 Tbsp, crushed
Candlenuts	4

GRAVY

Cooking oil	1½ Tbsp
Preserved soy bean paste	4 tsp
Onions	2, large, peeled and thinly sliced
Tamarind juice	500 ml (16 fl oz / 2 cups), extracted from 4 Tbsp tamarind pulp and 500 ml (16 fl oz / 2 cups) water
Salt	¾ tsp
Sugar	60 g (2 oz)
Peanuts	60 g (2 oz), toasted and pounded

GARNISH

Hard-boiled eggs	3, shelled and quartered
Cucumber	1, seeded and cut into thin strips
Red chillies	2, sliced
Calamansi limes	6, halved

1. Heat cooking oil in a wok and fry finely ground paste until fragrant. Put aside one-third of fried paste including the oil.

2. Add coconut cream to wok. Add prawns and fry for 2 minutes. Add fried bean curd, water and season well with soy sauce, anchovy stock granules, salt and sugar. Bring to the boil.

3. Add rice vermicelli and chives. Stir until well mixed. Add bean sprouts. Cook for 2 minutes, then remove from heat.

4. To prepare gravy, heat cooking oil and fry preserved soy beans until fragrant. Add reserved fried paste. Stir in onions and add tamarind juice. Season with salt and sugar. Simmer for 2 minutes, then add peanuts.

5. To serve, put rice vermicelli in individual bowls, add gravy and top with a garnish of eggs, cucumber, red chillies and limes.

THAI

Spicy Fried Noodles with Seafood

A light, tasty dish of flat rice noodles stir-fried with fresh seafood.

Seafood (squid, shelled prawns (shrimp), fish meat, steamed mussels)	500 g (1 lb 1½ oz)
Cooking oil	150 ml (5 fl oz / ³/₅ cup)
Garlic	3 Tbsp, peeled and crushed
Light soy sauce	2 Tbsp
Thick flat rice noodles	500 g (1 lb 1½ oz)
Fish sauce	3 Tbsp
Holy basil leaves	a handful, crisp-fried
Red chillies	3, roughly chopped
Ground white pepper	to taste

1. Cut seafood into pieces if necessary.
2. Heat 4 Tbsp oil and brown garlic. Sauté seafood for a few minutes in the same oil. Drain and set aside.
3. Add remaining oil to the wok and increase heat. Add soy sauce and noodles and sauté for 2–3 minutes. Add cooked seafood and fish sauce. Stir well.
4. Add basil leaves and chillies and stir. Add pepper to taste and cook for a minute more.
5. Serve hot, garnished with red chilli strips if desired.

Noodles 183

THAI

Beef Noodle Soup

Thai comfort food—thin rice noodles served in a bowl of warm beef stock with slices of beef.

Basic beef stock (page 19)	1.2 litres (40 fl oz / 5 cups)
Garlic	2 cloves + 1 Tbsp, peeled and chopped
Celery	2 stalks
Fish sauce	2 Tbsp
Light soy sauce	2 Tbsp
Ground white pepper	to taste
Beef fillet	300 g (11 oz), cut into thin strips
Flat rice noodles	500 g (1 lb 1½ oz)
Cooking oil	2 Tbsp
Coriander leaves (cilantro)	½ Tbsp, chopped
Spring onion (scallion)	½ Tbsp, chopped
Chilli powder	to taste
Lemon juice or vinegar	2 Tbsp

1. Heat stock with whole garlic cloves, celery, fish sauce, soy sauce and pepper. Cover and simmer for 10 minutes. Remove garlic and celery. Bring stock to the boil.

2. Place beef fillet in a straining spoon or strainer and hold in the boiling stock for 30 seconds. Remove and drain. Reduce heat.

3. Cook noodles in the simmering stock for 2 minutes, then remove and drain. Meanwhile heat oil and lightly brown chopped garlic.

4. Serve soup in individual bowls. First place noodles in each bowl and sprinkle with coriander, spring onion, browned garlic, chilli powder and pepper. Add meat, a few drops of lemon juice or vinegar and pour stock over.

THAI

Rice Vermicelli in Coconut Milk

Rice vermicelli, lightly flavoured with coconut milk, served with generous helpings of chicken, prawns and bean sprouts.

Tamarind pulp	55 g (2 oz)
Water	2 Tbsp
Boiled coconut cream*	250 ml (8 fl oz / 1 cup)
Shallots	6, peeled and chopped
Chicken fillet	100 g (3½ oz), thinly sliced
Tiger prawns (shrimps)	150 g (5⅓ oz), medium-size, peeled and deveined
Preserved soy bean paste	2 Tbsp
Sugar	2 Tbsp
Chilli powder	2 Tbsp
Rice vermicelli	250 g (9 oz), soaked for 15 minutes or until soft, drained
Fried bean curd	1, finely diced
Chinese chives	100 g (3½ oz), cut into 2.5-cm (1-in) lengths
Coriander leaves (cilantro)	50 g (1⅔ oz), cut into 1-cm (½-in) lengths
Eggs	2, beaten, fried into thin omelettes and cut into strips
Bean sprouts	300 g (11 oz), tailed
Lemons	2, cut in wedges
Banana blossom	1, tough outer layers discarded, shredded then blanched and drained

* BOUILED COCONUT CREAM

Water	435 ml (14 fl oz / 1¾ cups)
Grated coconut	500 g (1 lb 1½ oz)

1 Combine water and grated coconut. Squeeze to obtain coconut milk. Boil coconut milk until it separates and milk is reduced to 250 ml (8 fl oz / 1 cup).

2 Combine tamarind pulp, water and extract juice. Set aside. Heat boiled coconut cream for 5 minutes, add shallots and stir-fry until fragrant.

3 Add chicken and prawns and continue stir-frying for 2 minutes. Add preserved soy bean paste, sugar, chilli powder and tamarind juice and mix well into a sauce. Divide sauce into two portions and keep one aside.

4 Add rice vermicelli, bean curd and Chinese chives to one portion of the sauce and cook for 1 minute.

5 Transfer to serving dish and pour reserved sauce over vermicelli. Garnish with coriander leaves and omelette strips. Serve with bean sprouts, lemon wedges and blanched banana blossom.

Noodles with Meat Sauce

Thin egg noodles served with minced meat and a light sauce.

Dried egg noodles	500 g (1 lb 1½ oz)
Lettuce leaves	6
Cooking oil	150 ml (5 fl oz / ⅗ cup)
Garlic	1 tsp, peeled and chopped
Dark soy sauce	½ Tbsp
Shallot	2 Tbsp, peeled and chopped
Beef	400 g (14 oz), minced or ground
Water	125 ml (4 fl oz / ½ cup)
Curry powder	4 Tbsp
Light soy sauce	3 Tbsp
Plain (all-purpose) flour	½ tsp, blended with 2 Tbsp water
Salt	to taste
Ground white pepper	to taste

GARNISH
Coriander leaves (cilantro)	1 sprig, chopped

1. Cook noodles in boiling water according to the instructions on the packet. Drain.
2. Line a salad bowl with lettuce leaves and set aside.
3. Heat 90 ml (3 fl oz / ⅜ cup) oil and brown garlic. Add noodles and sauté for 1–2 minutes, adding dark soy sauce. Place noodles in prepared salad bowl.
4. Heat remaining oil and brown shallot. Add meat, water, curry powder and light soy sauce. Stir well. When sauce begins to boil, stir in blended flour and add salt and pepper to taste.
5. Simmer for a few minutes, before pouring mixture over noodles. Garnish with coriander leaves to serve.

VIETNAMESE

Traditional Chicken Noodle Soup

Served with rice noodles, this chicken soup is old-fashioned wholesome and comforting.

Basic chicken stock (page 19)	1 quantity
Chicken	1, about 1.5 kg (3 lb 4½ oz)
Sesame oil	as required
Flat rice noodles	2 kg (4 lb 6 oz)
Bean sprouts	200 g (7 oz), tailed if preferred
Chopped spring onions (scallions)	55 g (2 oz)
Onions	2, peeled and thinly sliced
Preserved soy bean paste	5 g (⅙ oz)
Chilli sauce	1 tsp
Limes	4, quartered

SEASONING

Salt	¼ tsp
Ground white pepper	¼ tsp
Chicken seasoning powder	¼ tsp

1. Prepare stock. When ready, lower in chicken and leave to boil over medium heat for about 30 minutes. Drain cooked chicken from stock, then lower it into a basin of water for 1 minute to cool down skin.

2. Smear sesame oil onto cooled chicken skin, then chop oiled chicken into bite-size pieces and set aside. Strain stock and discard solid ingredients. Return liquid to the boil, then add seasoning ingredients. Leave soup to simmer.

3. Put desired amounts of noodles and bean sprouts into a wire mesh strainer. Blanch in boiling hot water, drain and transfer to individual serving bowls.

4. Add desired amounts of cooked chicken pieces, chopped spring onions and onion slices on top of noodles in each bowl, then ladle boiling soup over.

5. Serve noodles with small saucers of preserved soy bean paste, chilli sauce, and lime quarters.

Noodles

VIETNAMESE

Quang Noodles

A satisfying meal of spicy pork slices and juicy prawns resting on a bed of yellow noodles and dusted with crushed crackers and peanuts.

Prawns (shrimps)	500 g (1 lb 1½ oz), washed, peeled but with tails intact and deveined
Chilli powder	1 tsp
Salt	½ tsp + 1 pinch
Spring onions (scallions)	55 g (2 oz), chopped
Cooking oil	100 ml (3½ fl oz / ⅖ cup)
Minced garlic	1 tsp
Minced onion	1 tsp
Pork thigh	300 g (11 oz), thinly sliced
Basic pork stock (page 19)	2 litres (64 fl oz / 8 cups)
Fish sauce	½ tsp + 2 Tbsp
Chicken seasoning powder	½ tsp
Fresh flat yellow noodles	500 g (1 lb 1½ oz)
Bean sprouts	100 g (3½ oz)
Mint leaves	55 g (2 oz)
Toasted sesame cracker	1, 30 x 30-cm (12 x 12-in), coarsely crushed
Skinned peanuts	100 g (3½ oz), toasted and coarsely ground
Red chillies	2, sliced
Limes	3, quartered and cored

1 Put prawns into a bowl. Add ½ tsp each of chilli powder and salt and spring onions. Mix well and set aside.

2 Heat oil in a pot. Fry garlic and onion until golden over medium heat. Add remaining chilli powder and pork slices. Stir-fry for 5 minutes. Add prawns and stir-fry for 5 minutes more.

3 Pour in stock then bring to the boil. Remove scum from liquid surface. Season with 1 pinch salt, ½ tsp fish sauce and seasoning powder.

4 Put desired amounts of noodles and bean sprouts into individual serving bowls. Top with desired amount of mint leaves. Ladle boiling soup over, then sprinkle on crushed crackers and ground peanuts.

5 Serve hot with 2 Tbsp fish sauce, chilli slices and lime quarters in separate small saucers.

VIETNAMESE

Crabmeat Noodle Soup

The sweetness of crabmeat is given centre stage in this noodle dish supported by straw mushrooms and a thickened pork stock.

Basic pork stock (page 19)	1 quantity
Cooking oil	1 Tbsp
Chopped garlic	2 Tbsp
Crabmeat	300 g (11 oz)
Salt	½ tsp
Ground white pepper	½ tsp
Fresh or canned straw mushrooms	200 g (7 oz), each halved
Thick round rice noodles	1.5 kg (3 lb 4½ oz)
Shallots	30 g (1 oz), peeled, sliced and crisp-fried
Spring onions (scallions)	50 g (1⅔ oz), chopped
Fish sauce	2 Tbsp
Sliced chillies	2 Tbsp
Limes	3, quartered and cores discarded

SEASONING

Chicken seasoning powder	½ tsp
Ground black pepper	½ tsp
Salt	½ tsp

1. Prepare stock.

2. Heat oil in a wok or frying pan. Add 1 Tbsp garlic and stir-fry until fragrant. Add crabmeat and sauté for a few minutes. Season crabmeat with salt and pepper. Dish out crabmeat to a plate.

3. Add remaining garlic to wok. When fragrant, sauté mushrooms for a few minutes, then dish out.

4. Put desired amounts of noodles into individual serving bowls and add some crabmeat and straw mushrooms on top. Ladle boiling soup over, then sprinkle on crispy fried shallots and chopped spring onions. Serve hot with some fish sauce, chilli slices and lime quarters in separate saucers.

Noodles 189

VIETNAMESE

Duck Noodle Soup

A hearty meal of bamboo shoot slices and duck pieces dusted with shallot slices and peanuts in a soupy bed of noodles.

Chicken bones	1 kg (2 lb 3 oz)
Duck	1, about 2 kg (4 lb 6 oz), washed, neck and feet discarded and halved lengthways
Lime juice	1 Tbsp
Minced ginger	1 Tbsp
Minced garlic	1 Tbsp
Chicken seasoning powder	3 tsp or more to taste
Dried or canned bamboo shoots	300 g (11 oz), soaked in water overnight and drained before use if dried and sliced if fresh
Salt	to taste
Shallots	100 g (3½ oz), peeled, sliced and crisp-fried
Skinned peanuts	100 g (3½ oz), coarsely ground
Fresh rice vermicelli	2 kg (4 lb 6 oz), or 500 g (1 lb 1½ oz) dried rice vermicelli soaked in water to soften and drained
Bean sprouts	300 g (11 oz)
Spring onions (scallions)	100 g (3½ oz), chopped
Polygonum (*laksa*) leaves	55 g (2 oz), washed, stems discarded and leaves coarsely chopped

DIPPING SAUCE (COMBINED)

Ginger and garlic paste	1 Tbsp finely chopped ginger + 1 tsp finely chopped garlic, pound until fine
Finely chopped chilli	1 tsp
Sugar	2 Tbsp
Lime juice	1 Tbsp
Fish sauce	1 Tbsp
Warm water	125 ml (4 fl oz / ½ cup)

1. Boil chicken bones in 3 litres (96 fl oz / 12 cups) water for 30 minutes. Strain and set aside.
2. Rub duck with combined lime juice and ginger combined to remove any unpleasant smell. Wash duck, drain and season with garlic and seasoning powder.
3. Return stock to the boil, then lower in duck. Leave to cook for 15–20 minutes, then drain and set aside.
4. Add bamboo shoot slices to stock and return to the boil. Adjust to taste with seasoning powder and salt if desired. Leave to simmer.
5. Chop cooked duck into bite-sized pieces and arrange on a plate. Sprinkle on some fried shallot slices and ground peanuts.
6. Blanch noodles and bean sprouts, then transfer to individual serving bowls. Add some duck pieces, fried shallot slices, chopped spring onions and polygonum leaves on top. Ladle boiling soup over.
7. Serve noodles with dipping sauce.

VIETNAMESE

Beef Noodles

This is a classic Vietnamese meal of beef slices and rice noodles bathed in a clear soup that belies its rich flavour.

Chicken bones	1 kg (2 lb 3 oz)
Beef thigh	400 g (14⅓ oz), with some ligaments, washed and dried
Beef fillet	400 g (14⅓ oz), washed and thinly sliced across grain
Thin flat rice noodles	2 kg (4 lb 6 oz)
Bean sprouts	200 g (7 oz), washed and drained well
Spring onions (scallions)	2–3 stalks, finely chopped
Onion	1, large, peeled and thinly sliced
Preserved soy bean paste	5 g (⅙ oz)
Chilli sauce	5 g (⅙ oz)
Limes	4, quartered

SEASONING

Salt	¼ tsp
Ground white pepper	¼ tsp
Chicken seasoning powder	¼ tsp

1. Boil chicken bones in 3 litres (96 fl oz / 12 cups) water for 30 minutes. Add beef thigh and simmer for 5 minutes or until ligaments soften. Drain beef thigh and thinly slice when cooled. Strain stock and discard solid ingredients. Return liquid to the boil, then add seasoning ingredients. Simmer.

2. Put desired amounts of noodles and bean sprouts into a wire mesh strainer and blanch in boiling water. Transfer to individual serving bowls.

3. On top of noodles in each bowl, arrange raw beef slices, cooked beef thigh slices, chopped spring onions and onion slices. Ladle boiling soup over and raw beef will cook in the meantime. Serve noodles with small saucers of preserved soy bean paste, chilli sauce and lime quarters.

MEAT

BALINESE
- *194* Balinese Lamb Stew
- *195* Braised Pork Ribs with Young Jackfruit
- *196* Minced Pork and Mushrooms in Banana Leaf

CHINESE
- *197* Pig's Trotters in Chinese Black Vinegar
- *198* Beef Patties in Tomato Sauce

FILIPINO
- *199* Beef Mechado
- *200* Filipino-style Meat Loaf
- *201* Beef Steak with Onions and Potatoes
- *202* Spanish Beef Roll

INDIAN
- *203* Mutton Pepper Fry

INDONESIAN
- *204* Saté with Sweet Soy Marinade
- *205* Beef Stew in Black Nut Sauce
- *206* Beef Braised in Coconut Milk

JAPANESE
- *207* Deep-fried Breaded Pork Cutlets
- *208* Braised Pork

KOREAN
- *209* Korean Beef Stir-fry
- *210* Braised Short Ribs
- *211* Beef Braised in Soy Sauce
- *212* Stir-fried Porkl

MALAYSIA
- *213* Sweet Princess Beef

THAI
- *214* Crab and Pork Stuffed Tomatoes
- *215* Pattaya-style Chilli Fried Beef
- *216* Beef Cutlet in Egg Net

VIETNAMESE
- *217* Vietnamese Beef Stew
- *218* Beef Cooked in Vinegar
- *219* Pork Stewed in Coconut Juice
- *220* Beef on Fire
- *221* Steamed Minced Pork with Duck Eggs

BALINESE

Balinese Lamb Stew

In Indonesia, goat meat is also used for this dish. Goat meat has a strong gamey flavour, which is why very pungent spices and vinegar are added to counter it. This recipe also works well with any kind of game or game birds.

Boned lamb leg or shoulder	800 g (1¾ oz), cut into 2-cm (1-in) cubes
Basic spice paste (page 14)	250 g (9 oz)
Cooking oil	2 Tbsp
Coriander seeds	1 Tbsp, crushed
Cardamoms	12, bruised and ground
Lemongrass	1 stalk, bruised
Salam leaves	3
Indonesian-style stock (page 20)	1 litre (32 fl oz / 4 cups)
Rice vinegar	1 Tbsp
Coconut milk	250 ml (8 fl oz / 1 cup)
Salt	a pinch or to taste
Crushed black pepper	a pinch

1. Combine meat and spice paste in a large bowl and mix well. Leave to marinate in a cool place for 1 hour.

2. Heat oil in a heavy saucepan. Add marinated meat, coriander seeds, cardamoms, lemongrass and *salam* leaves. Sauté over medium heat until meat changes colour.

3. Add half the stock and vinegar. Bring to the boil, reduce heat and simmer until meat is almost cooked. Frequently top up with more stock as it evaporates.

4. Pour in coconut milk. Return to the boil, reduce heat to very low and simmer until meat is tender and sauce shiny and creamy.

5. Season with salt and pepper.

BALINESE

Braised Pork Ribs with Young Jackfruit

The unusual combination of pork ribs and jackfruit is enhanced by the subtle fragrances of lemongrass, *salam* leaves and ginger.

Pork ribs	1 kg (2 lb 3 oz), cut into 3-cm (1½-in) pieces
Basic spice paste (page 14)	325 g (11⅔ oz)
Cooking oil	2 Tbsp
Lemongrass	2 stalks, bruised
Salam leaves	4
Ginger	50 g (1⅔ oz), peeled, sliced and bruised
Red chillies	2, large, left whole
Indonesian-style stock (page 20)	1.5 litres (48 fl oz / 6 cups)
Young jackfruit	400 g (14⅓ oz), peeled, cleaned and cut into 2.5 x 1-cm (1 x ½-in) pieces
Salt	to taste
Crushed black pepper	to taste
Kaffir lime leaves (optional)	1–2, finely chopped, for garnishing

1. Season pork ribs with 125 g (4½ oz) spice paste and set aside in a cool place for 1 hour.
2. Heat oil in a heavy stewing pan. Add remaining spice paste and sauté until fragrant.
3. Add pork ribs, lemongrass, *salam* leaves, ginger and chillies. Continue to sauté until pork ribs change colour.
4. Pour in half the chicken stock. Bring to the boil and simmer until ribs are almost cooked. Top up with more stock as it evaporates.
5. Meanwhile, cook jackfruit. Bring 3 litres (96 fl oz / 12 cups) of salted water to the boil and add jackfruit. Return to the boil and simmer for about 15 minutes or until almost cooked.
6. Drain and transfer jackfruit into iced water to cool, then drain well.
7. Add jackfruit to pork ribs and simmer until ribs are tender.
8. Season to taste with salt and pepper. Serve garnished with chopped kaffir lime leaves, if desired.

Meat

BALINESE

Minced Pork and Mushrooms in Banana Leaf

This recipe also can be prepared with chicken or duck. Replace basic spice paste with that for chicken.

Pork shoulder or neck	400 g (14⅓ oz), minced
Shiitake mushrooms	100 g (3½ oz), diced
Basic spice paste (page 14)	85 g (3 oz)
Bird's eye chillies	4, sliced and fried until golden
Crisp-fried shallots	2 Tbsp
Crisp-fried garlic	1 Tbsp
Palm sugar	1 tsp, chopped
Salt	a pinch
Crushed black pepper	a pinch
Coconut cream	85 ml (2½ fl oz / ⅓ cup)
Salam leaves	12
Banana leaf squares	12, each 12 x 12-cm (5 x 5-in)
Banana leaf strips	12, each 3.5 x 12-cm (1¾ x 5-in)
Bamboo skewers or cocktail sticks	

1. Mix minced pork, mushrooms, spice paste, chillies, fried shallots and garlic, palm sugar, salt, pepper and coconut cream together in a bowl until a smooth paste results.
2. Place 1 *salam* leaf onto the centre of a banana leaf square. Top with 1 Tbsp of prepared meat mixture.
3. Fold banana leaf in half by bringing 2 opposing edges together.
4. Fold in ends, then wrap a banana leaf strip around the parcel.
5. Secure with a bamboo skewer or cocktail stick and trim off excess leaf. Repeat until ingredients are used up.
6. Steam parcels for about 10 minutes or until well cooked.
7. Remove and unwrap to serve.

CHINESE

Pig's Trotters in Chinese Black Vinegar

A delicious dish of fried pig trotters simmered in black vinegar.

Pig trotters	2, cleaned and cut into 5-cm (2-in) pieces
Cooking oil	3 Tbsp
Soy bean paste	3¼ Tbsp, ground
Chinese black vinegar	3¼ Tbsp
Sugar	2 tsp
Water	1.5 litres (48 fl oz / 6 cups) or enough to cover trotters
Dark soy sauce	1 tsp

GROUND INGREDIENTS

Shallots	15, peeled
Garlic	15 cloves, peeled
Red chillies	6

1 Boil a large saucepan of water and scald trotters for 5 minutes. Drain.

2 Heat a saucepan or a deep claypot with oil until hot and stir-fry ground ingredients until fragrant.

3 Add ground soy bean paste and continue to stir-fry until aromatic. Put in trotters and fry for another 3 minutes. If necessary, sprinkle with a little water to prevent burning.

4 Add vinegar, sugar and enough water to cover trotters.

5 Cover pot and bring to the boil. Reduce heat and allow to simmer for 1½ hours until trotters are tender, stirring occasionally to prevent sticking.

6 When trotters are tender, stir in dark soy sauce. Dish out and serve hot.

CHINESE

Beef Patties in Tomato Sauce

Tasty beef patties shallow-fried and cooked in tomato sauce.

Minced beef	450 g (1 lb)
Green (mung) bean flour	2 Tbsp
Ground white pepper	a pinch
Salt	½ tsp
Cooking oil	6 Tbsp
Light soy sauce	1 Tbsp
Water	425 ml (14 fl oz / 1¾ cups)
Tomato sauce	2 Tbsp
Sugar	a pinch
Tomatoes	5, quartered
Worcestershire sauce	½ Tbsp

1. Season beef with flour, pepper and salt. Shape into patties.

2. Heat oil in a pan over medium heat and fry beef patties until golden brown. This will take about 5 minutes.

3. Pour soy sauce, water and tomato sauce over patties. Simmer for 30 minutes over very low heat. Add sugar and tomatoes. Add Worcestershire sauce just before serving.

FILIPINO

Beef Mechado

Mechado is a Spanish dish that traditionally uses fatty cuts of beef. The addition of crushed biscuits gives the gravy a unique texture, and the fatty cuts of beef keeps the stew moist and flavourful.

Stewing beef such as topside, brisket or chuck tender	1 kg (2 lb 3 oz), cut into 5-cm (2-in) cubes
Onion	1, large, peeled and quartered
Potatoes	5, medium, peeled and halved
Tomatoes	5, medium, finely diced
Red capsicum (bell pepper)	1, medium, cored, seeded and diced
Carrots	3, medium, peeled and cut into 7.5-cm (3-in) pieces
Light or sweet soy sauce	125 ml (4 fl oz / ½ cup)
Salt	to taste
Ground black pepper	1 tsp
Water	1.5 litres (48 fl oz / 6 cups)
Digestive biscuits	100 g (3½ oz), crushed into semi-fine pieces

STOCK

Light soy sauce	4 Tbsp
Distilled vinegar	4 Tbsp
Bay leaf	1, small
Garlic	2 cloves, peeled and crushed
Ground black pepper	1 tsp
Water	2 litres (64 fl oz / 8 cups)

1. Prepare stock. In a pot, combine ingredients and add beef. Bring to the boil over high heat, then reduce heat to medium, cover pot and simmer until beef is tender.

2. Remove beef and transfer to a clean saucepan. Strain stock and reserve 250 ml (8 fl oz / 1 cup).

3. Add reserved stock and remaining ingredients to beef, except for crushed digestive biscuits. Bring to the boil over high heat, then reduce heat to medium and simmer for 10–15 minutes, or until potatoes are tender. Stir occasionally to prevent burning.

4. Stir in crushed digestive biscuits. Taste and adjust seasoning, if necessary, stirring continuously until sauce has thickened.

5. Dish out and serve immediately, with plain rice or crusty bread.

Meat 199

Filipino-style Meat Loaf

This dish can be served hot or cold depending on your preference. It can be prepared ahead of time and frozen, as it keeps well. It is usually served during festive occasions.

Minced chicken or beef	500 g (1 lb 1½ oz)
Chorizo	3, chopped
Chicken or turkey ham	110 g (4 oz), diced
Red capsicum (bell pepper)	1, medium, cored, seeded, finely diced
Onion	1, large, peeled and finely diced
Celery	115 g (4 oz), finely diced
Carrot	1, finely diced
Pickles (gherkins)	55 g (2 oz)
Raisins	110 g (4 oz)
Cheddar cheese	100 g (3½ oz), grated
Olives	85 g (3 oz), pitted and sliced
Bread slices	4, torn into small pieces
Eggs	3, lightly beaten
Salt	2 tsp
Ground black pepper	1 tsp
Hard-boiled eggs	5, peeled, ends cut off

BRAISING STOCK

Cooking oil	4 Tbsp
Garlic	5 cloves, peeled and minced
Onion	1, medium, peeled and sliced
Tomato paste	55 g (2 oz)
Celery	1 stalk, roughly chopped
Water	2 litres (64 fl oz / 8 cups)

MEAT LOAF SAUCE

Cooking oil	4 Tbsp
Onion	1, medium, peeled and sliced
Plain (all-purpose) flour	55 g (2 oz)
Canned tomato sauce	3 Tbsp
Fresh milk	90 ml (3 fl oz / ⅜ cup)
Salt	to taste
Ground black pepper	to taste

1. In a mixing bowl, combine all ingredients except hard-boiled eggs. Mix well and divide into 2 equal portions.

2. Place 1 portion of mixture in the middle of a 30 x 30-cm (12 x 12-in) sheet of aluminium foil, and spread mixture out into a 20 x 10-cm (8 x 4-in) rectangle.

3. Arrange eggs on top in a row. Scoop remaining meat mixture over eggs. Fold up both sides of aluminium foil lengthwise and seal by tightly twisting together both ends of foil. Shape meat loaf by rolling it and twisting the ends of foil. Untwist the ends and fold in to seal. Set aside.

4. Prepare braising stock. In a large pot, heat oil over medium heat. Fry garlic until fragrant. Add onion and fry until soft, then add tomato paste and celery. Add water and stir to mix well. Carefully lower meat loaf into braising stock and bring mixture to the boil. Reduce heat, cover pot and simmer for 45 minutes to 1 hour.

5. Remove meat loaf and set aside to cool. Reserve braising stock. Place meat loaf on a roasting pan and unwrap one end of foil.

6. Roast meat loaf in a preheated oven at 180°C (350°F) for 25 minutes or until meat loaf is golden brown. Remove from heat and set aside to cool.

7. Meanwhile, prepare sauce. Heat oil in a saucepan over medium heat and fry onion until soft. Stir in flour and mix well. Add tomato sauce and reserved stock and increase heat. Bring to the boil, then reduce heat and leave to simmer for 3 minutes. Add milk, and season with salt and pepper. Leave to cook until sauce thickens.

8. Place meat loaf on a serving platter and garnish with fresh herbs, if desired. Serve warm or cold, with sauce on the side.

FILIPINO

Beef Steak with Onions and Potatoes

Simmered in a tangy marinade of soy sauce, lemon juice and pepper, *bistek*, a dish with Spanish and Mexican influences is considered to be one of the national dishes of the Philippines.

Sweet soy sauce	90 ml (3 fl oz / ⅜ cup)
Lemon juice	4 Tbsp
Ground black pepper	½ tsp
Beef sirloin or tenderloin	500 g (1 lb 1½ oz), sliced into 7 x ½-cm (3 x ¼-in) thick fillets
Water	375 ml (12 fl oz / 1½ cups), or more if necessary
Cooking oil	90 ml (3 fl oz / ⅜ cup)
Onions	2, large, peeled and sliced into rings
Light soy sauce	3 Tbsp
Potatoes	4, peeled and sliced into 4-cm (1½-in) thick wedges and fried until light brown
Salt	to taste
Corn flour (cornstarch)	2 tsp, mixed with 1 Tbsp water

1. In a mixing bowl, combine sweet soy sauce, lemon juice and pepper. Place beef slices in to steep and leave aside to marinate for at least 30 minutes. Reserve marinade.

2. Transfer beef slices and marinade to a frying pan or wok. Add water and bring mixture to the boil over high heat. Reduce heat to medium and simmer, uncovered, for 10 minutes. Remove beef slices and set aside. Reserve liquid.

3. In a clean frying pan, heat oil over medium heat and fry beef slices for 2 minutes. Add onions and light soy sauce and stir to mix well.

4. Add fried potatoes and reserved liquid. Stir-fry for 3–5 minutes, or until potatoes are tender.

5. Season with salt to taste and stir in corn flour mixture. Cook for 1 minute or until sauce thickens before removing from heat.

6. Dish out and serve immediately with plain rice and salad greens if desired.

Spanish Beef Roll

This is a dish that is associated with festive occasions because of its elaborate preparation. Once sliced, the myriad of colours from the stuffing gives the dish a festive appearance.

Beef flank, skirt or round cut	2 kg (4 lb 6 oz)
Light soy sauce	125 ml (4 fl oz / ½ cup)
Canned tomato sauce	125 ml (4 fl oz / ½ cup)
Ground black pepper	1 tsp
Salt	1 tsp
Sugar	2 Tbsp

STUFFING

Carrots	2, peeled and sliced into 0.5-cm (¼-in) thick strips
Pickles (gherkins)	55 g (2 oz), sliced into thin strips
Red capsicum (bell pepper)	1, small, cored, seeded and sliced into thin strips
Any type of sausage such as chorizo	2, diagonally sliced
Hard-boiled eggs	9, peeled and halved
Plain (all-purpose) flour	for dusting
Cooking oil	90 ml (3 fl oz / ⅜ cup)
Kitchen string	

BRAISING STOCK

Onion	1, large, peeled and quartered
Bay leaf	1, small
Sweet soy sauce	90 ml (3 fl oz / ⅜ cup)
Canned tomato sauce	125 ml (4 fl oz / ½ cup)
Sugar	2 Tbsp
Salt	1–2 tsp
Water	3 litres (96 fl oz / 12 cups)

1. Butterfly beef. Place beef on a flat surface and use a sharp knife to cut through the middle without slicing through completely. Split beef open. Beginning on one side of beef, make diagonal, continuous 0.5-cm (¼-in) cuts. Repeat for other side of beef.
2. Use a meat pounder to pound beef lightly to flatten, then slice into three 30 x 30-cm (12 x 12-in) pieces.
3. In a large bowl, combine soy sauce, tomato sauce, pepper, salt and sugar. Place beef pieces in to steep and leave aside to marinate for 10 minutes.
4. Place a piece of beef on a clean flat surface. On one end of beef, arrange one-third of stuffing ingredients except for eggs. Place 3 eggs on top of ingredients, then roll beef up and tie with string to secure stuffing. Repeat step for remaining ingredients.
5. Coat beef rolls with flour, dusting off any excess flour. In a frying pan, heat oil over medium heat and fry beef rolls until evenly browned.
6. Transfer beef rolls to a large pot. Add braising stock ingredients and stir to mix. Bring to the boil over high heat, then reduce heat to medium. Cover and simmer over low heat for 1½ to 2 hours until beef is tender.
7. Remove beef rolls and set aside to cool. Discard string and reserve braising stock for sauce. When beef rolls have cooled, place on a serving platter and slice into 2.5-cm (1-in) slices. Serve as a main dish, with sauce on the side.

Mutton Pepper Fry

This dish is fragrant with the aroma of freshly ground black pepper. Adjust the amount of black pepper to taste as desired.

Mutton	1.5 kg (3 lb 4½ oz), cut into small cubes
Water	
Cooking oil	90 ml (3 fl oz / ⅜ cup)
Dried red chillies	3
Mustard seeds	2 tsp
Curry leaves	3 stalks
Urad dhal	3 Tbsp
Shallots	500 g (1 lb 1½ oz), peeled and sliced
Chilli powder	3 Tbsp
Tomato paste	1½ Tbsp
Dark soy sauce	2 Tbsp (optional)
Freshly ground black pepper	1 Tbsp
Salt	to taste
Sugar	½ tsp
PASTE	
Garlic	10 cloves, peeled
Ginger	2.5-cm (1-in) knob, peeled
Salt	to taste

1. Prepare paste. Combine garlic, ginger and salt and grind into a paste. Rub paste into mutton and leave for 30 minutes.
2. Place mutton in a pot then add enough water to cover mutton. Bring to the boil for 20 minutes, stirring.
3. Heat oil in a wok and stir-fry dried red chillies. When chillies brown, add mustard seeds, curry leaves, urad dhal and sliced shallots. Fry until shallots are soft.
4. Add boiled mutton and stock, chilli powder, tomato paste, soy sauce and pepper. Stir well. Add salt and sugar. Cover and cook over medium heat, stirring occasionally, until meat is tender.
5. Serve with rice, chapatti or plain crusty bread.

INDONESIAN

Saté with Sweet Soy Marinade

Choose only one type of meat or soy bean cakes when preparing this recipe. If more is desired, increase spice paste quantities accordingly.

Leg of lamb, beef tenderloin or top round (topside) or chicken breast	600 g (1 lb 5⅓ oz), cut into 1.5-cm (¾-in) cubes or fermented soy bean cakes, cut into 2.5-cm (1-in) cubes
Limes	2, cut into wedges
SPICE PASTE	
Vegetable oil	3 Tbsp
Shallots	60 g (2¼ oz), peeled and sliced
Garlic	40 g (1⅓ oz), peeled and sliced
Red chillies	70 g (2½ oz), halved, seeded and sliced
Coriander seeds	1 Tbsp, toasted and crushed
Cumin	1 Tbsp
Lime juice	2 Tbsp
Palm sugar	1 Tbsp, chopped
Salt	1 tsp
Indonesian sweet soy sauce	4 Tbsp

1. Prepare spice paste. Combine all ingredients, except sweet soy sauce, in a stone mortar or blender and grind into a fine paste. Add sweet soy sauce and blend well.
2. Transfer spice paste to a heavy saucepan and place over medium heat. Sauté until fragrant, then remove from heat and allow to cool to room temperature.
3. Mix meat of choice or soy bean cakes with spice paste. Leave to marinate in a cool place for 30 minutes. Thread meat or soy bean cake onto bamboo skewers that have been pre-soaked in water.
4. Either oven-grill at very high heat or place over very hot charcoal, turning a few times. Remove when cooked. Serve with lime wedges and extra sweet soy sauce as a side dip.
5. Another serving suggestion is to serve saté with peanut sauce (page 17) and compressed rice cakes (page 21). To save time, ready-made rice cakes can be bought at Asian stores or supermarkets.

INDONESIAN

Beef Stew in Black Nut Sauce

Black nuts or *buah keluak* are an Indonesian speciality and their unique flavour is best brought out in a thick, meaty stew.

Vegetable oil	3 Tbsp
Lemongrass	1 stalk, bruised
Kaffir lime leaves	3, bruised
Beef brisket or shoulder	800 g (1¾ lb), cut into 2-cm (1-in) cubes
Indonesian-style stock (page 20)	1.5 litres (48 fl oz / 6 cups), hot
Salt	to taste
Ground black pepper	to taste
Crisp-fried shallots	for garnishing

SPICE PASTE

Red chillies	2, halved, seeded and sliced
Candlenuts	3, roasted
Turmeric	1 Tbsp, peeled and chopped
Galangal	1 Tbsp, peeled and chopped
Garlic	4, peeled and sliced
Shallots	8, peeled and sliced
Dried prawn (shrimp) paste	½ tsp, toasted
Coriander seeds	1 Tbsp, crushed
Indonesian sweet soy sauce	1 Tbsp
Palm sugar	1 Tbsp
Indonesian black nuts	3–4, shelled and blanched until tender
Tamarind pulp	1 Tbsp

1. Prepare spice paste. Combine all ingredients in a stone mortar or blender and grind coarsely.
2. Heat oil in heavy saucepan. Add spice paste, lemongrass and kaffir lime leaves and sauté over medium heat until fragrant and spice paste changes colour. Add beef cubes and continue to sauté until meat changes colour.
3. Add 500 ml (16 fl oz / 2 cups) beef stock and bring to the boil, then reduce heat and simmer until meat is very tender. Regularly check liquid level and add more stock as it reduces. Remove scum as it accumulates at the surface.
4. When the last of the stock has been added, simmer until sauce is thickened and shiny.
5. Season to taste with salt and pepper, then dish out, garnish as desired and serve.

INDONESIAN

Beef Braised in Coconut Milk

The delicious sauce that blankets these fork-tender cubes of beef is rich with spices and meat juices.

Beef shoulder or neck	800 g (1¾ lb)
Vegetable oil	3 Tbsp
Coconut milk	1.6 litres (52 fl oz / 6½ cups)
Lemongrass	2 stalks, bruised
Turmeric leaf	1, torn and knotted
Kaffir lime leaves	3, bruised
Salt	to taste

SPICE PASTE

Shallots	60 g (2¼ oz), peeled and sliced
Garlic	40 g (1¼ oz), peeled and sliced
Red chillies	100 g (3½ oz), halved, seeded and sliced
Turmeric	35 g (1¼ oz), peeled and sliced
Galangal	35 g (1¼ oz), peeled and sliced
Ginger	35 g (1¼ oz), peeled and sliced
Candlenuts	35 g (1¼ oz), toasted and crushed
Crushed black pepper	¾ tsp

1. Cut cleaned beef into 2.5-cm (1-in) cubes, then set aside. Prepare spice paste. Combine all ingredients in a stone mortar or blender and grind coarsely.

2. Heat oil in heavy saucepan, add spice paste and sauté over medium heat until fragrant and colour changes. Add coconut milk, lemongrass and turmeric and kaffir lime leaves. Bring to the boil.

3. Add beef cubes and return to the boil, then reduce heat and simmer until meat is tender and almost all the liquid has evaporated. Stir frequently.

4. Season to taste with salt and remove from heat when dish appears dry and oily.

Deep-fried Breaded Pork Cutlets

Although deep-fried breaded pork cutlets are commonly served at many Japanese restaurants, they are fairly simple to prepare at home.

Pork loin cutlets	4, boneless, each about 100 g (3½ oz), and 1.5-cm (¾-in) thick
Milk	100 ml (3½ fl oz / ²/₅ cup)
Sake	100 ml (3½ fl oz / ²/₅ cup)
Ground black pepper	to taste
Salt	to taste
Plain (all-purpose) flour	4 Tbsp
Egg	1, large, beaten
Dried bread crumbs	55 g (2 oz)
Cooking oil for deep-frying	

GARNISHING

Cabbage	300 g (11 oz), finely shredded, soaked in iced water and drained before use
Tomato	1, cut into wedges
Lemon	½, cut into wedges
Cucumber	½, diagonally sliced
Japanese hot mustard	to taste

SAUCE

Store-bought *tonkatsu* pork cutlet sauce	to taste
Ground toasted white sesame seeds	to taste

1. Make a few deep cuts on each cutlet. Marinate in milk and sake for about 10 minutes. Drain and pat dry with absorbent paper.
2. Tenderise cutlets briefly with a meat mallet, or the spine of a cleaver. Season with pepper and salt to taste.
3. Coat each cutlet with flour, shaking off any excess. Dip into beaten egg and coat well with bread crumbs.
4. Heat oil to 160–170°C (325–340°F). Deep-fry pork cutlets, 1–2 pieces at a time, for 5 minutes until golden. Remove and drain on absorbent paper. Repeat until all cutlets are deep-fried. Cut deep-fried cutlets crossways into 1.5-cm (¾-in) strips.
5. Arrange on individual serving plates, accompanied by some cabbage, tomato and lemon wedges, cucumber slices and a dollop of Japanese hot mustard on the side, if desired.
6. Serve hot, with individual bowls of ready-to-use *tonkatsu* dipping sauce, topped with ground sesame seeds.

JAPANESE

Braised Pork

This delicious dish has Chinese origins, but has been adapted with Japanese seasoning ingredients to add a Japanese twist to the dish.

Ladies fingers (*okra*)	12, washed and pat dry with absorbent paper
Salt	2 tsp
Pork belly	800 g–1 kg (1¾ lb–2 lb 3 oz)
Raw rice (any kind except Basmati or fragrant Thai)	2 Tbsp
Water	500 ml (16 fl oz / 2 cups)
Sake	200 ml (7 fl oz / ¾ cup)
Mirin	100 ml (3½ fl oz)
Sugar	60 g (2¼ oz)
Japanese spring onions (scallions)	2, green portion only
Mature ginger	7-cm (3-in) knob, left unpeeled, scrubbed and cut into 0.5-cm (¼-in) slices
Japanese dark soy sauce	4 Tbsp
Japanese hot mustard	(optional)

1. Sprinkle ladies fingers with salt, then lightly roll each ladies fingers on a chopping board with your hands to remove the fine hairs.
2. Blanch ladies fingers in boiling water for 1–2 minutes, then remove and soak in iced water to refresh. Set aside.
3. Heat a large pan and pan-fry pork belly over high heat until most of the fat is rendered and pork is lightly browned.
4. Rinse pork with hot water to remove oil, then drain and cut into 5-cm (2-in) pieces.
5. Place pork belly in a large pot and cover with water. Add rice and simmer over low heat for 2 hours until meat is completely tender. This will rid meat of any smell. Alternatively, simmer pork belly in a pressure cooker for about 20 minutes until tender.
6. Remove meat and discard cooking liquid with rice. Rinse pork belly under tap water. Drain and set aside.
7. Add water, sake, mirin and sugar to a large pot. Bring to the boil.
8. Add pork belly and spring onions, then lower heat and simmer with a drop-in lid, or baking paper trimmed to fit pot, for about 30 minutes. If using pressure cooker, simmer for 5 minutes.
9. Remove and discard spring onions, and add ginger and soy sauce. Cover and continue to simmer for another 15–20 minutes, until sauce has reduced by half. If using pressure cooker, simmer for 3–5 minutes.
10. To serve, drain and put ladies fingers into a deep serving dish. Transfer some pork belly to same dish. Add about ⅛ tsp Japanese hot mustard, if desired. Serve immediately.

KOREAN

Korean Beef Stir-fry

Tender and juicy beef marinated in light soy sauce.

Cooking oil	½ Tbsp
Minced garlic	3 Tbsp
Carrot	1, sliced
Spring onion (scallion)	1, sliced
Shiitake mushrooms	2, sliced
White sesame seeds	½ tsp, toasted
Sesame oil	a few drops

BEEF STIR-FRY

Teriyaki beef	500 g (1 lb 1½ oz)
Light soy sauce	3 Tbsp
Sugar	85 g (3 oz)
Ground black pepper	1 Tbsp
Canned pineapple rings	2
Canned pear juice or pineapple syrup	125 ml (4 fl oz / ½ cup)
Sesame oil	3 Tbsp
Onion	1½, peeled and minced
Mirin	125 ml (4 fl oz / ½ cup)

1. Combine beef stir-fry ingredients in a large mixing bowl. Mix well with your hands. Refrigerate overnight or for at least 2 hours.
2. Heat cooking oil and add garlic. When garlic is fragrant, stir-fry marinated beef with sliced carrot, spring onion and mushrooms.
3. Sprinkle with sesame seeds and sesame oil just before removing from heat. Serve hot.

KOREAN

Braised Short Ribs

Ribs simmered in soy sauce over low heat until tender and tasty.

Beef short ribs	1 kg (2 lb 3 oz), meaty parts scored
Water	2 litres (64 fl oz / 8 cups)
Dried shiitake mushrooms	8, soaked for 10 minutes, squeezed dry and sliced, discard stems
Carrots	2, medium, cut into small pieces
Chestnuts	6, peeled
Dried red dates	1–2 stoned and sliced

MARINADE

Light soy sauce	90 ml (3 oz / ⅜ cup)
Sugar	3 Tbsp
Crushed garlic	2 Tbsp
Sesame oil	1 Tbsp
Pineapple syrup or pear juice	150 ml (5 fl oz / ⅗ cup)
Cooking wine	2 Tbsp
Ground black pepper	1 Tbsp
Spring onions (scallions)	2, chopped

1. Soak ribs for 20 minutes. Change the water several times. Drain and trim off fat from ribs.
2. Combine marinade ingredients and place ribs in to marinate for 1 hour.
3. Place ribs in a heavy-based pot. Add water and cook over medium heat until ribs are tender. This will take about 30–40 minutes.
4. Add mushrooms, carrots and chestnuts then reduce heat to simmer for about 20–30 minutes. Serve hot, garnished with red dates.

KOREAN

Beef Braised in Soy Sauce

A comforting dish of beef braised in soy sauce. Serve hot with steamed white rice.

Garlic	4–5 cloves
Onion	½, peeled
Black peppercorns	2 tsp
Water	1.25 litres (40 fl oz / 5 cups)
Beef	500 g (1 lb 1½ oz)
Light soy sauce	180 ml (6 fl oz / ¾ cup)
Sugar	3 Tbsp
Hard-boiled eggs	2–3, peeled and halved
Sesame oil	a few drops

1. Put garlic, onion, and peppercorns in water and boil for 10 minutes.
2. Place beef in and boil for another 10–20 minutes.
3. Test to see if beef is cooked by piercing with a skewer. Drain beef and reserve stock. Discard garlic, onion and peppercorns.
4. Place beef and stock in a pot and add soy sauce and sugar. Bring to the boil for 10–15 minutes over medium heat. Remove from heat and leave to cool.
5. Slice beef into thin slices and serve in a small dish on a bed of hardboiled egg halves. Drizzle with sesame oil before serving.

KOREAN

Stir-fried Pork

Pork marinated with red chilli pepper paste and stir-fried.

Pork shoulder	1 kg (2 lb 3 oz), machine-sliced into teriyaki-thin strips
Hot chilli paste	4 Tbsp
Light soy sauce	2 Tbsp
Sugar	2 Tbsp
Ground black pepper	½ Tbsp
Crushed garlic	2 Tbsp
Ginger juice	1 tsp
Chilli powder	2 Tbsp
Pineapple syrup	125 ml (4 fl oz / ½ cup)
Onion	1, medium, peeled and sliced
White sesame seeds	1 tsp, roasted

1 Start preparations up to 6 hours ahead.
2 Combine all ingredients except onion, sesame seeds and sliced chilli. Leave pork to marinate for 6 hours.
3 Heat some cooking oil and pan-fry marinated pork until almost cooked. Add onion and continue to cook until well done.
4 Sprinkle sesame seeds over and garnish as desired before serving.

MALAYSIAN

Sweet Princess Beef

The beef cubes are simmered until tender in a thick tamarind sauce.

Ghee	55 g (2 oz)
Cinnamon stick	5-cm (2-in) piece
Cardamoms	3
Cloves	4
Curry leaves	3 sprigs
Garlic	3 cloves, peeled and finely chopped
Shallots	10, peeled and finely chopped
Ginger	1-cm (½-in) knob, peeled and finely chopped
Chilli paste	4 Tbsp
Ground coriander	1 Tbsp
Ground cumin	2 tsp
Ground fennel	1 tsp
Fresh blade, knuckle or beef cubes	500 g (1 lb 1½ oz)
Water	250 ml (8 fl oz / 1 cup)
Tamarind juice	4 Tbsp, extracted from 2 Tbsp tamarind pulp and 4 Tbsp water
Salt	to taste
Sugar	2 Tbsp
Potatoes	2, large, peeled, cut into wedges and deep-fried
Tomatoes	2, large, quartered
Onion	1, peeled and sliced into rounds

1. Heat ghee and fry cinnamon, cardamoms, cloves and curry leaves. Add garlic, shallots and ginger.
2. Add chilli paste, coriander, cumin and fennel. Fry until fragrant.
3. Add beef and water. Stir well and simmer for 30 minutes until beef is tender and the sauce thick.
4. Add tamarind juice, salt and sugar. Stir well before adding potatoes, tomatoes and onion. Cook for another 2 minutes. Serve.

THAI

Crab and Pork Stuffed Tomatoes

A colourful dish of stuffed tomatoes wrapped in egg net.

Tomatoes	10
Salt	as needed
Coriander (cilantro) roots	3, chopped
Garlic	4 cloves, peeled and chopped
Black peppercorns	10
Pork	250 g (9 oz), minced (ground)
Cooked or canned crabmeat	250 g (9 oz)
Onion	1, peeled and chopped
Sugar	1 tsp
Fish sauce	2 Tbsp
Eggs	5, beaten

1. Slice tops off tomatoes and set aside to be used as lids. Scoop out tomato flesh and coat inside of tomato shells lightly with salt. Stand upside down to allow excess water to drain.

2. Pound together coriander roots, garlic and peppercorns. Mix in pork, crab, onion, sugar, fish sauce and 1 egg.

3. Rinse and dry tomato shells. Stuff with the mixture and cover with reserved lids.

4. Cook in a preheated oven at 180°C (350°F) for 30 minutes.

5. Use remaining eggs to make egg net. Heat some cooking oil and sprinkle egg by hand in criss-cross lines to resemble a net. Make each net approximately 10 cm (4 in) in diameter. Lift the egg nets out with a wok ladle or spatula. Continue until egg is used up.

6. Roll cooked, stuffed tomatoes in egg net. Serve with a sauce of your choice.

Pattaya-style Chilli Fried Beef

A spicy dish of Chinese mushrooms, beef, onion, capsicum and bamboo shoots. Remove the seeds from the red chillies and reduce or omit the bird's eye chillies for a milder dish.

Peanut oil	3 Tbsp
Dried Chinese mushrooms	10, soaked and finely sliced
Beef tenderloin	500 g (1 lb 1½ oz), finely sliced
Oyster sauce	2 Tbsp
Sugar	1 Tbsp
Fish sauce	3 Tbsp
Onion	1, peeled and sliced in rounds
Green capsicum (bell pepper)	¼, cut into cubes
Red capsicum (bell pepper)	¼, cut into cubes
Canned sour bamboo shoots	140 g (5 oz), sliced
Thai sweet basil leaves	a handful
Corn flour (cornstarch)	1 tsp, mixed with 1 Tbsp water

PASTE

Red chillies	4
Bird's eye chillies	8
Garlic	3 cloves, peeled

GARNISH

Spring onion (scallion)	1, chopped

1. Combine paste ingredients and pound into a fine paste. Heat oil and fry the finely pounded paste until fragrant.
2. Add mushrooms and stir-fry until soft. Add beef, oyster sauce, sugar and fish sauce and stir-fry for another 3 minutes.
3. Add onion, green and red capsicums, bamboo shoots and basil leaves. Pour in the corn flour mixture and stir for a few minutes.
4. Garnish with spring onion and serve immediately.

THAI

Beef Cutlet in Egg Net

An attractive and colourful dish that is commonly served as an appetiser. Replace the beef with chicken or pork as desired.

Beef	350 g (12 oz), minced
Prawns (shrimps)	100 g (3½ oz), peeled and minced (ground)
Cooking oil	90 ml (3 fl oz / ⅜ cup)
Onion	1, large, peeled and finely diced
Garlic	1 Tbsp, peeled and minced
Toasted peanuts	70 g (2½ oz), ground
Coriander (cilantro) roots	1 Tbsp, chopped
Ground white pepper	1 tsp
Fish sauce	3 Tbsp
Sugar	1 Tbsp
Eggs	6, beaten
Coriander leaves (cilantro)	1 sprig, stalk removed
Red chilli	1, seeded and cut into thin strips
GARNISH	
Cucumber	1, peeled and sliced
Spring onion (scallion)	1, chopped
Carrot	1, peeled and chopped

1. Combine beef and prawns and mix well.
2. Heat two-thirds of the cooking oil and sauté onion and garlic. Add beef and prawns mixture. Stir-fry until slightly dry.
3. Add peanuts, coriander roots, pepper, fish sauce and sugar. Fry until meat is slightly dry. Set aside.
4. Heat some of the remaining cooking oil and sprinkle beaten egg by hand in criss-cross lines to resemble a net. Make each net approximately 10 cm (4 in) in diameter. Lift the egg nets out with a wok ladle or spatula. Continue until all the egg is used up.
5. Assemble each cutlet by placing 1 heaped Tbsp of cooked beef and prawn mixture, a few coriander leaves and red chilli strips on each egg net. Enclose ingredients with egg net. Continue until ingredients are used up.
6. Serve garnished with cucumber, spring onions and carrot.

VIETNAMESE

Vietnamese Beef Stew

Seemingly adapted for the tropics, this wholesome, hearty stew has a refreshingly tangy taste and is not overly rich or heavy.

Beef thigh	1 kg (2 lb 3 oz), cut into 2-cm (1-in) cubes or desired bite-size pieces
Cooking oil	4 Tbsp
Sliced shallots	1 Tbsp
Minced garlic	1 Tbsp
Minced lemongrass	1 Tbsp
Lemongrass stalks	4
Coconut juice	1 litre (32 fl oz / 4 cups)
Carrots	250 g (9 oz), cut into bite-sized pieces
White radish (daikon)	250 g (9 oz), cut into bite-sized pieces
Onions	2, peeled and cut into wedges
Tomato ketchup	2 Tbsp
Chilli sauce	2 Tbsp
Spring onions (scallions)	5, finely chopped or cut into 5-cm (2-in) lengths
Red chillies	2, sliced

SEASONING

Salt	to taste
Sugar	to taste
Chicken seasoning powder	to taste

MARINADE (COMBINED)

Five-spice powder	1 tsp
Minced garlic	2 Tbsp
Minced shallots	2 Tbsp
Minced lemongrass	2 Tbsp
Pounded ginger	1 Tbsp
Curry powder	2 Tbsp
Chicken seasoning powder	3 tsp

1. Marinate beef cubes for 30 minutes.
2. Heat oil in a large saucepan. Add shallot slices and minced garlic and lemongrass. Fry until fragrant.
3. Add marinated beef and fry until golden brown. Then, add lemongrass stalks and coconut juice. Bring to the boil.
4. Discard scum on liquid surface. Cover saucepan and simmer for 45 minutes to 1 hour or until meat is tender.
5. Add carrots and radishes and simmer for 10 minutes, then add onion wedges, then tomato and chilli sauces. Return to the boil over high heat. Adjust to taste with seasoning ingredients before removing from heat.
6. Garnish with spring onions and chilli slices and serve with dipping sauce (page 18).
7. Serve with sliced French loaf or with flat rice noodles.

Meat 217

VIETNAMESE

Beef Cooked in Vinegar

The vinegar stock and the pickled vegetables in this dish provide a more tangy and appetising taste.

Beef fillet	1 kg (2 lb 3 oz), sliced thinly and across grain to ensure tenderness
Onion	1, peeled and thinly sliced
Round rice papers	30 sheets, 15-cm (6-in) in diameter
Chinese lettuce	1 bunch, leaves separated, washed and drained
Cucumber	1, washed, peeled, cored and sliced into 5-cm (2-in) lengths
Pickled vegetables	1 jar, about 200 g (7 oz), consisting of cabbage, carrots and white radishes
Sour star fruits	2, washed, edges trimmed and sliced into star shapes
Green bananas (optional)	2, peeled, sliced into rounds
Fresh rice vermicelli	500 g (1 lb 1½ oz), or Indian string hoppers or thick round rice noodles

MARINADE (COMBINED)

Lemongrass	3 tsp, finely chopped
Ground white pepper	2 tsp
Sugar	1 tsp
Chicken seasoning powder	2 tsp
Garlic juice	2 tsp, extracted by pounding and squeezing garlic cloves

STOCK (COMBINED)

Vinegar	125 ml (4 fl oz / ½ cup)
Coconut juice	125 ml (4 fl oz / ½ cup)
Minced garlic	1 tsp
Ground white pepper	1 tsp
Salt	1 tsp
Sugar	2 tsp
Chicken seasoning powder	1 tsp

1. Marinate beef for 30 minutes to 1 hour.
2. Meanwhile, prepare stock. Bring combined stock ingredients to the boil, then reduce heat and leave to simmer.
3. Arrange beef slices flat on a serving plate or platter. Distribute onion slices on top.
4. Serve beef slices with complementary ingredients, dipping sauce (page 18) and hot stock.
5. To assemble, first take some beef slices and dip into hot stock to cook, then drain and set aside. Place 1 lettuce leaf at the lower end of a rice paper round already smeared with water to soften.
6. Layer on cucumber, pickled vegetables, star fruit and green banana, if used. Top with some rice vermicelli and cooked beef, then fold in left and right sides and roll up firmly.
7. Eat with rolls and dipping sauce.

VIETNAMESE

Pork Stewed in Coconut Juice

Aside from tender and smooth pork pieces, the hard-boiled eggs, in having absorbed the flavours of the gravy, also make tasty nourishment.

Pork thigh	1 kg (2 lb 3 oz), with some skin and fat intact
Eggs	3–4
Coconut juice	1 litre (32 fl oz / 4 cups)

MARINADE (COMBINED)

Fish sauce	125 ml (4 fl oz / ½ cup)
Salt (optional)	½ Tbsp
Brown sugar	4 tsp
Minced garlic	2 tsp

1. Wash and cut pork into bite-sized pieces, then marinate them for 1 hour.
2. Meanwhile, prepare hard-boiled eggs. When eggs are cooked, transfer them to a bowl of room-temperature water to cool, then shell them.
3. Cook pork and marinade in a pot until liquid is almost dried up. Stir occasionally.
4. Pour in coconut juice and add eggs. Return to the boil, all the while discarding scum from liquid surface to keep gravy clear. When liquid reaches the boil, reduce heat and simmer until pork is lightly golden.
5. When done, pork should be tender but not too soft; fat and skin would have separated a little from meat.

VIETNAMESE

Beef on Fire

A guaranteed spectacle if done at the table, this dish uses gentle cradling heat to cook beef slices to tender perfection.

Beef fillet	250 g (9 oz), slice thinly and across grain to ensure tenderness
Ginger	55 g (2 oz), peeled and cut into thin strips
Skinned peanuts	55 g (2 oz), toasted and roughly pounded
Coriander (cilantro) leaves	55 g (2 oz)
Rice wine	125 ml (4 fl oz / ½ cup), for burning only, at least 40% alcohol (80 proof)
Round rice paper	30 sheets, 15-cm (6-in) in diameter
Chinese lettuce	1 bunch, leaves separated and washed
Pineapple	½, peeled, cored, quartered lengthways and cut into 0.5-cm (¼-in) wide slices
Sour star fruits	2, washed, hard edges pared and sliced into star shapes
Green bananas (optional)	2, peeled, sliced into rounds
MARINADE	
Lemongrass	55 g (2 oz), chopped
Garlic	55 g (2 oz), peeled and chopped
Five-spice powder	½ tsp
Chicken seasoning powder	½ tsp
Light soy sauce	1 tsp
Sugar	½ tsp
Salt	½ tsp

1 Prepare marinade. First, fry lemongrass and garlic in a little oil until golden brown. Dish out and combine with remaining marinade ingredients. Marinate beef slices for 30 minutes.

2 Put marinated beef in a heatproof or clay bowl. Add ginger, peanuts and coriander on top. Place bowl into a larger heatproof or clay bowl containing the rice wine, then set rice wine alight.

3 When fire is extinguished, beef slices should be just cooked. Serve with remaining ingredients and dipping sauce (page 18).

4 To assemble, place 1 lettuce leaf at the lower end of a rice paper round already smeared with water to soften. Layer on slices of pineapple, star fruit and green banana, if used, and top with beef slices. Fold in left and right sides, then roll up firmly.

5 Serve rolls with dipping sauce.

VIETNAMESE

Steamed Minced Pork with Duck Eggs

A dish with Chinese roots, the Vietnamese version differs in using duck eggs, as well as glass noodles and black fungus for crunch.

Cooking oil	1 tsp
Garlic	1 clove, peeled and minced
Minced lean pork	300 g (11 oz)
Glass vermicelli	5 g (1/5 oz), soaked in water for 10 minutes, then drained and cut into 1-cm (1/2-in) pieces
Black (woodear) fungus	3, soaked to soften and hard stems discarded
Duck eggs	3, lightly beaten
Light soy sauce	2 Tbsp
Red chilli slices	2 Tbsp

SEASONING

Ground black pepper	1 tsp
Sugar	1 tsp
Salt	1/2 tsp
Cooking oil	1 tsp

1. Heat oil in a saucepan. Fry chopped garlic until golden brown. Dish out and set aside.
2. Combine minced pork, vermicelli, black fungus, eggs and fried garlic in a heatproof bowl. Mix well.
3. Add seasoning ingredients to meat mixture. Mix well again.
4. Steam for 30 minutes.
5. Serve dish with soy sauce in a small saucer and chilli slices in another.

POULTRY

BALINESE
224 Fried chicken
225 Shredded Chicken with Chillies and Lime

CHINESE
226 Chicken Stew with Fresh Chestnuts
227 Five-spice Crispy Chicken
228 Ginger Chicken in Earthen Pot
229 Teochew Duck

FILIPINO
230 Chicken Adobo
231 Chicken Apritada

INDIAN
232 Butter Chicken
233 Spicy Chicken Masala
234 Chicken Tikka

INDONESIAN
235 Chicken in Spiced Coconut Sauce
236 Spiced Chicken Stew with Potatoes
237 Minced Duck Saté

JAPANESE
238 Japanese-style Deep-fried Chicken

KOREAN
239 Seasoned and Simmered Chicken
240 Chicken Ginseng Stew

MALAYSIAN
241 Chicken Sate with Peanut Sauce

THAI
242 Spicy Chicken Salad
243 Stuffed Chicken Wings
244 Fried Chicken in Screwpine Leaves

VIETNAMESE
245 Fried Lemongrass Chicken
246 Steamed Chicken with Spring Onions
247 Fried Chicken Wings in Fish Sauce

BALINESE

Fried Chicken

An old favourite, fried chicken is given an aromatic Balinese twist here.

Spring chickens	4, each about 800 g (1¾ lb)
Chicken spice paste (page 15)	250 g (9 oz)
Salt	a pinch + more to taste
Crushed black pepper	a pinch + more to taste
Vegetable oil	2 Tbsp
Lemongrass	2 stalks, bruised
Salam leaves	3
Bird's eye chillies	3–4, bruised
Kaffir lime leaves	2, bruised
Indonesian-style stock (page 20)	1 litre (32 fl oz / 4 cups)
Coconut milk	250 ml (8 fl oz / 1 cup)
Rice flour	100 g (3½ oz)

1. Cut each chicken into 8 pieces and season with half the spice paste and a pinch each of salt and pepper. Cover and leave to marinate in refrigerator.

2. Heat oil in a heavy saucepan. Add remaining spice paste, lemongrass, *salam* leaves, bird's eye chillies and kaffir lime leaves. Sauté over medium heat for 2 minutes.

3. Add stock and bring to the boil, then add coconut milk and bring to a simmer.

4. Add chicken, reduce heat and simmer until about 75 per cent cooked. Turn chicken frequently when cooking.

5. Leave chicken in the sauce to cool to room temperature, then remove and drain well.

6. Combine 500 ml (16 fl oz / 2 cups) of sauce with rice flour and mix until a smooth batter results. Season to taste with salt and pepper.

7. Dust chicken pieces with flour, then coat with batter.

8. Deep-fry at 160–170°C (325°F–330°F) until golden and crispy. Drain and serve with lemon wedges if preferred.

BALINESE

Shredded Chicken with Chillies and Lime

Aromatic and slightly tangy, this light chicken dish will make a decent meal for two with a vegetable dish and some steamed rice.

Chicken	1 about 1.2 kg (2 lb 10 oz)
Salt	a pinch + more for seasoning
Finely crushed black pepper	a pinch + more for seasoning
Chicken spice paste (page 15)	250 g (9 oz)
Salam leaves	2
Lemongrass	2 stalks, bruised
Kaffir lime leaves	2
Bamboo or saté skewers	
Spiced tomato sauce (page 16)	45 g (1½ oz)
Lime juice	3 Tbsp
Crisp-fried shallots	2 Tbsp

BASTING LIQUID (COMBINED)

Chicken spice paste (page 15)	250 g (9 oz)
Vegetable oil	250 ml (8 fl oz / 1 cup)

1. Rub chicken inside and outside with salt and pepper.
2. Stuff chicken cavity with 3 Tbsp spice paste, *salam* leaves, lemongrass and kaffir lime leaves, then close opening with skewers.
3. Rub outside of chicken evenly with remaining spice paste.
4. Place chicken on a wire rack in an oven preheated to 220°C (430°F) and roast for 10 minutes.
5. Turn heat down to 160°C (325°F) and roast chicken until done and juices run clear, basting frequently. Remove cooked chicken from oven and leave to cool to room temperature.
6. Skin and debone cooled chicken and shred meat finely by hand. Reserve stuffing for making dressing later.
7. Combine chicken shreds with spiced tomato sauce, lime juice, crisp-fried shallots and chicken stuffing. Mix well and season to taste.
8. Serve at room temperature with steamed rice.
9. For variation, deep-fry seasoned chicken shreds in medium-hot oil (170°C (340°F)) until golden and crispy, then drain on paper towels. The Balinese call the resulting dish *abon ayam*.
10. For another variation, replace the spiced tomato sauce with 4 Tbsp shallot and lemongrass dressing (page 17) for a light, fresh chicken salad the Balinese call *ayam sambel matah*.

Poultry 225

CHINESE

Chicken Stew with Fresh Chestnuts

Chunky chicken pieces stewed in rice wine with mushrooms and fresh chestnuts.

Chicken	1, about 1.75 kg (3 lb 13½ oz)
Light soy sauce	½ tsp
Chestnuts	675 g (1 lb 8 oz)
Garlic	6 cloves
Preserved soy beans	2 Tbsp
Dried Chinese mushrooms	6
Cooking oil	4 Tbsp
Rice wine	1½ Tbsp
Water	800 ml (26 fl oz / 3¼ cups)
Brown sugar	a pinch
Salt	½ tsp
Green (mung) bean flour	1 Tbsp

1 Rub chicken with soy sauce. Dip chestnuts in boiling water for 2 seconds, remove and leave in cold water for 3 minutes. Shell and remove hairy membrane. Peel garlic and pound to a paste with preserved soy beans. Soak mushrooms in water to soften. Discard stems and cut into big pieces.

2 Fry pounded garlic and soy bean mixture in hot oil over medium heat for 3 minutes. Add chicken and turn briskly several times. Increase heat to brown chicken. Add rice wine, water, chestnuts, mushrooms, brown sugar and salt. Cover tightly and bring to the boil. Reduce heat and stew for 1 hour.

3 Remove chicken to a chopping board and cut into large pieces. Arrange pieces on a plate in the form of a chicken. Add flour mixed to a paste with water to thicken gravy. Bring to the boil. Pour hot gravy over chicken. Place chestnuts around chicken and mushrooms on top.

Five-spice Crispy Chicken

Crispy cornflake-coated chicken served with lettuce and cucumber.

Chicken	1 kg (2 lb 3 oz) or 4 chicken thighs, cut into large pieces
Cooking oil	for deep-frying
Lettuce or cucumber slices	

SEASONING

Sugar	1 Tbsp
Salt	1 tsp
Ground white pepper	1 tsp
Five-spice powder	½ tsp
Egg	1, lightly beaten
Water	2 Tbsp
Self-raising flour	2 Tbsp

FLOUR COATING MIXTURE (COMBINED)

Cornflakes	55 g (2 oz), finely ground
Self-raising flour	220 g (8 oz)
Salt	½ tsp
Ground white pepper	½ tsp
Bicarbonate of soda	¼ tsp

BATTER

Self-raising flour	55 g (2 oz)
Water or milk	180 ml (6 fl oz / ¾ cup)
Salt	¼ tsp
Ground white pepper	¼ tsp

1. Marinate chicken pieces with seasoning ingredients for 1–2 hours.
2. Just before frying, coat chicken pieces with flour coating mixture. Dip into batter mixture and drop into hot oil. Fry over high heat for 1 minute, then reduce heat to moderate and cook until chicken is golden in colour.
3. Drain well and serve with lettuce or cucumber slices.

CHINESE

Ginger Chicken in Earthen Pot

Bite-size chicken pieces cooked with mushrooms, carrots and bamboo shoots in a claypot.

Chicken	1, about 1 kg (2 lb 3 oz), cut into bite-sized pieces
Cooking oil	as needed
Firm bean curd	4 small squares, sliced into 1 x 2.5-cm (½ x 1-in) pieces
Ginger	6 slices, peeled
Garlic	4 cloves, peeled and sliced
Shallots	4, peeled and sliced
Dried Chinese mushrooms	5, soaked until soft and halved
Carrots	125 g (4 oz), peeled and sliced
Canned bamboo shoots	85 g (3 oz), sliced
Napa cabbage	220 g (8 oz), cut into 5-cm (2-in) lengths
Red chillies	2, sliced
Spring onions (scallions)	6, cut into 2.5-cm (1-in) lengths

SEASONING

Salt	1 tsp
Sugar	1 tsp
Dark soy sauce	1 tsp
Light soy sauce	2 tsp
Corn flour (cornstarch)	1 Tbsp

SAUCE (COMBINED)

Basic chicken stock (page 19)	375 ml (12 fl oz / 1½ cups)
Salt	½ tsp
Sugar	1 tsp
Ground white pepper	½ tsp
Light soy sauce	1 Tbsp
Oyster sauce	1 Tbsp
Dark soy sauce	1 tsp
Sesame oil	1 tsp

1 Marinate chicken with seasoning ingredients for 20 minutes. Heat oil in wok until hot and deep-fry bean curd pieces until golden. Remove and set aside. Deep-fry chicken for 5 minutes. Drain and place in an earthen pot.

2 Reheat a clean wok with 2 Tbsp oil and lightly brown ginger, garlic and shallots. Add mushrooms and stir-fry until fragrant. Add carrots, bamboo shoots and napa cabbage and fry for 3–5 minutes. Add sauce ingredients and bring to the boil.

3 Pour over chicken in clay pot, add chillies and when it returns to the boil, reduce heat, cover and simmer for 25 minutes or until chicken is tender.

4 Add bean curd pieces and spring onions and simmer for another 5–10 minutes. Thicken sauce with corn flour mixture and serve.

Teochew Duck

Deep-fried duck simmered in light soy sauce and served with hard-boiled eggs.

Duck	1, about 1.5 kg (3 lb 4½ oz)
Salt	2 tsp
Five-spice powder	2 tsp
Galangal	125 g (4½ oz), peeled and sliced
Cooking oil	for deep-frying
Sugar	2 Tbsp
Dark soy sauce	2 Tbsp
Water	1.25 litres (40 fl oz / 5 cups) or enough to cover more than half the duck
Light soy sauce	1 Tbsp
Hard-boiled eggs	6, peeled

1. Rub inside and outside of duck with salt and five-spice powder. Stuff duck with the galangal slices, keeping 3 slices aside. Let duck stand for at least 2 hours.
2. Heat deep-frying oil in a deep wok until hot and fry duck for 5 minutes until lightly browned. Remove duck and drain well. Pour off oil, leaving 2 Tbsp in the wok and add sugar and 3 galangal slices. When the oil turns dark golden, turn off heat. Add thick soy sauce. Return duck to wok and coat the whole duck with sauce.
3. Pour in water to cover more than half of the duck. Put in light soy sauce and hard-boiled eggs. Bring to the boil, cover and simmer for about 20 minutes. Remove eggs and set aside.
4. Turn duck and continue simmering over low heat for about 1½–2 hours, until duck is tender and sauce is thick. Turn duck occasionally while simmering.
5. Before serving, cut duck into serving size pieces and halve eggs. Place on a serving dish and pour sauce over.

FILIPINO

Chicken Adobo

Adobo is the national dish of the Philippines. It is usually made with chicken or pork, but other forms of poultry, such as quail may also be used.

Chicken	1, about 1.5 kg (3 lb 4½ oz), cut into 12 serving pieces
Light soy sauce	4 Tbsp
Apple cider vinegar or distilled vinegar	4 Tbsp
Bay leaf	1, small
Garlic	1 head + 2 cloves, peeled and crushed
Black peppercorns	2–3 Tbsp
Water	500 ml (16 fl oz / 2 cups), or more if necessary
Cooking oil	90 ml (3 fl oz / ⅜ cup)
Sweet soy sauce	90 ml (3 fl oz / ⅜ cup)
Salt	1–2 tsp
Spanish onion	1, large, peeled and sliced

1 Place chicken pieces in a saucepan. Add light soy sauce, vinegar, bay leaf, 2 cloves crushed garlic, 2 Tbsp peppercorns and enough water to cover chicken.

2 Bring mixture to the boil over high heat, then reduce heat to medium and leave to simmer, uncovered, until chicken is cooked and tender and liquid has reduced by half. Remove chicken pieces and set aside. Strain boiling liquid and reserve 375 ml (12 fl oz / 1½ cups).

3 In a large frying pan or wok, heat oil over medium heat. Fry remaining garlic until golden brown, then add chicken pieces and fry for 3 minutes or until light brown.

4 Add sweet soy sauce and remaining peppercorns. Stir to mix well and stir-fry for 2 minutes.

5 Add reserved boiling liquid and season with salt. Increase heat and bring to the boil, then reduce heat to medium and leave to simmer for 5 minutes. Add onion and stir to mix well. Leave for another 1–2 minutes to cook onion lightly.

6 Remove from heat and transfer to a serving dish. Serve with Filipino-style fried rice (page 138).

FILIPINO

Chicken Apritada

This is an easy dish of simmered chicken in a rich tomato sauce with fried potatoes and capsicum. Pork, or a combination of pork and chicken may be used as a variation of this recipe.

Chicken	1, about 1.2 kg (2 lb 10 oz), cut into serving size pieces
Garlic	6 cloves, peeled and crushed
Distilled vinegar	4 Tbsp
Light soy sauce	4 Tbsp
Bay leaf	1, small
Ground black pepper	2 tsp
Water	1.25 litres (40 fl oz / 5 cups)
Cooking oil	4 Tbsp
Spanish onion	1, peeled and sliced
Sweet or light soy sauce	3 Tbsp
Ripe tomatoes	300 g (11 oz), seeded and chopped
Potatoes	500 g (1 lb 1½ oz), peeled, quartered and fried
Salt	to taste
Red capsicum (bell pepper)	1, small, cored, seeded and cut into 2.5-cm (1-in) cubes
Green peas	100 g (3½ oz)

1. In a medium saucepan, combine chicken pieces, 2 cloves garlic, vinegar, light soy sauce, bay leaf, ½ tsp pepper and 750 ml (24 fl oz / 3 cups) water. Stir to mix well and bring to the boil over high heat, then reduce heat to medium and simmer, uncovered, for 12 minutes or until chicken pieces are tender. Remove chicken pieces, drain and set aside.

2. In a large frying pan or wok, heat oil over medium heat. Fry chicken pieces until light brown, then remove and drain on absorbent paper.

3. Reheat oil if necessary and fry remaining garlic until light brown. Add onion and cook until soft and translucent. Stir in sweet or light soy sauce and tomatoes. Mash tomatoes lightly with a spatula.

4. Return chicken to the wok. Add potatoes and remaining water and bring to the boil. Reduce heat and simmer, uncovered for 12 minutes or until chicken is cooked.

5. Season with salt and remaining pepper. Add capsicum and peas and cook for another 5 minutes before removing from heat.

6. Dish out and serve immediately, with plain rice.

Poultry 231

INDIAN

Butter Chicken

The evaporated milk used in this recipe gives it a really enjoyable creaminess.

Chicken thighs	10, washed, skinned and cut into serving-size portions
Cooking oil	2½ Tbsp
Butter	1 Tbsp
Onions	3, peeled and finely sliced
Curry leaves	2 stalks
Tomatoes	3, chopped
Chilli powder	1 Tbsp
Salt	to taste
Evaporated milk	4 Tbsp
Coriander leaves (cilantro)	2 sprigs, chopped
Cream	1 Tbsp

MARINADE

Red chillies	3
Onion	½, peeled and chopped
Garlic	5 cloves
Ginger	2.5-cm knob (1-in), peeled and chopped
Calamansi lime	1, juice extracted
Turmeric powder	½ tsp
Sugar	½ tsp
Kitchen king masala	1 tsp

1. Blend marinade ingredients and rub into chicken. Leave to marinate for at least 30 minutes.

2. Heat oil and butter in a wok until hot. The oil raises the smoking point of the butter and prevents it from burning. Add onions, curry leaves and tomatoes and fry until tomatoes are pulpy.

3. Add marinated chicken, chilli powder and salt. Cook over a medium-low flame for 30 minutes, stirring occasionally. Pour in evaporated milk and add coriander leaves. Mix well, and allow gravy to thicken. Remove from heat.

4. Drizzle with cream and garnish with coriander leaves. Serve hot with rice or chapattis.

Spicy Chicken Masala

This is a Kerala-style dish.

Cooking oil	125 ml (4 fl oz / ½ cup)
Curry leaves	3 stalks
Onions	2, peeled and sliced
Chicken	1, about 1.5 kg (3 lb 4½ oz), cut into serving-size pieces, washed and drained
Salt	to taste
Turmeric powder	¼ tsp
Potatoes	3–4, peeled and quartered (optional)
Fennel	2 tsp

PASTE

Cooking oil	1 Tbsp
Dried red chillies	20
Coriander	1 Tbsp
Black peppercorns	1 Tbsp
Cardamom	5 pods
Shallots	7, peeled
Curry leaves	2 stalks
Garlic	7 cloves, peeled and chopped
Ginger	1-cm (½-in) knob
Grated coconut	2½ Tbsp
Water	125 ml (4 fl oz / ½ cup)

1. Prepare paste. Heat oil in a wok and fry dried chillies, coriander, peppercorns and cardamom for 5 minutes. Remove and fry shallots, curry leaves, garlic, ginger and grated coconut until shallots brown lightly.
2. Put all paste ingredients except water into a blender. Add water bit by bit and blend mixture until very fine.
3. Heat oil in a wok. Add curry leaves, then onions. Cook until onions are brown. Add paste and fry until fragrant.
4. Add chicken pieces and stir-fry to coat completely.
5. When juices start sizzling, add salt and turmeric powder. Mix well. Add potatoes now, if using.
6. Cover wok with a lid and allow chicken to cook gently. Remember to stir occasionally. Cook until sauce is reduced and thickened.
7. Toast fennel, then grind into a powder using a mortar and pestle. Sprinkle over chicken and serve hot with rice or bread.

INDIAN

Chicken Tikka

This recipe has been adapted so it can be prepared at home even without a tandoor.

Boneless chicken breasts	500 g (1 lb 1½ oz)

MARINADE

Cream	125 ml (4 fl oz / ½ cup)
Yoghurt	3 Tbsp
Chilli powder	3 tsp
Garam masala	1 tsp
Cumin powder	½ tsp
Tomato paste	1 tsp
Sweet mango chutney	1 Tbsp
Yellow food colouring	½ tsp
Salt	to taste
Coriander leaves (cilantro)	1 sprig, minced
Olive oil	125 ml (4 fl oz / ½ cup)
Cooking oil	
Onions	3, peeled and sliced
Green chillies	3, chopped
Red and yellow capsicums (bell peppers)	1, each, sliced

GARLIC AND GINGER PASTE

Garlic	6 cloves, peeled and chopped
Ginger	2.5-cm (1-in) knob, peeled and chopped

1. Cut chicken breasts into cubes. Wash and drain well. Make sure chicken is dry when marinating or the flavour will be diluted. Combine marinade ingredients and blend.

2. Combine garlic and ginger paste ingredients and blend. Combine marinade and garlic and ginger paste, then marinate chicken for 4 hours. The addition of oil ensures that the grilled chicken remains moist.

3. Oil a flat pan and grill chicken in a preheated oven at 180°C (350°F). Grill for 15 minutes, then turn chicken over and grill other side for another 15 minutes. Sprinkle half the onions, chillies and capsicum slices over chicken. Drizzle olive oil. Turn chicken over and sprinkle with remaining onions, chillies and capsicums. Grill for another 10 minutes.

4. Alternatively, skewer chicken and capsicums using bamboo skewers and grill for 15 minutes before turning over to grill the other side for another 15 minutes. Serve with rice or bread and a fresh salad.

INDONESIAN

Chicken in Spiced Coconut Sauce

To save time, replace spice paste in this recipe with 190 g (6⁴/₅ oz) East Javanese Yellow Spice Paste (page 16). Finishing the sauce with lime juice helps to accentuate its complex blend of flavours.

Vegetable oil	2 Tbsp
Chicken thighs	600 g (1 lb 5⅓ oz), boned and cut into 2.5-cm (1-in) cubes
Indonesian-style stock (page 20)	150 ml (5 fl oz / ³/₅ cup)
Lemongrass	2 stalks, bruised
Salam leaves	2
Coconut cream	125 ml (4 fl oz / ½ cup)
Salt	to taste
Ground white pepper	to taste
Limes	as desired

SPICE PASTE

Coriander	1 Tbsp, roasted
Cumin	1 tsp
White peppercorns	½ tsp
Candlenuts	25 g (⁴/₅ oz), toasted and crushed
Galangal	30 g (1 oz), peeled and sliced
Shallots	55 g (2 oz), peeled and sliced
Garlic	30 g (1 oz), peeled and sliced
Palm sugar	15 g (½ oz), chopped
Ground toasted white sesame seeds	to taste

1. Prepare spice paste. Combine coriander, cumin and white peppercorns in a stone mortar and grind until very fine, then add all remaining ingredients and grind into a fine paste.
2. Heat oil in heavy saucepan. Add spice paste and sauté until fragrant.
3. Add chicken cubes and continue to sauté until they are evenly coated with spice paste and their colour has changed.
4. Add stock, lemongrass and *salam* leaves. Bring to the boil, reduce heat and simmer over low heat for 3 minutes.
5. Add coconut cream, return to the boil and simmer for 2 minutes more or until sauce thickens and chicken is tender.
6. Season to taste with salt and pepper, then add a generous squeeze of lime juice before serving.
7. Should sauce thicken too much during cooking, add splashes of stock to thin it down.

Poultry 235

INDONESIAN

Spiced Chicken Stew with Potatoes

Aromatic from garlic, shallots and galangal, this sweetish dish is simple to prepare and made hearty with the addition of fried potatoes.

Chicken thighs	800 g (1¾ lb), boned
Vegetable oil	3 Tbsp + enough for deep-frying
Garlic	20 g (⅔ oz), peeled and sliced
Shallots	30 g (1 oz), peeled and sliced
Galangal	20 g (⅔ oz), peeled, sliced and bruised
Indonesian-style stock (page 20)	500 ml (16 fl oz / 2 cups)
Potatoes	200 g (7 oz), peeled, sliced and deep-fried until golden
Salt	a pinch or to taste
Ground white pepper	¼ tsp or to taste

SEASONING

Indonesian sweet soy sauce	3 Tbsp
Indonesian salty soy sauce	2 Tbsp
Oyster sauce	1 Tbsp
Sweet chilli sauce	2 Tbsp

GARNISHING

Crisp-fried shallots
Lime wedges
Finely chopped kaffir lime leaves

1. Cut chicken thigh meat into 2.5-cm (1-in) cubes. Set aside.
2. Heat sufficient oil for deep-frying chicken to 180°C (350°F), then fry for 1 minute. Remove and place on a wire rack to drain.
3. Heat 3 Tbsp oil in heavy saucepan. Add garlic, shallots and galangal. Sauté over medium heat until fragrant.
4. Add all seasoning ingredients and continue to sauté until solid ingredients are evenly coated and glazed.
5. Add stock, bring to the boil and simmer for 1 minute, then add chicken and return to the boil.
6. Reduce heat and simmer, stirring continuously, until chicken is tender.
7. Remove chicken from sauce and keep warm, then reduce sauce to a syrupy consistency. Continue to simmer sauce until slightly thickened.
8. Mix in fried potatoes and chicken. Season to taste with salt and pepper.
9. Dish out, garnish as desired and serve.

INDONESIAN

Minced Duck Saté

A welcome variation from the usual beef, mutton or chicken saté, this recipe also works well with pork or game meat.

Minced duck meat	600 g (1 lb 5⅓ oz)
Grated coconut	125 g (4½ oz)
Bird's eye chillies	4, finely chopped
Crisp-fried shallots	2 Tbsp
Crisp-fried garlic	1 Tbsp
Chopped palm sugar	1 tsp
Salt	a pinch
Freshly crushed black pepper	a pinch
Bamboo skewers or trimmed lemongrass stalks	

SPICE PASTE

Red chillies	55 g (2 oz), halved seeded and sliced
Shallots	55 g (2 oz), peeled and sliced
Garlic	30 g (1 oz), peeled
Galangal	20 g (⅔ oz), peeled and sliced
Turmeric	30 g (1 oz), peeled and sliced
Ginger	20 g (⅔ oz), peeled and sliced
Candlenuts	20 g (⅔ oz), crushed
Dried prawn (shrimp) paste	¼ tsp, roasted
Coriander seeds	¼ tsp, crushed
Freshly crushed black pepper	a pinch
Grated nutmeg	a pinch
Cloves	2
Vegetable oil	3 Tbsp

1. Prepare spice paste. Combine all ingredients, except oil, in a stone mortar or blender and grind into a fine paste.
2. Heat oil in a heavy saucepan. Add spice paste and sauté over low heat until fragrant and colour has changed. Remove from heat and set aside to cool completely before using or storing.
3. Combine all ingredients, except skewers or lemongrass stalks, in a mixing bowl. Add 4 Tbsp spice paste and mix into a smooth paste.
4. Mould 1 heaped Tbsp mixture around one end of a bamboo skewer or the bulbous end of a lemongrass stalk. Repeat until ingredients are used up.
5. Prepare a basting mixture. Mix 2 Tbsp spice paste with 2 Tbsp vegetable oil until well blended.
6. Either grill prepared saté over very hot charcoal or oven-grill until golden brown, basting and turning frequently.

Poultry 237

Japanese-style Deep-fried Chicken

This crispy chicken dish is absolutely delicious. It is popular with children and adults alike.

Boneless chicken thighs	500g (1 lb 1½ oz)
Japanese dark soy sauce	2 Tbsp
Sake	1 Tbsp
Mirin	1 Tbsp
Ginger juice	2 tsp
Potato flour (potato starch)	5 Tbsp
Vegetable oil	for deep-frying
Lemon wedges	

1. Pierce each piece of chicken with a metal or bamboo skewer several times to enable meat to fully absorb seasoning ingredients. Cut into 4 x 5-cm (1¾ x 2-in) pieces and place in a large bowl.

2. Marinate chicken pieces with soy sauce, sake, mirin and ginger juice. Set aside for about 30 minutes.

3. Drain marinated chicken and pat dry thoroughly with absorbent paper.

4. Coat with potato flour, shaking off any excess, then deep-fry in small batches in hot oil at 170°C (330°F) for 5–7 minutes, until brown and crisp. Drain on absorbent paper.

5. Serve hot with lemon wedges on the side.

KOREAN

Seasoned and Simmered Chicken

A sweet and spicy chicken dish with onions, carrots and potatoes.

Cooking oil	½ Tbsp
Whole chicken	1,800 g–1 kg (1¾ lb–2 lb 3 oz), cleaned and cut into 4-cm (2-in) pieces
Big onions	300 g (11 oz), peeled and cut into 3-cm (1½-in) cubes
Carrots	100 g (3½ oz), cut into 3-cm (1½-in) cubes
Potatoes	200 g (7 oz), peeled and cut into 3-cm (1½-in) cubes
Leek slices	
Green chilli slices	
SEASONING	
Light soy sauce	2 Tbsp
Crushed garlic	2 Tbsp
Hot chilli paste	1 Tbsp
Chilli powder	2 Tbsp
Ginger juice	1 Tbsp
Ground black pepper	2 tsp
Sugar	2 Tbsp
Sesame oil	1 tsp (optional)
Water	125 ml (4 fl oz / ½ cup)

1. Combine seasoning ingredients adding water last and mix well. Set aside. Heat oil until hot but not smoking and fry chicken for about 7 minutes.
2. Pour in half the seasoning mixture and bring to the boil for 10 minutes.
3. Add onions, carrots and potatoes and remaining seasoning mixture. Continue boiling until chicken is tender but vegetables are not mushy.
4. Lower heat to simmer for 20 minutes.
5. Garnish with leek and green chilli. Serve hot with steamed rice.

Chicken Ginseng Stew

Chicken stuffed with ginseng, glutinous rice and garlic then stewed to perfection.

Chicken	1, about 1–1.5 kg (2 lb 3 oz–3 lb 4½ oz)
Korean ginseng	8-cm (3-in) piece
Glutinous rice	85 g (3 oz), soaked for 1 hour
Garlic	6 cloves, peeled
Water	3 litres (96 fl oz / 12 cups)
Dried red dates	2
Chestnuts	2, peeled
Salt	to taste
Ground white pepper	to taste

1. Clean chicken and discard organs. Cut off and discard head, feet, wing tips and neck. Leave body whole. Clean and wash thoroughly.
2. Skewer neck with toothpicks or bamboo skewers then stuff chicken with ginseng, rice and garlic.
3. Sew rear end of chicken up to hold stuffing in.
4. Put stuffed chicken into a pot. Add water, cover and bring to the boil.
5. Lower heat and add red dates and chestnuts. Simmer until chicken is tender.
6. Remove toothpicks or skewers and serve hot. Add salt and pepper to taste.

MALAYSIAN

Chicken Sate with Peanut Sauce

These grilled chicken skewers are excellent for barbecues, and can be prepared ahead of time.

Chicken breast	800 g (1¾ lb), skinned and cut into 0.5 x 2.5-cm (¼ x 1-in), or deboned drumsticks pieces
Thick coconut cream	5 Tbsp, extracted from 125 g (4½ oz) grated coconut
Salt	1½ tsp
Sugar	70 g (2½ oz)
Bamboo skewers	soaked in water for 1 hour
Peanut sauce (page 17)	1 quantity

FINELY GROUND PASTE

Shallots	9, peeled
Garlic	3 cloves, peeled
Candlenuts	3
Fresh mature turmeric	3.5-cm (1¾-in) knob, peeled
Young galangal	2.5-cm (1-in) knob, peeled
Lemongrass	1 stalk, sliced
Dried prawn (shrimp) paste	1 tsp, crushed

TOASTED AND FINELY POUNDED SPICES

Coriander	1½ Tbsp
Cumin	½ tsp
Fennel	½ tsp

BASTING LIQUID (BLENDED)

Cooking oil	4 Tbsp
Water	4 Tbsp
Coconut cream	2 Tbsp, extracted from 60 g (2¼ oz) grated coconut

GARNISH (MIXED)

Cucumbers	2, cut into small chunks
Onions	2, peeled and cut into wedges
Light soy sauce	4 Tbsp
Lime juice	1½ Tbsp
Red chillies	3, thinly sliced

1. Rub finely ground paste into chicken, add coconut cream and season with salt and sugar. Sprinkle toasted and finely pounded spices over chicken and mix thoroughly. Marinate for 3 hours.
2. Thread chicken through bamboo skewers and grill on a griddle pan or under a hot electric grill. Constantly baste with basting liquid to keep chicken sate moist.
3. Serve chicken sate with peanut sauce and garnish as desired.

Poultry 241

THAI

Spicy Chicken Salad

A light and refreshing salad that can be served as part of a main meal or as an appetiser.

Bird's eye chillies	10, coarsely pounded
Fish sauce (*nam pla*)	2 Tbsp
Palm sugar (jaggery)	1 Tbsp, crushed or brown sugar
Lemon or lime juice	3 Tbsp
Coconut milk	60 ml (2 fl oz / ¼ cup)
Chicken breast	250 g (9 oz), boiled for 10 minutes or until tender, then sliced
Lemon grass	6 stalks, ends trimmed, tough outer leaves removed and finely sliced
Kaffir lime leaves	4, finely sliced
Coriander leaves (cilantro)	50 g (1⅔ oz), finely sliced
Mint leaves	100 g (3½ oz), finely sliced + extra for garnishing

ROASTED CHILLI PASTE

Cooking oil	750 ml (24 fl oz / 3 cups)
Shallots	280 g (10 oz), peeled and sliced
Garlic	280 g (10 oz), peeled and sliced
Dried prawns (shrimps)	280 g (10 oz), soaked and drained
Dried prawn (shrimp) paste (*kapi*)	2.5-cm (1-in) piece, roasted and crushed
Dried chillies	170 g (6 oz), seeded, soaked and drained
Palm sugar (jaggery)	140 g (5 oz), crushed or brown sugar
Fish sauce (*nam pla*)	60 ml (2 fl oz / ¼ cup)
Tamarind juice	60 ml (2 fl oz / ¼ cup), from 2 Tbsp tamarind pulp and 60 ml (2 fl oz / ¼ cup) water
Salt	2 tsp

GARNISH

Lettuce leaves	10
Tomatoes	2, cut into wedges
Red chillies	3, seeded and cut into strips
Cucumber	1, cut in half and finely sliced
Radish	1, peeled and sliced

1 Prepare roasted chilli paste. Heat oil over medium heat and fry shallots and garlic until golden brown. Remove from heat and drain, reserving oil. Using reserved oil, fry dried prawns, prawn paste and chillies for 3 minutes until golden brown. Remove from heat and drain. Reserve oil and leave aside to cool.

2 Combine fried ingredients with palm or brown sugar and pound into a fine paste. Add fish sauce, tamarind juice, salt and cooled oil. Blend to get a fine paste. Store in an airtight jar until needed.

3 Blend bird's eye chillies, 2 Tbsp roasted chilli paste, fish sauce, palm or brown sugar, lemon or lime juice and coconut milk into a salty-sour dressing. Set aside.

4 Mix chicken with lemon grass, kaffir lime leaves, coriander leaves and mint. Add dressing and mix well. Serve on a dish lined with lettuce leaves and garnish with tomatoes, red chilli strips, mint leaves, cucumber and radish.

Stuffed Chicken Wings

A dish of fried chicken wings taken a step further by removing the bones and stuffing with additional minced meat.

Chicken wings	8–12
Coriander (cilantro) roots	5, chopped
White peppercorns	10
Garlic	3 cloves, peeled
Minced pork	400 g (14⅓ oz)
Light soy sauce	2 Tbsp
Cooking oil	250 ml (8 fl oz / 1 cup)
Coriander leaves (cilantro)	a handful
SAUCE	
Chilli sauce	2 Tbsp
Tomato sauce	3 Tbsp
Sugar	1 Tbsp
GARNISH	
Lettuce leaves	5
Tomatoes	2

1. Debone chicken wings leaving the tips intact. Be careful not to tear the skin.
2. Pound together coriander roots, peppercorns and garlic. Mix in pork and sprinkle with a little soy sauce.
3. Stuff chicken wings with pork mixture. Heat oil over medium heat and fry stuffed chicken wings until golden. Sprinkle in coriander leaves while frying. Remove cooked chicken wings and drain.
4. To make the sauce, pour chilli sauce, tomato sauce, sugar and remaining soy sauce into oil used for frying. Bring to the boil and simmer for 2 minutes.
5. Serve chicken wings with the sauce on the side. Garnish as desired.

THAI

Fried Chicken in Screwpine Leaf

The screwpine leaves give additional fragrance and adds a unique touch to this delightful dish.

Chicken fillet	500 g (1 lb 1½ oz), cut into small pieces
Sugar	1 Tbsp
Sesame oil	1 Tbsp
Fish sauce	2 Tbsp
Dark soy sauce	1 tsp
Screwpine leaves	15
Cooking oil	500 ml (16 fl oz / 2 cups)

PASTE
Garlic	4 cloves, peeled
Ground white pepper	1 tsp
Coriander leaves (cilantro)	3 sprigs, chopped
Shallots	4, peeled
Lemongrass	1 stalk, thinly sliced
Preserved soy bean paste	1 Tbsp

1. Combine paste ingredients and blend until fine.
2. Mix chicken with finely ground paste. Add sugar, sesame oil, fish sauce, dark soy sauce and marinate for 30 minutes.
3. Wrap marinated chicken in screwpine leaves.
4. Deep-fry wrapped chicken for 10–12 minutes or until screwpine leaves turn a dark green.
5. Remove from oil and drain. Serve wrapped.

Fried Lemongrass Chicken

Chicken pieces are dyed bright yellow by turmeric and flavoured by aromatic lemongrass and garlic.

Chicken pieces	1 kg (2 lb 3 oz), washed and cut into bite-sized pieces
Cooking oil	125 ml (4 fl oz / ½ cup)
Minced garlic	1 tsp

MARINADE (COMBINED)

Minced lemongrass	3 Tbsp, use hard stalk parts, bruised
Chicken seasoning powder	3 tsp
Turmeric powder	½ tsp
Minced red chilli	1 tsp
Salt	2 tsp

1. Marinate chicken pieces for 30 minutes to 1 hour.
2. Heat oil in a frying pan until hot, then add garlic and fry until fragrant.
3. Add marinated chicken and cook until golden brown.
4. Garnish if desired and serve.

VIETNAMESE

Steamed Chicken with Spring Onions

The natural flavours of the chicken are enhanced ever so subtly and yet so indispensably by ginger, sesame seed oil and spring onions.

Chicken	1, whole, about 2 kg (4 lb 6 oz)
Ginger	10 g (1/3 oz), peeled and finely shredded
Chicken seasoning powder	3 tsp
Salt	2 tsp
Sesame oil	2 tsp
Spring onions (scallions)	300 g (11 oz), peeled and cut into 15-cm (6-in) lengths, use hard stalk parts only

DIPPING SAUCE (COMBINED)

Lime juice	1 Tbsp
Salt	2 tsp
Ground black pepper	1 tsp

1. Season chicken with ginger, seasoning powder and salt. Set aside for about 1 hour.
2. Steam chicken for about 40 minutes or until cooked. Smear sesame seed oil onto skin of cooked chicken.
3. Blanch spring onions for about 1 minute, then drain and set aside.
4. Chop chicken into bite-sized pieces and arrange neatly on a serving plate. Place spring onion lengths on top. Alternatively, divide chicken pieces into desired serving portions and garnish.
5. Serve with dipping sauce.

VIETNAMESE

Fried Chicken Wings in Fish Sauce

A favourite among many, the deep-fried chicken wings here are given a Vietnamese twist.

Chicken wings	1 kg (2 lb 3 oz), washed and each cut into 2 pieces
Minced garlic	3 tsp
Chicken seasoning powder	3 tsp
Salt	½ tsp
Cooking oil	500 ml (16 fl oz / 2 cups)
Fish sauce	125 ml (4 fl oz / ½ cup)
Sugar	1½ Tbsp

DIPPING SAUCE (COMBINED)

Lime juice	1 Tbsp
Salt	2 tsp
Ground black pepper	1 tsp

1. Season chicken wings with minced garlic, seasoning powder and salt. Set aside for 30 minutes.
2. Heat oil in a wok or deep-fryer. Add chicken wings and deep-fry over medium heat until golden brown. Drain.
3. In a wok or cooking pan, cook fish sauce and sugar over low heat until sugar is completely dissolved and liquid thickens.
4. Add fried chicken wings to thickened fish sauce and mix well. When wings are well coated with sauce, remove from heat.
5. Transfer sauce-coated wings to a serving plate. Serve with dipping sauce.

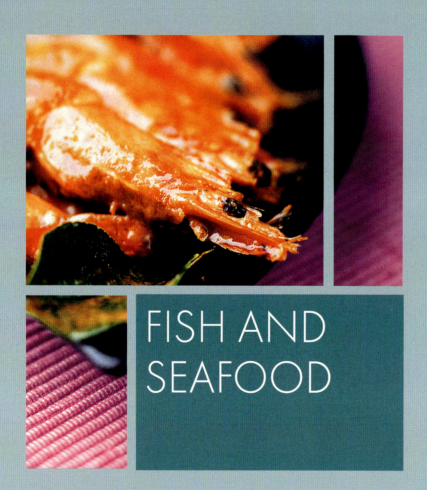

FISH AND SEAFOOD

BALINESE
250 Grilled Fish in Banana Leaf
251 Marinated Grilled Seafood
252 Minced Seafood Saté
253 Tuna Salad with Shallot and Lemongrass Dressing

CHINESE
254 Stir-fried Sichuan-style Squid
255 Chilli Oyster Crabs
256 Sea Bass with Spicy Black Vinegar Sauce

FILIPINO
257 Sweet and Sour Fish
258 Grilled Squid
259 Prawn Fritters in Sweet and Sour Sauce
260 Mexican Stew with Aubergine Sauce

INDIAN
261 Prawns in Spicy Masala
262 Fenugreek Fried Fish
263 Kerala Fish Curry

INDONESIAN
264 Crab in Turmeric Sauce
265 Prawns with Coconut Flesh
266 Tuna Salad with Green Mangoes

JAPANESE
267 Savoury Egg Custard
268 Deep-fried Seafood and Vegetables
269 Salt-grilled Horse Mackerel

KOREAN
270 Pan-fried Seafood with Spring Onion
271 Fried Sea Bream
272 Chilled Jellyfish with Cucumber

MALAYSIAN
273 Chilli Fried Clams
274 Cockle Rendang

STRAITS CHINESE
275 King Prawn with Spicy Prawn Paste

THAI
276 Thai Pineapple Prawn Curry
277 Thai Steamed Fish Mousse
278 Stuffed Crabs
279 Savoury Golden Cups with Seafood Filling

VIETNAMESE
280 Fish and Pineapple Stew
281 Fried Crab in Tamarind Sauce
282 Steamed Fish with Sugar Cane
283 Stuffed Squid

BALINESE

Grilled Fish in Banana Leaf

With only light cooking, this dish of mildly spiced fish is delicious and easy to prepare.

Fish fillet	600 g (1 lb 5⅓ oz), skinned, boned and cut into 1.5-cm (¾-in) cubes
Salt	a pinch
Crushed black pepper	a pinch
Seafood spice paste (page 15)	125 g (4½ oz)
Salam leaves	4
Banana leaves	4, cut into 15 cm (6-in) squares
Tomatoes	2, quartered
Lemon basil	8 sprigs
Bamboo skewers or cocktail sticks	

1. Season fish with salt and pepper, then mix with seafood spice paste.

2. Place 1 *salam* leaf onto the centre of a banana leaf. Top with 1 Tbsp marinated fish, 2 tomato pieces and 2 sprigs lemon basil.

3. Fold one-third of banana leaf over ingredients and roll up tightly. Secure ends with skewers or cocktail sticks. Repeat until ingredients are used up.

4. Cover parcels and leave to marinate in a cool place for 30 minutes. Parcels can be cooked in a few ways—steamed over rapidly boiling water for 7 minutes, grilled over very low heat for 9 minutes or baked in an oven preheated to 180°C (350°F) for 9 minutes.

5. Alternatively, steam for 4 minutes, then place over charcoal heat or under a grill and cook for 3 minutes until banana leaves are evenly browned.

6. Perhaps the most common way in Bali is to place the parcels on a dry, heated iron plate or a frying pan and cook until done. It is important that the parcels are not overcooked because the fish dries out very quickly. Instead, undercook them slightly, then leave them to rest in a warm place for 5 minutes to cook in the residual heat.

BALINESE

Marinated Grilled Seafood

The combination of sweet seafood juices and a smoky charcoal-grilled flavour makes this a memorable dish.

Assorted seafood	1 kg (2 lb 3 oz), use fish fillets, prawns (shrimps), clams, mussels, or 1 whole fish, 1 kg (2 lb 3 oz), use snapper, trevally, mackerel, etc.
Lime juice	2 Tbsp
Salt	1 tsp
Black peppercorns	1 tsp, finely crushed
Seafood spice paste (page 15)	200 g (7 oz)

BASTING PASTE (COMBINED)
Seafood spice paste (page 15)	125 g (4½ oz)
Vegetable oil	125 ml (4 fl oz / ½ cup)

1. If using assorted seafood, mix well with lime juice, salt, pepper and spice paste. Leave to marinate.
2. If using whole fish, halve butterfly style; start at the head and work towards the tail. Make 4 slits, each about 1-cm (½-in) deep, on the side with the bones. The seasoning will penetrate better and the fish will cook more evenly.
3. Season both sides of fish with lime juice salt and pepper. Evenly spread spice paste all over.
4. Brush assorted seafood or whole fish with a little basting paste before grilling over medium charcoal heat. Turn and baste frequently.
5. Serve with white rice accompanied by desired portions of spiced tomato sauce (page 16) and shallot and shallot and lemongrass dressing (page 17) on the side.

Fish and Seafood 251

BALINESE

Minced Seafood Saté

An interesting variation of saté, which is usually meat-based, seafood saté makes for a lighter meal and more delicate flavours.

Snapper fillet	600 g (1 lb 5⅓ oz), skinned, boned, finely minced
Freshly grated coconut	125 g (4½ oz)
Coconut cream	125 ml (4 fl oz / ½ cup)
Seafood spice paste (page 15)	125 g (4½ oz)
Bird's eye chillies	3–5, very finely chopped
Kaffir lime leaves	5, finely chopped
Ground black pepper	a pinch
Salt	a pinch
Palm sugar	1 Tbsp
Lemongrass stalks or large bamboo skewers	

1. Combine all ingredients except lemongrass or bamboo skewers and mix thoroughly until a uniformly sticky paste results.
2. Mould 1 heaped Tbsp mixture around the trimmed bulbous end of a lemongrass stalk or a bamboo skewer. Repeat until ingredients are used up.
3. Grill over very hot charcoal until golden brown.
4. For variation, replace half the amount of minced fish used with minced prawns (shrimps).

BALINESE

Tuna Salad with Shallot and Lemongrass Dressing

Serve this as a main course at room temperature with steamed rice, or as a cocktail snack on top of deep-fried prawn or seafood crackers.

Tuna steaks	4, each about 150 g (5⅓ oz)
Seafood spice paste (page 15)	65 g (2½ oz)
Salt	½ tsp or more to taste
Ground black pepper	a pinch or more to taste
Lime juice	1 Tbsp
Vegetable oil	2 Tbsp
Shallot and lemon grass dressing (page 17)	125 g (4½ oz)
Kaffir lime leaf	1 or to taste, finely chopped
Crisp-fried shallots	2 Tbsp
Red chilli (optional)	1, sliced and fried until golden
Lime (optional)	1, cut into wedges and seeded

1. Season tuna steaks with seafood spice paste, salt, pepper and lime juice.
2. Heat oil in frying pan. Fry tuna steaks over medium high heat, turning frequently until desired doneness is achieved; do not overcook. Dish out and set aside to cool.
3. In a mixing bowl, flake tuna into small chunks. Add shallot and lemongrass dressing and kaffir lime leaf. Mix well. Adjust to taste with salt and pepper.
4. Transfer tossed ingredients to a serving plate or bowl. Garnish with crisp-fried shallots and fried chilli slices, if used. Serve with lime wedges, if desired.

Fish and Seafood   253

CHINESE

Stir-fried Sichuan-style Squid
Large fresh squid stir-fried with hot bean paste, celery and chilli.

Fresh large squid	600 g (1 lb 5⅓ oz), cleaned, score the inner body and cut into thick slices, about 2 x 5-cm (1 x 2-in)
Salt	½ tsp
Ground white pepper	½ tsp
Cooking oil	3 Tbsp, preferably lard
Garlic	3 cloves, minced
Hot bean paste	1 Tbsp
Tender young celery	1 stalk, sliced
Red chillies	2, sliced

SAUCE (COMBINED)

Basic chicken stock (page 19) or water	375 ml (12 fl oz / 1½ cups)
Light soy sauce	1 Tbsp
Chinese wine	1 Tbsp
Sesame oil	1 tsp
Sugar	1 tsp
Ground white pepper	¼ tsp
Salt	¼ tsp
Corn flour (cornstarch)	2 tsp

1 Season squid with salt and pepper for 15 minutes. Blanch seasoned squid in boiling salted water for 30–60 seconds. Drain well.

2 Heat wok with oil until hot and stir-fry garlic and hot bean paste until fragrant. Add celery and stir-fry for 1½ minutes.

3 Stir in sauce ingredients and bring to the boil. When sauce thickens, add squid and chillies, and very briefly toss the mixture.

4 Transfer to serving dish and serve hot.

CHINESE

Chilli Oyster Crabs

Delicious chilli crabs given a twist with oyster sauce and Chinese wine.

Crabs	3 kg (6 lb 9 oz)
Cooking oil	250 ml (8 fl oz / 1 cup)
Ginger	55 g (2 oz), peeled and cut into strips
Garlic	7 cloves, peeled and sliced
Shallots	7, peeled and sliced
Red chillies	10, seeded, blended with 125 ml (4 fl oz / ½ cup) water
Eggs	5, beaten lightly
Spring onions (scallions)	6, cut into 5-cm (2-in) lengths
Coriander leaves (cilantro)	2 sprigs, cut into 5-cm (2-in) lengths

SAUCE

Chinese rice wine	3 Tbsp
Chilli sauce	3 Tbsp
Oyster sauce	4 Tbsp
Sugar	8 tsp
Sesame oil	1 tsp
Ground white pepper	¼ tsp

1. Clean crabs, remove and crack pincers with a nut cracker. Trim legs and cut into 4 pieces.
2. Heat oil in a large wok and stir-fry ginger, garlic and shallots until fragrant. Put in chillies and fry for 2 minutes.
3. Add crabs and stir briskly. Cover wok for approximately 4–5 minutes. Uncover and stir briskly once again, then add sauce ingredients. When crabs are bright red and nearly cooked, pour in beaten eggs. Add spring onions, stirring to mix with sauce.
4. Dish out, garnish with coriander leaves and serve hot with rice or toasted bread.

Fish and Seafood

CHINESE

Sea Bass with Spicy Black Vinegar Sauce

Fried sea bass served with black vinegar sauce and a dash of chilli.

Sea bass or any freshwater fish	500–600 g (1 lb 1½ oz–1 lb 5⅓ oz)
Salt	1 tsp
Ground white pepper	½ tsp
Corn flour (cornstarch)	for coating fish
Cooking oil	as needed
Garlic	2 large cloves, peeled and thinly sliced
Ginger	2.5-cm (1-in) knob, peeled and thinly sliced
Red chilli	1
Spring onions (scallions)	2
Corn flour (cornstarch)	2 tsp, mixed with 2 Tbsp chicken stock or water

SAUCE (COMBINED)

Chicken stock	165 ml (5½ fl oz / ⅔ cup)
Light soy sauce	¾ Tbsp
Dark soy sauce	¼ tsp
Sugar	55 g (2 oz)
Black vinegar	2 Tbsp
Salt	a pinch

1. Use a sharp knife and deeply score both sides of the fish, starting 4-cm (1½-in) from the gill opening. Lightly cut a criss-cross pattern on the tail end.
2. Marinate fish with salt and pepper and set aside for 15 minutes. Coat fish with corn flour, making sure to coat the slits.
3. Heat 3 Tbsp oil in a non-stick frying pan and fry fish on both sides, covered, until batter is crisp and golden brown for about 10 minutes. Place fish on serving dish.
4. Reheat pan with 2 Tbsp cooking oil. Add garlic and ginger and stir-fry for 20 seconds until fragrant. Stir in chilli and sauce ingredients and bring to a rapid boil. Add spring onions. Thicken sauce with corn flour mixture, then pour over fish.

FILIPINO

Sweet and Sour Fish

Escabeche, which means "pickled" in Spanish, is a mixture of vinegar and spices used to marinate fresh or cooked fish and vegetables that are left to chill in the refrigerator overnight before serving. However, in the Philippines, *escabeche* refers to this Chinese-style dish.

Fish such as grouper, sea bass or perch	1, medium, about 600 g (1 lb 5⅓ oz), cleaned, scaled and gutted
Salt	2½ tsp
Cooking oil	for deep-frying
Distilled vinegar	4 Tbsp
Sweet soy sauce	1 Tbsp
Sugar	85 g (3 oz)
Water	250 ml (8 fl oz / 1 cup)
Cooking oil	4 Tbsp
Garlic	5 cloves, peeled and finely chopped
Young ginger	15 g (½ oz), peeled and sliced into thin strips
Carrot	1, small, peeled and sliced into thin strips
Red capsicum (bell pepper)	1, small, cored, seeded and sliced into thin strips
Onion	1, large, peeled and sliced into rings
Corn flour (cornstarch)	1 Tbsp, mixed with 2 Tbsp water

1. Using a knife, score diagonal cuts on one side of fish. Season by rubbing 2 tsp salt all over fish. Set aside.

2. In a wok, heat oil for deep-frying over medium to high heat. Gently lower in fish and deep-fry for 7–10 minutes or until golden brown and crisp. Remove from heat and drain well. Place fish on a serving platter and set aside.

3. In a mixing bowl, combine vinegar, soy sauce, sugar, water and remaining salt. Stir to mix well and set aside.

4. In a frying pan, heat oil over medium heat. Fry garlic until light brown, then add ginger, carrot and capsicum and fry for 2 minutes. Add onion and fry until soft.

5. Add vinegar mixture. Without stirring, increase heat and bring mixture to the boil. Reduce heat and stir in corn flour mixture. Leave to simmer for 2 minutes or until sauce thickens.

6. Taste and adjust seasoning, if necessary. Remove from heat and spoon sauce over fish. Serve immediately.

FILIPINO

Grilled Squid

This dish of tenderly grilled squid marinated in a combination of tangy, salty flavours is tasty and filling, without being overly oily.

Large squid	10
Lemon juice	1 Tbsp
Light soy sauce	85 ml (2½ fl oz / ⅓ cup)
Salt	1 tsp
Ground white pepper	1½ tsp
Tomatoes	2, large, diced
Spanish onions	2, medium, peeled and diced
Cooking oil	1 Tbsp

GARLIC-VINEGAR DIP

Distilled vinegar	125 ml (4 fl oz / ½ cup)
Water	4 Tbsp
Garlic	4 cloves, peeled and crushed
Salt	½ tsp
Ground white pepper	¼ tsp
Sugar	1 Tbsp
Red and green bird's eye chillies	3, crushed

1. Prepare garlic-vinegar dip. In a saucepan, combine vinegar and water over medium heat. Without stirring, bring mixture to the boil for a few seconds. Remove from heat and add remaining ingredients. Set aside.

2. Clean squid. Separate squid heads from tubes. Remove innards and ink sac. Peel away skin. Rinse well and set aside. In a mixing bowl, combine lemon juice, soy sauce, ½ tsp salt and 1 tsp pepper. Add squid and leave to marinate for 30 minutes. Reserve marinade.

3. In a bowl, combine tomatoes, onions and remaining salt and pepper and mix well. Fill squid tubes with tomato mixture until almost full, then stuff heads in and secure with toothpicks. Lightly brush squids with oil, then score several cuts on one side of tubes.

4. Lightly grease a frying pan. In several batches, grill squid for 3–5 minutes on each side over medium-high heat until squid is tender and lightly charred. Brush with reserved marinade while grilling. Serve immediately with garlic-vinegar dip on the side.

Prawn Fritters with Sweet and Sour Sauce

This is a Filipino dish with a Spanish name, but with a Chinese style of preparation.

Calamansi or lemon juice	2 tsp
Salt	½ tsp
Ground white pepper	½ tsp
Prawns (shrimps)	500 g (1 lb 1½ oz), peeled and deveined, leaving tails intact
Cooking oil	for deep-frying

BATTER

Plain (all-purpose) flour	220 g (8 oz)
Corn flour (cornstarch)	110 g (4 oz)
Baking powder	1 tsp
Egg white	1
Iced water	180 ml (6 fl oz / ¾ cup)

SAUCE

Cooking oil	4 Tbsp
Onion	1, medium, peeled and quartered
Green and red capsicums (bell peppers)	1 each, small, cored, seeded and cut into strips
Tomato ketchup	2 Tbsp
Oyster sauce	2 tsp
White vinegar	2 Tbsp
Sugar	55 g (2 oz)
Water	125 ml (4 fl oz / ½ cup)
Salt	1 tsp
Ground white pepper	½ tsp
Corn flour (cornstarch)	2 tsp, mixed with 3 Tbsp water

1. In a mixing bowl, combine calamansi or lemon juice, salt and pepper. Place prawns in to steep and leave aside in the refrigerator until ready to use.
2. Prepare batter. In a bowl, combine all ingredients and whisk until smooth. Place batter in the refrigerator to rest for at least 2 hours.
3. In a wok, heat oil for deep-frying over medium to high heat. Coat prawns with batter, then deep-fry until golden brown and crisp, 5–6 pieces at a time, depending on how large the wok is. Do not put in too many prawns as this will cause the oil temperature to decrease and cause prawns to lose their crispness. Remove prawns from heat and drain on absorbent paper.
4. Prepare sauce. In a saucepan, heat oil over medium heat. Fry onion and capsicum for 1 minute, then add remaining ingredients except for corn flour mixture. Increase heat and bring mixture to the boil. Stir in corn flour mixture and cook until sauce thickens. Remove from heat.
5. Transfer prawns to a serving platter. Spoon sauce over or serve on the side. Serve immediately.

FILIPINO

Mexican Stew with Aubergine Sauce

Known as *puchero*, this stew is considered to be a one pot-meal. It is Spanish in origin and is normally cooked with beef and chicken, but fish makes a delicious substitute.

Cooking oil	for deep-frying
Fish such as grouper, sea bass, perch or snake head	1 kg (2 lb 3 oz) cleaned, scaled, gutted and diagonally sliced into steaks
Baby potatoes	3, peeled, quartered and fried until light brown
Plantain bananas	2, about 200 g (7 oz), peeled and sliced on the diagonal
Garlic	2 cloves, peeled and chopped
Onion	1, large, peeled and sliced
Tomatoes	500 g (1 lb 1½ oz), diced
Water	1 litre (32 fl oz / 4 cups)
Salt	2 tsp or to taste
Ground white pepper	1 tsp
Chorizo or any spicy sausage	200 g (7 oz), sliced on the diagonal into 2.5-cm (1-in) pieces
Cabbage	1, small, cored and quartered into wedges
Chinese cabbage	200 g (7 oz)
Canned chickpeas	200 g (7 oz), drained
Milk	90 ml (3 fl oz / ⅜ cup)

AUBERGINE SAUCE

Aubergines (brinjals/eggplants)	2, medium
Vinegar	4 Tbsp
Garlic	2 cloves, peeled and minced
Salt	to taste
Ground black pepper	to taste
Sugar	1 Tbsp

1. Prepare aubergine sauce. Grill aubergines for 15–20 minutes on each side until charred. Set aside to cool. Peel aubergines and discard skin. Place in a mixing bowl. Add remaining ingredients and mash. Set aside.

2. In a wok, heat oil for deep-frying over medium to high heat. Deep-fry fish for 3 minutes on each side or until half cooked. Remove from heat, drain and set aside. Reserve 90 ml (3 fl oz / ⅜ cup) oil.

3. In a saucepan, heat reserved oil over medium heat. Fry potatoes until golden brown. Remove from heat, drain and set aside.

4. Using the same saucepan, fry bananas over medium heat until light brown. Remove from heat, drain and set aside.

5. In a clean wok, heat oil over medium heat. Fry garlic until golden brown. Add onion and fry until soft and translucent. Add tomatoes and cook for 3 minutes.

6. Add water and stir to mix well. Increase heat and bring mixture to the boil. Add fried potatoes and reduce heat to medium. Leave to simmer for 5 minutes and season with salt and pepper.

7. Add fish, bananas and remaining ingredients and return mixture to the boil. Simmer for 5 minutes or until vegetables are tender.

8. Dish out and serve immediately, with aubergine sauce and plain rice on the side.

INDIAN

Prawns in Spicy Masala

This is a typical South Indian dish with prawns. It is spicy and goes well with rice and a simple stir-fried vegetable dish.

Cooking oil	4 Tbsp
Onion	1, peeled and sliced
Green chillies	3
Tomatoes	2, chopped
Tiger prawns (shrimps)	1 kg (2 lb 3 oz), peeled and deveined
Green mango	1, peeled, pitted and sliced
Tamarind pulp	50 g (1⅔ oz)
Water	125 ml (4 fl oz / ½ cup)
Salt	to taste
Curry leaves	2 stalks

PASTE

Dried red chillies	10
Grated coconut	55 g (2 oz)
Toasted cumin powder	½ tsp
Black peppercorns	1 tsp
Curry leaves	2 stalks
Shallots	5, peeled
Tamarind pulp	1 tsp
Garlic	2 cloves, peeled
Tomato	1, chopped
Fenugreek seeds	½ tsp

1. Prepare paste. In a wok, dry-roast dried chillies until smoky. Remove and grind to a paste with all other paste ingredients. Add some water if necessary to get a smooth paste.

2. Heat oil in a wok. Sauté onion, green chillies and tomatoes until soft. Add ground paste and keep cooking until fragrant.

3. Add prawns and green mango. Sauté for 10 minutes.

4. Combine tamarind pulp and water then strain. Add tamarind juice, salt and curry leaves to wok. Cook until prawns are done. Serve hot with rice or Indian breads.

Fish and Seafood

INDIAN

Fenugreek Fried Fish

Fenugreek and fish go very well together. This recipe uses fenugreek powder that leaves an irresistible aroma in your kitchen.

Fish (Spanish mackerel or threadfin bream)	4 thick slices, each about 100 g (3½ oz)
Calamansi limes	2, squeezed for juice
Salt	to taste
Fish curry powder	½ Tbsp
Chilli powder	½ Tbsp
Fenugreek powder	½ tsp
Turmeric powder	½ tsp
Toasted cumin powder	½ tsp
Chopped curry leaves	1 tsp
Cooking oil	for deep-frying
PASTE	
Shallots	10, peeled
Garlic	10 cloves, peeled
Ginger	2.5-cm (1-in) knob, peeled

1 Rub fish with lime juice and salt. Set aside to marinate.
2 Grind shallots, garlic and ginger into a paste.
3 Mix fish curry powder, chilli, fenugreek, turmeric and cumin powders, curry leaves and paste together then rub all over fish. Set aside for 30 minutes.
4 Heat oil and deep-fry fish to a golden brown.
5 Drain fish and serve hot with a fresh garden salad of your choice.

INDIAN

Kerala Fish Curry

This recipe works best when the fish is very fresh. You can also use a large meaty fish head if preferred. If you don't have a claypot, use an enamel pot.

Meaty fresh fish	600 g (1 lb 5⅓ oz), cut into chunks
Ground black pepper	1 tsp
Salt	½ Tbsp
Chilli powder	1 Tbsp
Turmeric powder	½ tsp
Cumin powder	1 tsp, toasted
Ginger	2.5-cm (1-in) knob, peeled and minced
Curry leaves	2 sprigs
Green mangoes	3, peeled and sliced, pits reserved
Curry leaves	5 stalks
Tamarind pulp	50 g (1⅔ oz)
Water	250 ml (8 fl oz / 1 cup)
Cooking oil	1 Tbsp
Fenugreek seeds	½ tsp, toasted then finely ground

PASTE A
Dried red chillies	15
Shallots	6, peeled

PASTE B
Grated coconut	55 g (2 oz)
Cumin	1 tsp
Garlic	6 cloves, peeled

1. Place fish in a bowl and add pepper, salt, chilli, turmeric and cumin powders and ginger. Rub seasoning into fish.
2. Scatter 2 stalks of curry leaves into the base of a seasoned claypot. Layer with sliced mangoes and pits and top with fish. Set aside. Combine tamarind pulp and water and strain.
3. Grind paste A ingredients together and mix with tamarind juice. Grind paste B ingredients together and set aside.
4. Pour paste A over fish and simmer on low heat. When mixture comes to the boil, add paste B. Give claypot a gentle shake and cook for 15 minutes more over low heat. Do not stir with a ladle or spoon or the fish will break up. Use kitchen mittens or a tea towel when handling hot pots.
5. Drizzle oil into curry then sprinkle fenugreek powder over. Add remaining curry leaves and shake pot again to mix. Adjust seasoning to taste.
6. Let curry stand for at least 30 minutes before serving.

INDONESIAN

Crab in Turmeric Sauce

To save time, replace spice paste in this recipe with 250 g (9 oz) Seafood spice paste (page 15).

Mud crabs	2 kg (4 lb 6 oz), large
Indonesian-style stock (page 20)	750 ml (24 fl oz / 3 cups)
Tomatoes	4, peeled, seeded and sliced
Sour star fruit	2, sliced
Salt	to taste
Freshly crushed black pepper	to taste
Lime juice	

SPICE PASTE

Red chillies	150 g (5⅓ oz), halved, seeded and sliced
Shallots	55 g (2 oz), peeled and sliced
Garlic	30 g (1 oz), peeled and sliced
Turmeric	55 g (2 oz), peeled and sliced
Ginger	30 g (1 oz), peeled and sliced
Candlenuts	45 g (1½ oz)
Coriander seeds	1 tsp, toasted and crushed
Dried prawn (shrimp) paste	1 tsp, roasted
Tamarind pulp	1 Tbsp, seeds discarded
Vegetable oil	4 Tbsp
Salam leaves	2
Kaffir lime leaves	2, bruised
Lemongrass	2 stalks, bruised

1. Bring 5 litres (160 fl oz / 20 cups) heavily salted water to the boil.
2. Cook crabs one at a time. With each addition, ensure that water returns to the boil and boil for 1 minute before removing.
3. Plunge each boiled crab into iced water and leave to chill for 5 minutes, then drain and dry well.
4. With each crab, break off pincers and crush shell evenly with a pestle or kitchen mallet. Dislodge top shell and rinse clean under running water. Quarter remaining body of crab.
5. Prepare spice paste. Combine all ingredients, except salam and lime leaves and lemongrass, in a stone mortar or blender and grind into a fine paste.
6. Transfer paste to a heavy saucepan and add all remaining ingredients. Place over medium heat and cook until paste is fragrant and takes on a golden colour.
7. Add crab pieces and stir until they are evenly coated with spice paste.
8. Add stock and bring to the boil, then reduce heat and simmer for 1 minute.
9. Add tomatoes and sour star fruit. Mix well and return to the boil. Season to taste with salt and pepper and add a generous squeeze of lime juice.
10. Dish out and garnish, if desired, with finely chopped kaffir lime leaves. Serve warm.

INDONESIAN

Prawns with Coconut Flesh

The use of tender coconut flesh in this dish is unusual, and it helps to counter the spiciness of the bird's eye chillies.

Prawns (shrimps)	600 g (1 lb 5⅓ oz), peeled and deveined
Lime juice	3 Tbsp
Vegetable oil	2 Tbsp
Salt	to taste
Freshly crushed white pepper	to taste
Indonesian-style stock (page 20)	100 ml (3½ fl oz / ⅖ cup)
Kaffir lime leaves	4, bruised
Turmeric leaf	½, sliced
Lemongrass	2 stalks, bruised
Tender coconut flesh	200 g (7 oz), sliced

SPICE PASTE

Shallots	70 g (2½ oz), peeled and sliced
Ginger	30 g (1 oz), peeled and sliced
Turmeric	30 g (1 oz), peeled and sliced
Bird's eye chillies	15 g (½ oz), sliced
Vegetable oil	3 Tbsp

1. Place prawns in a mixing bowl. Add lime juice, oil and salt and pepper to taste. Mix well and refrigerate or leave in a cool place for 30 minutes.

2. Meanwhile, prepare spice paste. Combine all ingredients, except oil, in a stone mortar or blender and grind into a fine paste.

3. Heat oil in a saucepan and add spice paste. Sauté over low heat until fragrant, adding 3 Tbsp stock during sautéing to prevent sticking.

4. Add prawns and all remaining ingredients. Increase heat to medium and sauté until prawns are cooked.

5. Adjust seasoning to taste before dishing out to serve. Garnish, if desired, with finely chopped red chillies and kaffir lime leaves.

INDONESIAN

Tuna Salad with Green Mangoes

Although tamed, the green mango shreds still retain some tanginess and acidity, which makes this dish a great appetiser.

Tuna steaks	4, each about 150 g (5 oz)
Green mangoes	2, about 200 g (7 oz), peeled and coarsely shredded
Salt	1 Tbsp
Shallots	50 g (1⅔ oz), peeled and sliced
Coconut cream	125 ml (4 fl oz / ½ cup)
Salt (optional)	to taste
Pepper (optional)	to taste

SEASONING
Salt	½ tsp
Freshly crushed black pepper	½ tsp
Lime juice	1 Tbsp

GARNISHING
Finely chopped red chillies
Finely chopped kaffir lime leaves

1 Rub tuna steaks with seasoning ingredients, then oven-grill or pan-fry over low heat until medium-well done.

2 Remove cooked tuna and leave to cool to room temperature before flaking into small pieces.

3 Place shredded mangoes in a bowl, add 1 Tbsp salt and mix well, then set aside for 10 minutes.

4 Squeeze mango shreds to remove the sour juices, then rinse mango thoroughly under running water to remove salt.

5 Drain shredded mango well and squeeze again until very dry.

6 Combine tuna, mangoes, shallots and coconut cream in a large bowl. Toss until well mixed and adjust seasoning to taste with salt and pepper if desired.

7 Transfer to a platter to serve or divide among individual serving plates, then garnish as desired.

JAPANESE

Savoury Egg Custard

In Japan, this dish is prepared in traditional *chawan mushi* cups with lids. If you do not have these cups, use porcelain rice bowls or ramekins.

Chicken thighs	50 g (1⅔ oz), skinned and boned, fat removed and cubed
Sake	1 tsp
Salt	a pinch
Eggs	3, lightly beaten
Salt	1 tsp
Japanese light soy sauce	1 tsp
Prawns (shrimps)	8, large, peeled and deveined
Gingko nuts	8, shelled
Fresh shiitake mushrooms	2, stems discarded and finely sliced
Pink-swirled fish paste cake or fish paste of choice	4 slices, each 0.5-cm (¼-in) thick
Trefoil (*mitsuba*)	4 stalks, finely sliced
Flower-shaped flour pieces	

DASHI

Water	600 ml (20 fl oz / 2½ cups)
Dried kelp (*konbu*)	8-cm (3¼-in) piece
Bonito flakes	20 g (⅔ oz)

1. Prepare dashi (page 19).
2. Marinate chicken with sake and salt for 10 minutes.
3. Mix together lightly eggs, salt, light soy sauce and dashi. Strain mixture using a fine sieve.
4. Divide chicken, prawns, gingko nuts, shiitake mushrooms and fish paste cake equally among 4 heatproof cups or bowls.
5. Gently pour an equal amount of egg mixture into each cup or bowl, then top with 1 flower-shaped flour piece.
6. Cover cups with lids or aluminium foil if lids are unavailable; custard will have a smooth surface when steamed.
7. Steam over high heat for 1 minute, then reduce heat to low and steam for about 12 minutes until egg mixture is set. Remove from heat and serve hot.

Fish and Seafood

JAPANESE

Deep-fried Seafood and Vegetables

Tempura originated from Europe about 400 years ago, but has become one of the most popular Japanese culinary delights in the world today.

Prawns (shrimps)	4, large, shelled and deveined, tails intact
Squid	1, about 200 g (7 oz) cleaned and cut into 3 x 4-cm (1⅓ x 1¾-in) pieces
Japanese aubergine (brinjal/eggplant)	1, medium, halved lengthways, then cut crossways into 3 pieces
Carrot	1, small, peeled and cut into thick matchsticks
Sweet potato	½, peeled and cut into 0.7-cm (⅓-in) rounds, then soaked in water before use
Fresh shiitake mushrooms	4, stems discarded
Ladies fingers (okra)	4, medium, washed and pat dry
Green perilla (*oba*) leaves	4, rinsed and pat dry
Japanese whiting	4, small, gutted, cleaned and butterflied
Plain (all-purpose) flour	for dusting
Salt	to taste
Cooking oil	for deep-frying
Grated white radish (daikon)	150 g (5⅓ oz), drained of juice
Grated mature ginger	10 g (⅓ oz)
Sea salt	(optional)

BATTER

Ice-cold water	200 ml (7 fl oz / ¾ cup)
Egg yolk	1
Plain (all-purpose) flour	125 g (4½ oz), sifted

DIPPING SAUCE

Mirin	3 Tbsp
Japanese dark soy sauce	3 Tbsp

DASHI

Water	250 ml (8 fl oz / 1 cup)
Dried kelp (*konbu*)	5-cm (2-in) piece
Bonito flakes	15 g (½ oz)

1. Prepare dashi (page 19). Place 200 ml (7 fl oz / ¾ cup) dashi, mirin and soy sauce in a saucepan. Boil for 1 minute. Remove from heat and set aside.
2. Prepare dipping sauce. Make dashi (page 19). Place 200 ml dashi, mirin and soy sauce in a saucepan. Bring to boil for 1 minute. Remove from heat and set aside.

3. Make 3 incisions across the belly of each prawn and straighten bodies. Make a few diagonal slits on both sides of each squid; this prevents them from curling when cooked. Make a few parallel cuts diagonally at one end of each piece of aubergine for it to spread out like a fan.
4. Dust each kind of seafood and vegetable with flour lightly, except perilla leaves.
5. Prepare batter. Put water and egg yolk into a mixing bowl. Mix lightly. Using chopsticks or a fork, fold in flour lightly to form a lumpy batter. Do not beat.
6. Heat oil to 170°C (340°F). Use a deep-fry thermometer to check temperature. Deep-fry vegetables first. Dip aubergine in batter and place in hot oil. Deep-fry 2–3 pieces at a time until crisp. Remove and drain on absorbent paper.
7. Deep-fry carrot. Gather 4–5 matchsticks into a bunch each time, then dip in batter and fry in hot oil until crisp. Remove and drain on absorbent paper. Repeat in small batches until ingredients are used up.
8. Heat oil to 180°C (350°F). Dip some prawns in batter and place in hot oil. Deep-fry in small batches until crisp. Remove and drain on absorbent paper. Repeat until remaining seafood is used up.
9. Transfer tempura to a serving dish or traditional tempura basket. Serve crisp and hot, with bowls of dipping sauce. Mix small mounds of grated radish and a little ginger into dipping sauce when eating. Alternatively, dip tempura in sea salt instead of dipping sauce when eating, if desired.

JAPANESE

Salt-grilled Horse Mackerel

Grilling is a popular cooking method for fish in Japanese cuisine. Many kinds of fish can be grilled including Spanish mackerel, bream, Pacific saury and sardine. Sardine and Pacific saury do not have to be gutted before cooking.

Horse mackerel	4, medium
Salt	1 Tbsp
White radish (daikon)	10-cm (4-in) length, peeled and grated
Japanese dark soy sauce	to taste
Lemon juice	(optional)

GARNISHING
Big green perilla (*oba*) leaves
Sliced lemon

1. Remove gills and gut fish, then rinse and pat dry with absorbent paper. Place cleaned fish on a flat sieve over a metal bowl to drain well. Just before grilling, sprinkle salt all over fish and coat tail and fins with salt. Heat grill pan over medium heat on gas hob until smoking, then grill fish on each side for 1–2 minutes until brown.

2. Place grated radish in a fine sieve, then rinse briefly under tap water. Press radish with the back of a spoon to drain away bitter juice.

3. Arrange fish, a small mound of drained radish drizzled with soy sauce to taste, perilla leaves and lemon slices on a large serving plate.

4. Sprinkle a little lemon juice over fish just before serving, if desired.

Pan-fried Seafood with Spring Onion

A seafood pancake lightly fragranced with spring onion.

Oysters	10, shucked
Prawns (shrimps)	5, medium, peeled
Clams	10, shelled
Salt	a pinch
Ground white pepper	a pinch
Ginger juice	½ tsp
Spring onions (scallions)	100 g (3½ oz), cut into equal lengths, white portions lightly bruised
Plain (all-purpose) flour	for sprinkling
Vegetable oil	4 Tbsp

BATTER

Plain (all purpose) flour	130 g (4½ oz)
Rice flour	65 g (2½ oz)
Water	375 ml (12 fl oz / 1½ cups)
Egg	1

VINEGAR SOY SAUCE (COMBINED)

Light soy sauce	4 Tbsp
Vinegar	2 Tbsp
Chilli powder	2 tsp
Sesame oil	2 tsp

1. Wash oysters, prawns and clams in brine (mix 625 ml (20 fl oz / 2½ cups) water with 1 tsp salt) and drain well.
2. Season oysters, prawns and clams with a pinch of salt and pepper and ginger juice. Leave refrigerated for 30 minutes. Drain well then chop into smaller pieces.
3. Beat batter ingredients with a whisk into a light batter.
4. Sprinkle spring onion lengths with some flour. Lower them into batter to coat lightly.
5. Transfer spring onion lengths to an oiled pan to cook. Pour some more batter over. Top with seafood. When batter is almost set, pour on remaining batter.
6. Flip pancake over and cook other side. Continue to flip and cook until both sides are golden brown in colour.
7. Slice and serve with vinegar soy sauce.

KOREAN

Fried Sea Bream

Deep-fried sea bream seasoned with sweet soy sauce.

Sea bream (or red snapper)	1, about 700 g (1½ lb), cleaned
Salt	1 Tbsp
Ground white pepper	2 tsp
Ginger juice	2 tsp
Corn flour (cornstarch)	55 g (2 oz)
Cooking oil	250 ml (8 fl oz / 1 cup)
Green capsicum (bell pepper)	1, cored and cut into thin strips
Leek	1, cut into 2.5-cm (1-in) lengths
Onion	1, peeled and cut into thin strips
Carrot	1, peeled and cut into thin strips

SAUCE

Cooking wine	2 Tbsp
Crushed garlic	½ Tbsp
Ground white pepper	1 tsp
Light soy sauce	5 Tbsp
Sugar	2 Tbsp
Maltose	2 Tbsp
Water	125 ml (4 fl oz / ½ cup)
Mirin	125 ml (4 fl oz / ½ cup)

1. Make 3 shallow cuts on each side of fish. Do not cut through. Sprinkle salt, pepper and ginger juice on fish and leave for 2 hours.
2. Combine ingredients for sauce and mix well with a blender.
3. Drain fish and dry using absorbent paper. Sprinkle corn flour over.
4. Heat cooking oil in a pan and cook fish on one side first. Then turn fish over to cook the other side.
5. In another pan, heat 3 Tbsp cooking oil and add sauce. When sauce comes to the boil, lower fish in. Reduce heat to simmer.
6. Top fish with capsicum, leek, onion and carrot and ladle sauce over fish repeatedly even as sauce simmers. Allow sauce to reduce before serving hot.

Fish and Seafood

KOREAN

Chilled Jellyfish with Cucumber

This is a cold appetiser of jellyfish and cucumber mixed in a mustard sauce.

Jellyfish	300 g (11 oz)
Vinegar	3 Tbsp
Salt	2 tsp
Sugar	2 Tbsp
Mustard	2 Tbsp
Crushed garlic	½ Tbsp
Lemon	2 slices
Large prawns (shrimps)	4
White sesame seeds	½ tsp, toasted
Cucumber skin	from 1 cucumber, cut into thin strips

1. Rinse jellyfish in several changes of cold water to remove sea salt.
2. Place jellyfish in a sieve and pour hot water at a temperature of 90°C (194°F) over. Leave to cool then squeeze out with your hands.
3. Combine vinegar, salt, sugar, mustard and garlic in a mixing bowl. Add jellyfish and refrigerate for 2 hours.
4. In a small pot, bring some water to the boil and add lemon and prawns. When prawns turn colour and are cooked, remove and rinse in cold water.
5. Peel then slice each prawn lengthwise into two. Set aside.
6. In a mixing bowl, toss jellyfish and white sesame seeds, then transfer to a plate. Serve cold with prawns and garnish with cucumber shreds.

MALAYSIAN

Chilli Fried Clams

The clams are best served with gravy and chilli all over.

Peanut oil	4 Tbsp
Lemongrass	2 stalks, bruised
Yellow or black preserved soy beans	2 Tbsp
Oyster sauce	2 Tbsp
Clams	500 g (1 lb 1½ oz), washed and drained
Fish stock or water	250 ml (8 fl oz / 1 cup)
Corn flour (cornstarch)	1 tsp, mixed with 1 Tbsp water
Spring onions (scallions)	6, cut into 2-cm (1-in) lengths
Sugar	½ tsp
Red chilli	sliced, for garnishing

PASTE (FINELY POUNDED)

Red chillies	5
Garlic	4 cloves, peeled
Ginger	2-cm (1-in) knob, peeled

1. Heat oil. Sauté lemongrass and finely pounded paste until fragrant.
2. Add preserved soy beans, oyster sauce and clams. Stir well and cover tightly.
3. After 2–3 minutes, remove lid and discard any clams that are unopened. Pour in fish stock or water and stir in corn flour mixture and spring onions. Season with sugar and bring gravy to a simmer.
4. When gravy thickens, remove from heat.
5. Serve immediately, garnished with chilli.

Fish and Seafood 273

MALAYSIAN

Cockle Rendang

Cockles cooked in coconut milk with a spicy paste.

Cooking oil	4 Tbsp
Coconut milk	1 litre (32 fl oz / 4 cups), extracted from 1½ grated coconuts and 1 litre (32 fl oz / 4 cups) water
Dried sour fruit slices (*asam gelugor*)	3 pieces
Turmeric leaf	1, finely sliced
Kaffir lime leaf	1, finely sliced
Cockle meat	600 g (1 lb 5⅓ oz)
Salt	to taste
Sugar	to taste
Grated coconut or desiccated coconut	55 g (2 oz), toasted and pounded

RENDANG PASTE

Dried chillies	10, seeded, soaked in water and drained
Bird's eye chillies	5
Lemongrass	2 stalks, finely sliced
Shallots	5, peeled
Garlic	1 clove, peeled
Ginger	1-cm (½-in) knob, peeled
Galangal	1-cm (½-in) knob, peeled
Turmeric	1-cm (½-in) knob, peeled

1. Heat oil and sauté finely ground paste until almost dry.
2. Pour in coconut milk and add sour fruit, turmeric leaf and kaffir lime leaf. Simmer until gravy thickens.
3. Add cockle meat and season with salt and sugar. Simmer until cockle meat is cooked.
4. Add coconut and simmer for 5 minutes over medium heat.

STRAITS CHINESE

King Prawns with Spicy Prawn Paste

Cooked with a spicy prawn paste, these prawns are very fragrant and go well with plain rice.

Cooking oil	500 ml (16 fl oz/ 2 cups)
King prawns (shrimps)	500 g (1 lb 1½ oz), feelers trimmed, seasoned with ¼ tsp salt and ¼ tsp sugar for 1 hour
Bottled sambal *belacan*	125 g (4½ oz)
Kaffir lime leaves	2
Anchovy stock granules	½ tsp
Calamansi lime juice	2 tsp

1. Heat cooking oil until very hot and deep-fry prawns for 30 seconds. Remove from heat and set aside.
2. Reserve 150 ml (5 fl oz / ⅗ cup) oil in the wok and stir-fry sambal *belacan* for 30 seconds.
3. Add prawns, kaffir lime leaves and anchovy stock granules.
4. When prawns are cooked, switch off heat and add calamansi juice. Dish out and serve immediately.

THAI

Thai Pineapple Prawn Curry

A spicy prawn curry sweetened with the addition of pineapple.

Cooking oil	3 Tbsp
Coconut milk	500 ml (16 fl oz / 2 cups)
Kaffir lime leaves	3
Fish sauce	2 Tbsp
Salt	to taste
Sugar	to taste
Pineapple	350 g (12 oz), sliced
Freshwater prawns (shrimps)	700 g (1½ lb), medium-sized, legs and feelers removed
Thai sweet basil	a handful

PASTE
Red chillies	10
Lemongrass	2 stalks, finely sliced
Galangal	1-cm (½-in) knob, peeled
Coriander leaves (cilantro)	3 sprigs
Kaffir lime leaves	2 tsp, chopped
Black peppercorns	10
Ground cumin	2 tsp
Dried prawn (shrimp) paste	1 tsp
Ground turmeric	2 tsp

1. Combine paste ingredients and grind until fine.
2. Heat oil and sauté finely ground paste until fragrant. Stir in coconut milk.
3. Add kaffir lime leaves, fish sauce, salt, sugar and pineapple. Simmer until the oil starts separating. Add prawns and basil leaves and simmer for 3 minutes.
4. Dish out and serve immediately.

Thai Steamed Fish Mousse

A popular Thai dish of steamed spicy fish paste. Serve hot as part of a main meal.

Coconut milk	500 ml (16 fl oz / 2 cups)
Rice flour	1 tsp
Spanish mackerel	600 g (1 lb 5⅓ oz), deboned and minced
Egg	1, beaten
Fish sauce	2 Tbsp
Sugar	1 tsp
Banana leaf cups	15–20, each about 7.5-cm (3-in) wide
Thai sweet basil	1 sprig
Kaffir lime leaves	3, finely sliced
Coriander leaves (cilantro)	2 Tbsp, chopped
Red chilli	1, finely sliced in strips

CURRY SPICES

Dried chillies	5, seeded, soaked and drained
Shallots	7, peeled
Garlic	3 cloves, peeled
Galangal	2 Tbsp, peeled and finely sliced
Lemongrass	2 Tbsp finely sliced
Coriander (cilantro) root	1 Tbsp, chopped
Ground white pepper	1 tsp
Salt	1 tsp
Dried prawn (shrimp) paste	1 tsp

1. Mix half the coconut milk with rice flour and cook over medium heat until it boils and forms a paste. Remove from heat and set aside.
2. Combine curry spices and grind until fine. In a large mixing bowl, combine the ground curry spices with remaining coconut milk, mackerel, egg, fish sauce and sugar. Stir well.
3. Line bottom of each banana leaf cup with basil leaves then fill with fish mixture. Steam for 15–20 minutes.
4. Remove from heat. Pour some coconut paste on each cup of fish mousse and sprinkle kaffir lime leaves, coriander leaves and chilli strips over. Steam for another minute before serving.

THAI

Stuffed Crabs

Crab shells stuffed with a seasoned minced pork mixture, then steamed to seal in the juices and deep-fried to achieve an attractive golden colour.

Garlic	1 Tbsp, peeled and chopped
Coriander (cilantro) root	1 Tbsp, chopped
Black peppercorns	10
Shallots	2, peeled and chopped
Fish sauce	1 Tbsp
Minced pork	200 g (7 oz)
Cooked or canned crabmeat	500 g (1 lb 1½ oz), mashed
Coriander leaves (cilantro)	4–6 sprigs
Egg yolks	2
Cooking oil	for deep-frying
Crab shells	4–6

1. Pound together garlic, coriander root, peppercorns and shallots with the fish sauce. Mix in pork, then knead in mashed crabmeat.

2. Fill crab shells with mixture. Place in a steamer over boiling water and steam for 15 minutes, then top with coriander leaves and coat with egg yolk.

3. Heat enough oil to deep-fry stuffed shells. When oil is hot, drop in stuffed shells, and cook until tops turn brown. Serve with Thai chilli sauce, if desired.

Savoury Golden Cups with Seafood Filling

An attractive appetiser of deep-fried spring roll wrappers filled with seafood, cashew nuts and button mushrooms.

| Spring roll wrappers | 6, cut into 7.5-cm (3-in) squares |
| Cooking oil | for brushing |

SEAFOOD FILLING

Squid	150 g (5⅓ oz), cleaned and finely diced
Tiger prawns (shrimps)	200 g (7 oz), peeled, deveined and finely diced
Crabmeat	50 g (1⅔ oz), shredded
Fish sauce	4 Tbsp
Cooking oil	90 ml (3 fl oz / ⅜ cup)
Cashew nuts	100 g (3½ oz), coarsely chopped
Garlic	2 cloves, peeled and finely chopped
Red chilli	1, finely sliced
Kaffir lime leaves	2, torn into pieces
Canned button mushrooms	100 g (3½ oz), finely sliced
Palm sugar	1 Tbsp, crushed or brown sugar
Lemon or lime juice	2 tsp
Corn flour (cornstarch)	1 Tbsp, blended with 2 Tbsp water

1. Brush a sheet of spring roll wrapper with a little cooking oil and place another sheet over it so that an eight-sided 'star' is formed.
2. Gently press it into a small fluted muffin tin or aluminium jelly mould. Hold it down by stacking with another tin or mould.
3. Repeat with remaining spring roll wrappers.
4. Transfer tins or moulds onto a baking tray and bake in a preheated oven at 200°C (400°F) for 12–15 minutes or until light brown and crisp. Set aside.
5. Marinate squid, prawns and crabmeat in fish sauce for 5–10 minutes. Heat cooking oil and stir-fry cashew nuts until slightly brown. Drain and set aside.
6. In the same oil, sauté garlic, chilli and kaffir lime leaves for 3 minutes. Add marinated seafood and mushrooms and stir-fry for 2–3 minutes.
7. Add cashew nuts and mix well before adding palm sugar or brown sugar and lemon or lime juice. Stir in corn flour mixture to thicken.
8. Spoon filling into baked spring roll cups and serve immediately.

VIETNAMESE

Fish and Pineapple Stew

Tangy pineapple slices tame the pungent taste of fish sauce in this dish, while the bird's eye chillies impart fiery spiciness.

Tuna	1 kg (2 lb 3 oz), cut into 1-cm (½-in) thick pieces
Minced garlic	2 tsp
Chicken seasoning powder	3 tsp
Ground black pepper	1 tsp
Cooking oil	5 Tbsp
Pineapple	1, peeled, quartered lengthways, cored and cut into 0.5-cm (¼-in) thick slices
Bird's eye chillies	5, halved
Fish sauce	50 ml (1⅔ fl oz) or more to taste
Coconut juice	500 ml (16 fl oz / 2 cups)
Spring onions (scallions)	5, peeled and cut into 5-cm (2-in) lengths

1. Season fish with garlic, seasoning powder and pepper. Set aside for 30 minutes to 1 hour.
2. Heat oil in a frying pan. Add seasoned fish and cook until golden brown. Dish out and set aside.
3. Use a clay or heavy-based pot to stew. Arrange a layer of pineapple pieces to cover base of vessel, followed by a layer of fish on top. Arrange a second layer of pineapple atop fish, followed by a second layer of fish.
4. Arrange alternating layers until the 2 ingredients are used up. Chillies will be placed last and right on top.
5. Pour in fish sauce and coconut juice to cover ingredients. Simmer over low heat for 30 minutes or until liquid thickens.
6. Garnish as desired with spring onions before serving.

VIETNAMESE

Fried Crab in Tamarind Sauce

A quaint rendition of the sweet-and-sour formula, this crab dish has a delightfully balanced and appetising flavour.

Cooking oil	500 ml (16 fl oz / 2 cups)
Crab(s)	1–2, about 1 kg (2 lb 3 oz), washed, top shell(s) and grey crab curd underside reserved, pincers separated and cracked and remaining crab(s) quartered
Onion	1, peeled and cut into wedges
Minced garlic	2 tsp
Minced shallots	2 tsp
Tamarind pulp	55 g (2 oz), soaked in root beer or sarsaparilla
Root beer or sarsaparilla	250 ml (8 fl oz / 1 cup)
Watercress	100 g (3½ oz)
French loaf	1

SEASONING
Salt	¼ tsp
Ground black pepper	¼ tsp
Sugar	¼ tsp
Chicken seasoning powder	¼ tsp or to taste

DIPPING SAUCE (COMBINED)
Lime juice	1 Tbsp
Salt	2 tsp
Ground black pepper	1 tsp

1. Heat oil in a wok. Add crab pincers and fry for 4 minutes, then add crab quarters and cook for 5 minutes. Lastly, add top shell(s) and cook for 3 minutes. Drain and set aside.
2. Remove the bulk of oil, leaving about 4 Tbsp in wok. Add onion wedges and stir-fry briefly, then dish out and set aside.
3. In the same oil, stir-fry garlic and shallots until fragrant. Add tamarind, root beer and fried onion wedges. Cook over medium heat until liquid reaches the boil.
4. Add crab pieces and cover with lid to cook. Stir occasionally.
5. When liquid is thickened, add crab curd and mix well. Then, add seasoning ingredients. Adjust to taste if necessary before removing from heat.
6. Transfer to a serving plate or bowl with watercress on the side.
7. Eat with French loaf slices and dipping sauce.

Fish and Seafood

VIETNAMESE

Steamed Fish with Sugar Cane

With all the natural juices sealed in during stewing, the fish meat here is succulent and brushed with sugar cane sweetness.

Sugar cane	5 sticks, each 10-cm (4-in), washed, peeled and quartered lengthways
Sardines	1 kg (2 lb 3 oz), 9–10 fishes, washed in salted water and drained well, or 1 kg (2 lb 3 oz) chubb mackerel
Water	500 ml (16 fl oz / 2 cups)
Round rice papers	10 sheets, 20 cm (8 in) in diameter
Sweet potato	1, steamed, peeled and sliced into 6 pieces lengthways
Water convolvulus (*kang kong*)	1 kg (2 lb 3 oz), roots discarded, washed and cut into 10-cm (4-in) sections

1. Line bottom of a pot with a layer of sugar cane strips, followed by a layer of sardines on top. Arrange a second layer of sugar cane strips atop fish, followed by a second layer of fish.

2. Continue to arrange alternating layers of sugar cane and fish until both ingredients are used up.

3. Pour water into pot and cook over high heat for 20 minutes.

4. Turn off heat and transfer fish to a serving plate, along with sweet potato slices and water convolvulus.

5. To assemble, place a sheet of rice paper on a plate. Smear on water to soften, then put half a sardine, a sweet potato slice and some water convolvulus on top. Fold lower edge over ingredients, then fold in left and right sides and roll up firmly.

6. Serve rolls with dipping sauce (page 18).

VIETNAMESE

Stuffed Squid

A versatile dish, the deep-fried stuffed squids here can be one of several dishes served at mealtimes, a starter or a tasty afternoon snack.

Pork	100 g (3½ oz)
Prawns (shrimps)	200 g (7 oz), washed, peeled and deveined
Minced onion	1 tsp
Minced garlic	1 tsp
Salt	1 tsp
Chicken seasoning powder	2 tsp
Squids	500 g (1 lb 1½ oz), heads separated, hard strips discarded, bodies thoroughly washed and skinned
Cooking oil	2 Tbsp + enough for deep-frying
Minced shallot	1 tsp
Tomato sauce (ketchup)	3 Tbsp
Ground black pepper	1 tsp
Sugar	½ tsp
Egg	1
Plain (all-purpose) flour	100 g (3½ oz)
Iceberg or Chinese lettuce	about 20 leaves, separated and washed
Chilli sauce	as required

1. Cut pork and peeled prawns into smaller pieces. Then, blend them together with onion and garlic until pasty. Transfer paste to a bowl.
2. Season paste with ½ tsp salt and 1 tsp seasoning powder. Then, stuff into squid bodies. Sew up open ends to secure.
3. Heat oil in a wok. Fry shallot until fragrant. Add tomato sauce and stir well. Remove sauce and season with remaining salt and seasoning powder, as well as pepper and sugar.
4. Beat egg well. Dip squids in, then coat with flour.
5. Heat sufficient oil in a clean wok for deep-frying, then cook coated, stuffed squids until done.
6. Arrange lettuce and cooked squids on serving plate, then pour on prepared sauce.
7. Serve with chilli sauce.

Fish and Seafood 283

SNACKS

CHINESE
286 Deep-fried Pork Rolls
287 Fried Meat and Vegetable Dumplings

FILIPINO
288 Deep-fried Spring Rolls
289 Prawns in Garlic Sauce
290 Spanish Meat Pies
291 Salted Beef Slices

INDIAN
292 Urad Dhal Dumplings with Yoghurt
293 Fried Bread

KOREAN
294 Sweet Glutinous Rice
295 Sweet and Sour White Radish

THAI
296 Thai Money Bags
297 Steamed Rice Pancakes with Pork
298 Spicy Red Curry Fishcake
299 Steamed Glutinous Rice with Banana and Kidney Beans

VIETNAMESE
300 Fresh Spring Rolls
301 Squid Cakes
302 Deep-fried Spring Rolls
303 Hanoi Prawn Fritters
304 Prawn Paste on Sugar Cane
305 Beef Rolls

Deep-fried Pork Rolls

Young bamboo shoots and Chinese mushrooms rolled in deep-fried pork make a tasty appetiser.

Boneless pork loin	250 g (9 oz), lightly frozen to facilitate slicing
Carrot	5-cm (2-in) piece, peeled and cut into strips
Canned bamboo shoots	5-cm (2-in) piece, cut into strips
Dried Chinese mushrooms	2 large pieces, soaked and shredded
Breadcrumbs	45 g (1½ oz)
Cooking oil	for deep-frying

SEASONING

Salt	½ tsp
Sugar	½ tsp
Ground white pepper	¼ tsp
Chinese rice wine	2 tsp
Egg	1, beaten
Corn flour (cornstarch)	1 Tbsp

1. Double the size of the sliced meat so that it will be large enough to cover the vegetables. To do this, cut a 0.25-cm (¼-in) thick slice across the grain without cutting through. Cut the next slice completely through 0.25-cm (¼-in) from the first cut. Continue to do this with the whole piece of meat.

2. Open up each slice of meat and beat lightly with the blunt edge of a cleaver to tenderise. Marinate meat with seasoning for 30 minutes.

3. Open and spread out each piece of meat on a flat surface and place 2 strips each of carrot, bamboo shoots and dried mushrooms.

4. Roll up meat, enclosing vegetables. Coat well with breadcrumbs.

5. Heat oil for deep-frying in a wok. Deep-fry pork rolls for about 5 minutes or until golden. Drain well.

6. Arrange pork rolls on a serving dish and garnish as desired.

Fried Meat and Vegetable Dumplings

Meat and vegetable pastry served with vinegar and ginger dip.

Minced pork or chicken	180 g (6½ oz)
White cabbage	2 leaves, about 125 g (4½ oz), finely chopped
Chinese chives	30 g (1 oz), finely chopped
Spring onion (scallion)	1, finely chopped
Cooking oil	2 Tbsp
Basic pork stock (page 19) or water	185 ml (6 fl oz / ¾ cup)

SEASONING

Sugar	1 tsp
Salt	¾ tsp
Ground white pepper	¼ tsp
Light soy sauce	1 tsp
Chinese rice wine	1 tsp
Sesame oil	1 tsp
Cooked oil or shallot oil	1 Tbsp

PASTRY

Plain (all-purpose) flour	125 g (4½ oz)
Salt	¼ tsp
Boiling water	165 ml (5½ fl oz / ⅔ cup)

VINEGAR AND GINGER DIP

Vinegar	2 Tbsp
Sugar	1 tsp
Ginger	30 g (1 oz), shredded

1. Mix minced meat with seasoning. Set aside. Place chopped cabbage in a muslin cloth and squeeze to remove excess liquid. Add to minced pork with chives and spring onion. Mix to a smooth paste.
2. Lift mixture with hand and slap it against a bowl or chopping board continuously for 1 minute to improve texture of meat. Refrigerate for 1 hour.
3. To make pastry, sieve flour into mixing bowl and add salt. Pour boiling water into flour and quickly mix into a stiff dough with a spoon.
4. Form dough into a round ball and leave to rest, covered with a dry towel, for 30 minutes. Knead dough on a lightly floured board for 3–5 minutes until smooth. Shape into a long sausage roll and divide equally into 18 pieces. Form each piece into a ball and roll out into a thin circle about 7-cm (3-in) in diameter. Put 1 tsp of meat mixture, slightly off centre on each circle. Pleat one half of the wrapper and press against the unpleated side to seal and form a half-moon shape dumpling.
5. Heat a flat pan with 2 Tbsp oil until hot, reduce heat and place dumplings in a circle close together. Fry for 1 minute until bottom of dumpling is golden brown.
6. Pour chicken stock into the pan, cover and simmer dumplings on low heat for 4–5 minutes until cooked through. Drain off remaining liquid and transfer dumplings onto a serving dish. Serve hot with vinegar and ginger dip or chilli sauce. To prepare the vinegar and ginger dip, heat combined vinegar and sugar. Stir until sugar dissolves and pour immediately over ginger Leave, covered, for 1–2 hours before serving.

FILIPINO

Deep-Fried Spring Rolls

Piping hot spring rolls are favoured as a *mirienda*, or snack in the Philippines. They are incredibly addictive and one is seldom enough. Omit the chicken and prawns if a vegetarian version is preferred.

Spring roll or egg roll wrappers	12–15 pieces
Corn flour (cornstarch)	1 Tbsp, mixed with 2 Tbsp water
Cooking oil	for deep-frying

FILLING

Cooking oil	4 Tbsp
Garlic	4 cloves, peeled and chopped
Onion	1, medium, peeled and sliced
Fish sauce	1 Tbsp
Chicken fillet	200 g (7 oz), diced
Prawns (shrimps)	110 g (4 oz), peeled
Water	125 ml (4 fl oz / ½ cup)
Sweet potato	55 g (2 oz), peeled and sliced into strips
French beans	100 g (3½ oz), diagonally sliced into strips
Carrot	55 g (2 oz), peeled and sliced into strips
Bean sprouts	200 g (7 oz), tailed, rinsed and drained
Salt	½ tsp or to taste
Ground white pepper	½ tsp

GARLIC-VINEGAR DIPPING SAUCE

Distilled vinegar	125 ml (4 fl oz / ½ cup)
Water	4 Tbsp
Garlic	4 cloves, peeled and lightly crushed
Salt	¼ tsp
Ground black pepper	¼ tsp
Sugar	1 Tbsp
Bird's eye chillies	3, crushed

1. Prepare filling. In a wok, heat oil over medium heat and fry garlic until golden brown. Add onion and fry until onion is soft and translucent.
2. Add fish sauce and stir to mix. Add chicken and prawns and fry until they change colour and are cooked.
3. Add water, then add sweet potato and fry until slightly tender.
4. Add French beans and carrot and fry for 3 minutes. Add bean sprouts and toss gently to mix well. Season with salt and pepper. Remove from heat and strain filling through a colander to drain excess liquid. Set aside to cool.
5. Place a spring roll or egg wrapper on a flat work surface with a corner facing you. Spoon 2–3 Tbsp filling in a line near the corner facing you.
6. Fold in left and right corners over filling, then fold bottom corner over and roll up tightly. Dab with a little corn flour mixture to seal. Repeat with remaining ingredients.
7. In a wok, heat oil for deep-frying over medium to high heat. Gently lower in spring rolls and deep-fry until light golden brown. Remove from heat and drain well.
8. Prepare garlic-vinegar sauce. In a saucepan, combine vinegar and water. Without stirring, bring to the boil over medium heat for a few seconds. Remove from heat and leave aside to cool completely. Add remaining ingredients and set aside to cool before serving.
9. Serve springs rolls immediately, with garlic-vinegar dipping sauce on the side.

Prawns in Garlic Sauce

Said to originate from the northwest of Spain, this is a favourite tapa, or appetiser in the Philippines.

Olive oil	90 ml (3 fl oz / ⅜ cup)
Garlic	1 head, peeled and chopped
Prawns (shrimps)	500 g (1 lb 1½ oz) medium-size, peeled and deveined, with tails left intact
Bird's eye chillies	3, crushed, or use 1 tsp chilli flakes
Tomato paste	1 Tbsp
Paprika	1 tsp
Worcestershire sauce	2 tsp
Dry white wine (optional)	2 Tbsp
Sugar	1 tsp
Salt	½ tsp
Ground black pepper	½ tsp

1. In a frying pan, heat oil over medium heat and fry garlic until golden brown.
2. Add prawns and increase heat to medium-high. Stir-fry until prawns turn pink. Add remaining ingredients and toss to mix well. Remove from heat and set aside.
3. If desired, lightly grease a hot plate with a little oil and heat over an open flame. Transfer prawns to hot plate and serve immediately.

FILIPINO

Spanish Meat Pies

Introduced by the Spaniards from the Iberian Peninsula, this popular snack is similar to Italian calzones, or Malay curry puffs.

Plain (all-purpose) flour	225 g (8 oz)
Sugar	30 g (1 oz)
Salt	a pinch
Butter	85 g (3 oz), softened and cut into small cubes
Vegetable shortening	55 g (2 oz)
Egg	1, lightly beaten
Iced water	2 Tbsp
Cooking oil	for deep-frying

FILLING

Cooking oil	4 Tbsp
Garlic	2 cloves, peeled and chopped
Onion	1, large, peeled and sliced
Chicken breast	300 g (11 oz), skinned, deboned, boiled and diced
Carrot	1, peeled and diced
Red capsicums (bell pepper)	110 g (4 oz), cored, seeded and finely diced
Potatoes	500 g (1 lb 1½ oz), peeled, diced and fried until light brown
Curry powder	1 tsp
Milk	125 ml (4 fl oz / ½ cup)
Basic chicken stock (page 19)	125 ml (4 fl oz / ½ cup)
Sugar	30 g (1 oz)
Salt	2 tsp or to taste
Ground black pepper	1 tsp
Raisins	85 g (3 oz)
Hard-boiled eggs	3–4, peeled and cut into 3–4 wedges each

1 Prepare filling. In a large frying pan or wok, heat oil over medium heat. Fry garlic until golden brown, then add onion and cook until soft and translucent.

2 Add chicken, carrot, capsicum and potatoes. Fry for 5 minutes, then add curry powder, milk, stock and sugar. Stir to mix well and leave to simmer for 3–5 minutes.

3 Season with salt and pepper. Add raisins and toss gently to mix well. Leave to simmer for a few minutes more or until vegetables are tender. Remove from heat and set aside to cool completely.

4 In a mixing bowl, combine flour, sugar and salt. Cut in butter and shortening until mixture resembles fine bread crumbs.

5 Add egg and stir lightly to combine. Gradually add water and using a fork, mix until dough starts to come together. Using your fingertips, lightly knead dough until smooth. Do not overwork dough. Roll into a ball and cover with plastic wrap. Refrigerate for 30 minutes.

6 On a lightly floured work surface, roll out dough to a 0.5 cm (¼-in) thick sheet. Using a 10-cm (4-in) round cutter, cut out dough circles.

7 Spoon 1 Tbsp filling onto the centre of dough. Fold up both sides of each dough circle. Top with a wedge of egg and fold dough up into a semi-circle to enclose filling. Crimp edges to seal. If desired, the prepared, uncooked meat pies may be stored in an airtight container and kept frozen up to one month. If freezing, omit hard-boiled eggs as they do not keep well.

8 In a wok or large frying pan, heat oil for deep-frying over medium to high heat. Deep-fry meat pies until golden brown. Remove from heat and drain well.

9 Alternatively, bake pies. Arrange pies on a prepared baking tray and brush with egg wash made from 1 egg yolk combined with 2 Tbsp milk. Bake in a preheated oven at 200°C (400°F) for 20–25 minutes or until golden brown. Serve hot.

Salted Beef Slices

This Filipino adaptation of beef jerky is popularly for breakfast in the Philippines, together with garlic fried rice, fried egg and tomato salsa.

Salt	½ Tbsp
White sugar	55 g (2 oz)
Brown sugar	30 g (1 oz)
Beef fillet or sirloin	500 g (1 lb 1½ oz), thinly sliced into 10 x 12-cm (4 x 5-in) pieces of 0.2-cm (⅛-in) thickness
Pineapple juice	125 ml (4 fl oz / ½ cup)
Cooking oil	4 Tbsp

1. Prepare a day in advance.
2. In a bowl, combine salt and both types of sugar. Add beef slices and rub mixture in thoroughly.
3. Add pineapple juice, cover and refrigerate overnight.
4. In a frying pan, heat oil over medium to high heat. Fry beef until light brown and tender.
5. Serve immediately on its own or as a side dish with Filipino-style fried rice (page 138).

INDIAN

Urad Dhal Dumplings with Yoghurt

These dumplings are eaten with cold yoghurt and piquant chutney. This dish is popular in Mumbai's many *chaat* outlets.

Urad dhal	100 g (3½ oz)
Rice	½ Tbsp
Water	125 ml (4 fl oz / ½ cup)
Salt	
Cooking oil for deep-frying	
Thick yoghurt	375 ml (12 fl oz / 1½ cups)
Sugar	1 Tbsp
Chilli powder	a pinch
Toasted cumin powder	a pinch
Turmeric powder	a pinch

TAMARIND CHUTNEY

Tamarind pulp	100 g (3½ oz)
Water	300 ml (10 fl oz / 1¼ cups)
Salt	to taste
Dark brown sugar	300 g (11 oz)
Chilli powder	1 tsp

GARNISH

Coriander leaves (cilantro)	1 Tbsp minced
Curry leaves	1 stalk, minced
Fine *muruku*	
Pomegranate seeds	

1. Soak urad dhal and rice for at least 2 hours and drain well. Pour urad dhal and rice into a blender then add water and blend to a paste.
2. Pour paste into a bowl, add a pinch of salt and mix vigorously.
3. Heat oil for deep-frying. Drop spoonfuls of batter into oil and fry to a golden brown. Remove and drop into a basin of water. Leave for about 20 minutes then drain, squeeze and set aside.
4. Whisk yoghurt, a pinch of salt and sugar in a large bowl. Place dumplings in to soak for 30 minutes.
5. Prepare tamarind chutney. Mix tamarind pulp and water and strain. Combine tamarind water with remaining ingredients. Bring to the boil then lower heat and simmer until a thick consistency (similar to pancake batter) is achieved. This chutney can be kept indefinitely if stored in the refrigerator.
6. Serve dumplings with a good helping of yoghurt. Sprinkle chilli, cumin and turmeric powders and coriander and curry leaves over. Drizzle with tamarind chutney and garnish with *sev* and pomegranate seeds.

INDIAN

Fried Bread

This bread goes well with spicy curries. The vegetable shortening gives the bread a light and flaky texture. If you are unable to obtain vegetable shortening, substitute with ghee (clarified butter).

Plain (all-purpose) flour	250 g (9 oz)
Bicarbonate of soda	½ tsp
Sugar	1 Tbsp
Salt	to taste
Vegetable shortening	1 Tbsp
Yoghurt	3 Tbsp
Warm water	250 ml (8 fl oz / 1 cup)
Ghee (clarified butter)	1 Tbsp, melted
Cooking oil	for deep-frying

1. Sift flour with bicarbonate of soda, sugar and salt. Rub shortening into mixture until it resembles fine bread crumbs.
2. Warm yoghurt over a low flame. This will sour the yoghurt.
3. Pour warmed yoghurt a little at a time into flour mixture while kneading. When yoghurt has been used up, add warm water a little at a time and continue to knead for another 5 minutes.
4. Add ghee and knead to a fine, smooth dough. Cover with a dry cloth and set aside for at least 1 hour.
5. Divide dough into 10 lemon-sized balls and dust generously with some flour. Dust rolling board and rolling pin with flour. Roll dough balls into discs.
6. Heat oil in a wok. When oil is hot, fry dough balls one at a time until they bloat up and are golden brown in colour. Drain in a colander lined with absorbent paper.
7. Serve hot with a spicy curry.

Snacks   293

KOREAN

Sweet Glutinous Rice

Glutinous rice steamed with chestnuts, dried red dates, sugar, pine nuts and cinnamon.

Glutinous rice	600 g (1 lb 5⅓ oz)
Molasses	200 g (7 oz)
Water	500 ml (16 fl oz / 2 cups)
Light soy sauce	2 Tbsp
Ground cinnamon	1 tsp
Sesame oil	4 Tbsp
Dried red dates	10, stoned and sliced
Chestnuts	10, peeled and sliced
Pine nuts	1 Tbsp

1. Soak glutinous rice in water for at least 3 hours.
2. Melt molasses in an uncovered pressure cooker over low heat with water, soy sauce, ground cinnamon and sesame oil.
3. Drain glutinous rice. Add to pressure cooker with dried red dates, chestnuts and pine nuts.
4. Cover pressure cooker and increase heat.
5. When pressure cooker starts to steam, switch it off and leave covered for another 3–5 minutes. When all the steam has escaped from the pressure cooker, open the lid and remove glutinous rice.
6. Portion rice into desired moulds and turn out onto a serving plate. Serve hot or at room temperature.

Sweet and Sour White Radish

A refreshing appetiser of marinated radish.

Water	250 ml (8 fl oz / 1 cup)
Salt	1 Tbsp
Sugar	1 Tbsp
White radish	½, peeled and thinly sliced into rounds
Cucumber skin	from 1 cucumber, juilenned
Pear	1, juilenned
Carrot	½, peeled and juilenned

MARINADE
Vinegar	2 Tbsp
Water	500 ml (16 fl oz / 2 cups)
Sugar	2 Tbsp
Salt	1 tsp

1. Start preparations up to a day ahead.
2. Combine water, salt and sugar in a bowl. Put radish slices into bowl and leave for 6 hours.
3. Drain radish and pat dry using absorbent paper.
4. Place a few strips of cucumber skin, pear and carrot on each slice of radish and roll up.
5. Combine marinade ingredients and sprinkle over radish rolls. Refrigerate for at least 12 hours before serving.

Thai

Thai Money Bags

Deep-fried pouches of diced chicken, Chinese mushrooms, water chestnuts, prawns and glass noodles.

Cooking oil	4 Tbsp + more for deep-frying
Garlic	4 cloves, peeled and finely chopped
Boneless chicken	200 g (7 oz), finely diced
Oyster sauce	2 Tbsp
Light soy sauce	1 tsp
Ground white pepper	½ tsp
Sesame oil	½ tsp
Dried Chinese mushrooms	6, soaked in hot water and finely chopped
Water chestnuts	6, peeled and finely diced
Prawns (shrimps)	200 g (7 oz), small, shelled and deveined
Glass noodles	55 g (2 oz), soaked in hot water and drained
Spring onions (scallions)	2, finely chopped
Corn flour (cornstarch)	1 tsp, mixed with 1 Tbsp water
Spring roll wrappers	10–12 sheets, each about 10 x 10-cm (4 x 4-in)
Dried spring onions (scallions)	10–12

1. To make the filling, heat oil and add garlic, chicken, oyster sauce, soy sauce, pepper and sesame oil. Sauté until chicken is cooked. Add mushrooms, water chestnuts and prawns and cook for 1 minute.

2. Add glass noodles and chopped spring onions. Mix well. Stir in corn flour mixture and cook until sauce is thick. Leave to cool.

3. Take a sheet of spring roll wrapper and top with 4 Tbsp filling. Bring the edges of the spring roll wrapper together and secure with a length of dried spring onion to resemble a small pouch. Neaten pouch top with a pair of scissors. Repeat until ingredients are used up.

4. Heat oil for deep-frying and fry pouches until golden brown. Drain. Serve hot with Thai chilli sauce.

Steamed Rice Pancakes with Pork

A light snack of steamed rice flour pancakes with a savoury filling.

PANCAKE BATTER

Rice flour	250 g (9 oz)
Tapioca flour	4 Tbsp
Water	450 ml (15 fl oz / $1^{4}/_{5}$ cups)

FILLING

Cooking oil	2 Tbsp
Garlic	1 Tbsp, peeled and crushed
Coriander (cilantro) root	1 Tbsp, chopped
Ground white pepper	1 tsp
Minced pork	200 g (7 oz)
Palm sugar	3 Tbsp
Fish sauce	2 Tbsp
Turnip	125 g (4½ oz), peeled and grated
Water	4 Tbsp
Shallots	1, peeled and finely sliced
Peanuts	55 g (2 oz), crushed
Coriander leaves (cilantro)	a few sprigs, to taste

1. Prepare pancake batter. Mix rice and tapioca flour with water. Set aside.
2. For the filling, heat oil and brown crushed garlic and coriander root. Add pepper and pork and sauté for 3–4 minutes until browned. Remove pork mixture and reserve.
3. In the same frying pan, mix palm sugar, fish sauce, turnip and water. Bring to the boil and stir until mixture boils down and becomes drier. Add cooked pork mixture, shallots and peanuts and mix well. Cook for another 5 minutes. Remove from heat.
4. The only successful way to cook rice pancakes is by steaming. Half-fill a fairly deep, heatproof container or saucepan with water. Stretch a piece of muslin or cotton over the top like a drum and tie down tightly with string. Place over medium heat. When steam appears through the material, spread a fine layer of batter over it. Cover with a lid for 1 minute to cook pancake.
5. Place 1 Tbsp of pork mixture in the centre of pancake. Top with coriander leaves, then fold sides of pancake over to form a square parcel.
6. Repeat with remaining batter and pork mixture.

THAI

Spicy Red Curry Fishcake

A light and tasty deep-fried fish cake of minced fish and red curry paste.

Red curry paste (page 18)	140 g (5 oz)
Red snapper fillet	500 g (1 lb 1½ oz), minced
Egg	1, small, about 70 g (2½ oz)
Fish sauce	3 Tbsp
Coriander leaves (cilantro)	1 sprig, chopped
Palm sugar	1 Tbsp, crushed or brown sugar
Long beans	85 g (3 oz), thinly sliced
Cooking oil	750 ml (24 fl oz / 3 cups)

SPECIAL CHILLI SAUCE

Sugar	200 g (7 oz)
Salt	2 tsp
Vinegar	125 ml (4 fl oz / ½ cup)
Water	2 Tbsp
Garlic	5 cloves, peeled and finely ground
Red chillies	2, finely ground
Shallots	3, peeled and sliced
Cucumber	1, quartered lengthways and thinly sliced
Toasted peanuts	3 Tbsp, pounded

1. Combine red curry paste and fish with egg, fish sauce, coriander leaves, palm sugar or brown sugar and long beans. Knead into a soft dough.
2. Shape 2 Tbsp of dough into a ball and flatten slightly. Deep-fry fishcakes until golden brown. Drain. Serve with special chilli sauce.
3. Prepare chilli sauce. Boil sugar, salt, vinegar and water until sugar is dissolved.
4. Add garlic, red chillies, shallots, cucumber slices, peanuts and mix well.

Steamed Glutinous Rice with Banana and Kidney Beans

Sticky glutinous rice topped with banana slices and boiled kidney beans, sealed in a banana leaf parcel.

Coconut milk	750 ml (24 fl oz / 3 cups)
Salt	1 tsp
Sugar	125 g (4½ oz)
Glutinous rice	450 g (1 lb), washed, soaked for 3–4 hours and drained
Semi-ripe bananas	2, peeled and finely sliced
Kidney beans	125 g (4½ oz), washed and boiled until soft
Banana leaves	5, cut into 10 x 15-cm (4 x 6-in) pieces
Bamboo toothpicks	10

1. Combine coconut milk with salt and sugar and stir well until sugar has dissolved. Strain coconut milk through a muslin cloth.

2. Bring to the boil and add glutinous rice. Stir constantly over medium heat until liquid is absorbed. Remove from heat and set aside to cool.

3. Place 1 Tbsp glutinous rice on a piece of banana leaf and flatten rice slightly. Layer with a few slices of banana, another tablespoonful of glutinous rice and some kidney beans.

4. Fold up the lengths of the banana leaf to enclose the filling. Secure the two open ends with toothpicks. Repeat until ingredients are used up.

5. Steam parcels over rapidly boiling water for 20–25 minutes. Serve hot or cold.

VIETNAMESE

Fresh Spring Rolls

The combination of Chinese lettuce, mint leaves and garlic chives gives this Vietnamese classic an unmistakably light and fresh taste.

Round rice papers	30 sheets, 20 cm (8 in) in diameter
Warm boiled water	as required
Chinese lettuce leaves	300 g (11 oz), washed and drained
Mint leaves	55 g (2 oz), washed and stalks discarded
Fresh rice vermicelli	1 kg (2 lb 3 oz), or Indian string hoppers or thick round rice noodles
Chinese chives	200 g (7 oz), washed and cut into 12-cm (5-in) lengths
Lean pork	300 g (11 oz), boiled for 15 minutes or until cooked then thinly sliced
Freshwater prawns (shrimps)	500 g (1 lb 1½ oz), boiled and peeled

DIPPING SAUCE (COMBINED)

Preserved soy bean paste	5 Tbsp
Coconut juice	2 Tbsp
Chopped lemongrass	1 Tbsp
Light soy sauce	1 Tbsp
Skinned peanuts	2 Tbsp, pounded
Sugar	2 tsp
Minced chilli	2 tsp
Minced garlic	2 tsp

1. Lay 1 sheet of rice paper on a round tray or plate. Smear on warm, boiled water to soften.
2. Put 1 lettuce leaf and 1 mint leaf at lower end of rice paper, followed by some rice vermicelli on top.
3. Fold in left and right sides of rice paper, resulting length should be about 10-cm (4-in).
4. Position 1 chive stalk along length of roll, leaving about 2-cm (1-in) to stick out on 1 side.
5. Put 1 piece of pork and 2 prawns on top of other ingredients, then roll up firmly. Dampened rice paper will stick to seal.
6. Repeat process until ingredients are used up. Serve rolls with dipping sauce.

VIETNAMESE

Squid Cakes

Delight in the tastier relative of fish cakes, especially when eaten with lettuce and mint leaves and a sweet-and-sour dipping sauce.

Squid	1 kg (2 lb 3 oz), washed, cleaned and skinned
Minced garlic	½ tsp
Minced shallot	1 tsp
Green (mung) bean powder	½ tsp
Cooking oil	125 ml (4 fl oz / ½ cup)
Chinese lettuce leaves	200 g (7 oz), washed and drained
Mint leaves	as required

SEASONING

Chicken seasoning powder	3 tsp
Ground white pepper	1 tsp
Sugar	1 tsp
Salt	1 tsp

1. Cut squid tubes into small pieces. Blend squid pieces to a fine paste. Transfer to a mixing bowl.
2. Season squid paste with minced garlic and shallot, mung bean powder and seasoning ingredients.
3. Shape squid paste into balls about 5-cm (2-in) in diameter. Flatten them into round-shaped patties about 0.5-cm (¼-in) thick.
4. Heat oil in a wok or frying pan. Cook squid patties until golden brown.
5. For presentation, cut squid cakes into diamond shapes and arrange on a plate. Garnish as desired with leaves and squid-cake trimmings.
6. Serve squid cakes with lettuce and mint leaves, as well as dipping sauce (page 18).

Snacks 301

VIETNAMESE

Deep-fried Spring Rolls

The Vietnamese version of a favourite among many, is richly stuffed with pork, crabmeat, yam and black fungus for crunch.

Minced pork	300 g (11 oz)
Crabmeat	300 g (11 oz), coarsely chopped and mashed, or minced prawn (shrimp) meat
Yam (taro)	300 g (11 oz), washed, peeled and finely shredded
Black (woodear) fungus	5, soaked to soften and finely shredded
Minced shallots	2 tsp
Minced garlic	1 tsp
Round rice papers	30 sheets, 15-cm (6-in) in diameter
Coconut juice	125 ml (4 fl oz / ½ cup)
Cooking oil	500 ml (16 fl oz / 2 cups)
Chinese lettuce leaves	
Mint leaves	

SEASONING

Chicken seasoning powder	4 tsp
Ground black pepper	1 tsp
Salt	2 tsp

1. Prepare stuffing. Combine pork, crabmeat, yam, black fungus, shallots and garlic in a large bowl. Mix in seasoning ingredients. Set aside.

2. Lay 1 sheet of rice paper on a round tray. Smear on coconut juice to soften. Put 1 Tbsp stuffing onto lower end of rice paper. Then, fold in left and right sides and roll up firmly. Each roll should be 3–4-cm (1½–2-in) long. Repeat process until ingredients are used up.

3. Heat oil in a wok or deep-fryer. Deep-fry spring rolls over medium heat until golden brown.

4. Serve hot with some lettuce and mint leaves, as well as dipping sauce (page 18).

VIETNAMESE

Hanoi Prawn Fritters

Traditionally, prawns for the dish were not peeled because of the calcium the shells contained. The shells also help maintain crispness.

Prawns (shrimps)	1 kg (2 lb 3 oz), small (50–60 pieces), washed
Limes	as required
Water	as required
Potatoes	500 g (1 lb 1½ oz), peeled, washed and cut into thin strips
Cooking oil	500 ml (16 fl oz / 2 cups)
Chinese lettuce leaves (optional)	100 g (3½ oz), washed and drained well
Mint leaves (optional)	100 g (3½ oz), washed and drained well

BATTER

Eggs	3
Plain (all-purpose) flour	500 g (1 lb 1½ oz)
Rice flour	250 g (9 oz)
Turmeric powder	2 tsp
Chicken seasoning powder	4 tsp
Salt	2 tsp
Hot water	as required

1. Peel prawns if desired, but leave tails intact.
2. Make sufficient lime water to soak potato strips until required. To make lime water, squeeze the juice of 1 lime into 1 litre (32 fl oz / 4 cups) water, increasing proportionately.
3. Prepare batter. In a bowl, beat eggs, then mix in flours. Add turmeric powder, seasoning powder and salt, then continue to beat until mixture is smooth. Add some hot water if the mixture is too thick.
4. Combine batter, prawns and drained potato shreds in a larger bowl.
5. Heat oil in a wok or frying pan. Use a ladle to scoop batter (containing at least 2 prawns and some potato shreds) to lower into hot oil. Make sure that fritters do not stick together while frying. Cook until golden brown.
6. Serve fritters with dipping sauce (page 18). For a lighter experience, eat fritters with some lettuce and mint leaves.

Snacks

VIETNAMESE

Prawn Paste on Sugar Cane

Succulent prawn meat on lengths of sweet sugar cane are bound to delight both the family and guests.

Prawns (shrimps)	1 kg (2 lb 3 oz)
Sugar cane	5 sticks, each 10-cm (4-in), washed and peeled
Lard	100 g (3½ oz), washed and cut into 1.5-cm (¾-in) wide pieces
Sugar	3 tsp
Garlic	10 cloves, peeled
Salt	1 tsp

1. Wash, peel and devein prawns. Set aside.
2. Quarter each sugar cane piece lengthways, then pare the pointed edge down to make rounder.
3. Combine lard and sugar in an ovenproof bowl, then leave in oven preheated to 120°C (250°F) for about 30 minutes.
4. In the meantime, blend prawns and garlic together until well mixed.
5. In a bowl, combine prawn paste and lard, then add salt.
6. Take 1 Tbsp paste and press around central portion of a sugar cane length, covering roughly two-thirds of stick. Repeat until ingredients are used up.
7. Deep-fry, barbecue or oven grill prepared sugar cane lengths.
8. Serve with dipping sauce (page 18) or bottled chilli sauce.

VIETNAMESE

Beef Rolls

Deeply aromatic and rich with meat juices, this starter will please any meat-lover.

Beef fillet	1 kg (2 lb 3 oz)
Brandy	1 tsp
Lean pork or chicken breast	450 g (1 lb), minced
Crabmeat	100 g (3½ oz)
Straw mushrooms	200 g (7 oz), finely chopped
Cooking oil	2 Tbsp
Chinese lettuce leaves	300 g (11 oz), washed and drained

SEASONING

Chicken seasoning powder	4 tsp
Ground white pepper	1 tsp
Salt	1 tsp

1. Cut beef into thin slices, about 3 x 6-cm (1½ x 3-in). When done, put beef slices in a bowl and add brandy. Mix and set aside for 30 minutes.

2. Prepare filling. Combine minced pork or chicken, crabmeat and mushrooms in a bowl. Mix in seasoning ingredients and set aside.

3. Heat cooking oil in a frying pan. Add filling and stir-fry for 10 minutes or until meat is cooked. Dish out and leave to cool for about 10 minutes.

4. Put about 2 tsp filling onto a beef slice and roll up firmly. Repeat until beef slices are used up.

5. Skewer 3–4 rolls onto each skewer and grill them over charcoal heat. The rolls should be cooked after 10 minutes of grilling or when they turn golden on the outside. Alternatively, bake in oven preheated to 160°C (325°F) for about 8 minutes, turning once or twice.

6. Remove rolls from skewers and put on serving plate. Serve rolls with lettuce. To eat, wrap each beef roll with a lettuce leaf, then eat with dipping sauce (page 18).

Snacks 305

DESSERTS

BALINESE
- 308 Black Rice Pudding
- 309 Coconut Pancakes
- 310 Steamed Jackfruit Cake
- 311 Iced Fruit in Coconut Dressing
- 312 Fried Bananas

CHINESE
- 313 Sweet Dumplings
- 314 Gingko Nut and Water Chestnut Dessert
- 315 Sweet Yam Paste
- 316 Peanut Crème

FILIPINO
- 317 Young Coconut Pie
- 318 Filipino Crème Caramel
- 319 Corn Pudding

INDIAN
- 320 Cream of Jackfruit and Sago
- 321 Green Mung Payasam
- 322 Indian Bread and Butter Pudding
- 323 Steamed Jackfruit Turnover

INDONESIAN
- 324 Fried Coconut Cakes
- 325 Coconut Almond Pudding
- 326 Fried Mung Bean Balls
- 327 Dumplings in Sweet Ginger Soup

JAPANESE
- 328 Rice Ball Skewers
- 329 Agar-agar, Glutinous Rice Balls and Red Bean Paste with Syrup
- 330 Pancakes with Red Bean Paste
- 332 Candied Sweet Potatoes

KOREAN
- 333 Sweet Rice Cake
- 334 Cinnamon Punch with Dried Persimmon

MALAYSIAN
- 335 Sugar-coated Tapioca Rings

STRAITS CHINESE
- 336 Sesame Puffs
- 337 Nyonya-style Pancakes

THAI
- 338 Water Chestnut Cake with Coconut Cream Topping
- 339 Red Rubies
- 340 Coconut Bananas

VIETNAMESE
- 341 Sweet Yam Dessert
- 342 Peanut and Sago Dessert
- 343 Tapioca Cake

BALINESE

Black Rice Pudding

A classic dessert of black and white glutinous rice, this is substantial enough to double-up as an afternoon snack.

Black glutinous rice	250 g (9 oz)
White glutinous rice	85 g (3 oz)
Water	1.25 litres (40 fl oz / 5 cups)
Screwpine leaf	1
Palm sugar	175 g (6¼ oz) or to taste
Salt	a pinch or to taste
Coconut cream	375 ml (12 fl oz / 1½ cups)

1. Rinse black and white glutinous rice well under running water. Soak overnight and drain before using.

2. Combine 750 ml (24 fl oz / 3 cups) water, both types of glutinous rice and screwpine leaf in a heavy pan. Simmer over medium heat for about 45 minutes, adding more water if necessary.

3. Add palm sugar and continue to cook until most liquid has evaporated. Season to taste with salt. Remove from heat and leave to cool.

4. Serve at room temperature topped with desired amounts of coconut cream.

BALINESE

Coconut Pancakes

Coconut pancakes are like soft, sweet spring rolls when served. They can be served as an after-meal dessert or a tea-time snack.

Rice flour	100 g (3½ oz)
Sugar	30 g (1 oz)
Salt	a pinch
Eggs	3
Coconut milk	250 ml (8 fl oz / 1 cup)
Vegetable oil	2 Tbsp

PALM SUGAR SYRUP

Palm sugar	375 g (13²/₅ oz), chopped
Water	250 ml (8 fl oz / 1 cup)

COCONUT FILLING

Palm sugar syrup	125 ml (4 fl oz / ½ cup)
Grated coconut	125 g (4½ oz)
Screwpine leaf	1, bruised

1. Prepare pancakes. Combine all ingredients in a large bowl and mix well. Stir well with a balloon whisk until lump-free, then strain. Batter should be very liquid in consistency.
2. Heat a non-stick pan over low heat. Add 4 Tbsp batter to form a very thin pancake.
3. Turn over when batter has set. Repeat until mixture is used up. Leave pancakes to cool to room temperature.
4. Prepare palm sugar syrup. Combine palm sugar and water in a saucepan and bring to the boil. Simmer for 10 minutes, then remove from heat and leave to cool before using.
5. Prepare coconut filling. Heat palm sugar syrup in a frying pan. Add grated coconut and screwpine leaf and mix well. Cook over low heat for 2 minutes.
6. Place 1 Tbsp filling along the centre of a pancake. Fold in left and right sides, then roll up. Repeat until ingredients are used up.
7. Serve at room temperature.

Desserts

BALINESE

Steamed Jackfruit Cake

The unique taste of jackfruit is balanced by the mild fragrance of banana leaf and robust flavour of coconut milk in this pleasant and light dessert.

Rice flour	180 g (6½ oz)
Sugar	80 g (2⅘ oz)
Coconut milk	500 ml (16 fl oz / 2 cups)
Salt	a pinch
Banana leaf squares	12, each 15 x 15-cm (6 x 6-in)
Jackfruit segments	12, halved

1. Combine rice flour, sugar, coconut milk and salt in a large bowl. Mix well and until lump-free.
2. Slowly bring mixture to the boil in a non-stick pan. Simmer until mixture thickens, stirring continuously until smooth and lump-free. Remove from heat and leave to cool.
3. Place 1 heaped Tbsp cooked mixture onto a banana leaf square. Top with a slice of jackfruit and cover with 1 Tbsp mixture.
4. Fold banana leaf in thirds lengthways, then fold down left and right ends so the weight of the parcel rests on them. Repeat until ingredients are used up.
5. Steam parcels for about 20 minutes or until cooked. Remove and leave to cool.
6. Serve at room temperature.

BALINESE

Iced Fruit in Coconut Dressing

An exciting mix of tropical fruits with a creamy coconut dressing that is sweetened by palm sugar and brushed with subtle screwpine fragrance.

Palm sugar	375 g (13²/₅ oz), chopped
Water	250 ml (8 fl oz / 1 cup)
Screwpine leaf	1, bruised
Sweet potatoes	200 g (7 oz), peeled and diced
Palm fruit	200 g (7 oz)
Diced mixed fruit of choice	200 g (7 oz), use pineapple, mango, jackfruit and/or bananas
Coconut cream	50 ml (1¾ oz)
Lime juice	2 Tbsp

RICE FLOUR DUMPLINGS

Glutinous rice flour	150 g (5⅓ oz)
Tapioca flour	55 g (2 oz)
Salt	a pinch
Water	180 ml (6 fl oz / ¾ cup)

1. Prepare rice flour dumplings. Combine both flours and salt in a bowl. Gradually mix in water and knead until a smooth dough is formed. The dough should be soft, elastic and not dry. Shape dough into 1-cm (½-in) dumplings.

2. Bring 4 litres (128 fl oz / 16 cups) lightly salted water to the boil. Add dumplings, return to the boil and simmer for 5 minutes. Drain dumplings and lower into a bowl of iced water to cool.

3. Bring palm sugar, water and screwpine leaf to the boil and simmer for 5 minutes. Add sweet potatoes and palm fruit. Simmer until almost soft.

4. Add mixed fruit and dumplings. Return to the boil and simmer for 2 minutes.

5. Mix in coconut cream, return to the boil and simmer 1 minute more. Finish by adding lime juice, then remove from heat and leave to cool.

6. Serve at room temperature or chilled and topped with ice.

BALINESE

Fried Bananas

Sweet and fragrant bananas with crispy outer coatings, fries bananas, or has been unfailingly popular with the whole family. It also could not be easier to prepare.

Rice flour	100 g (3½ oz)
Plain (all-purpose) flour	50 g (1⅔ oz)
Water	160 ml (5¾ oz)
Salt	a pinch
Finger bananas	8, peeled and halved lengthways, or 4 large bananas, peeled and sliced
Cooking oil	for deep-frying

PALM SUGAR SAUCE
Palm sugar	375 g (13⅖ oz), chopped
Water	250 ml (8 fl oz / 1 cup)

1 Prepare palm sugar syrup. Combine palm sugar and water in a saucepan and bring to the boil. Simmer for 10 minutes, then remove from heat and leave to cool before using.

2 Combine both types of flour, water and salt in a mixing bowl. Whisk until batter is smooth and slightly thick. Dip banana slices into batter and coat generously.

3 Heat oil for deep-frying to 160°C (325°F). Place battered bananas into hot oil one at a time to prevent them from sticking.

4 Deep-fry over low heat until battered bananas are golden brown and very crispy.

5 Drain well on absorbent paper towels. Serve with palm sugar syrup.

6 For a variation known as *jaja pulung biu*, mash 400 g (14⅓ oz) very ripe bananas, then add 100 g (3½ oz) plain (all-purpose) flour, 160 ml (5⅓ oz / ⅔ cup) water, 30 g (1 oz) sugar and a pinch of salt and mix until a soft elastic dough results. Deep-fry tablespoonfuls of dough in 160°C (325°F) oil until crisp and golden, then drain on absorbent paper and serve with palm sugar syrup.

CHINESE

Sweet Dumplings

Fried glutinous rice balls filled with delicious red bean paste.

Glutinous rice flour	225 g (8 oz)
Canned red bean paste	225 g (8 oz)
Corn or vegetable oil (optional)	as needed

1. Stir 225 ml ($7^{3}/_{5}$ fl oz / $^{4}/_{5}$ cup) cold water gradually into the flour and work it into a smooth dough. There is no need to knead.
2. Take a small piece of dough about the size of a chestnut and shape it into a round. Press a thumb into the round.
3. Insert 1 tsp bean paste and work dough over bean paste completely: Roll dumpling between the palms to make it round. Repeat until all the dough and bean paste are used.
4. Bring 1.5 litres (48 fl oz / 6 cups) water to the boil in a large saucepan. Add about half of the dumplings, one by one, and bring water to the boil. Move dumplings once or twice with a wooden spoon to prevent them from sticking to the pan.
5. Reduce the heat but continue to boil for 5–6 minutes or until dough looks transparent.
6. Lift out dumplings with a slotted spoon, drain them, and put them onto a warmed serving plate. Cook the rest of the dumplings in the same way, draining them thoroughly and putting them on the serving plate.
7. Serve hot as they are or, if desired, when they are drained, fry them in a little oil over medium low heat, gently stirring, until they begin to brown; this gives the sticky dumplings a delicious crisp outer coating.
8. Dumplings can be frozen after step 3. It takes 8–9 minutes to cook them from frozen in boiling water and, again, they can be fried if wished.

CHINESE

Gingko Nut and Water Chestnut Dessert

A sweet dessert made with gingko nuts and water chestnuts.

Water	1.5 litres (48 fl oz / 6 cups)
Rock sugar	300 g (11 oz)
Gingko nuts	180 g (6½ oz), peeled and bitter shoot removed
Water chestnuts	22, skinned and diced into 0.5-cm (¼-in) cubes
Sweet potato flour	3 Tbsp
Corn flour (cornstarch)	1 Tbsp
Water	125 ml (4 fl oz / ½ cup)
Egg whites	2, lightly beaten

1. In a large saucepan, bring water and rock sugar to a slow boil. When rock sugar dissolves, put in gingko nuts. Boil over low heat for 10 minutes, then add water chestnuts. Simmer for another 10 minutes.

2. Combine sweet potato flour, corn flour and water, and strain mixture.

3. Slowly drizzle and stir egg white into soup. Repeat with flour solution. When it boils again, remove from heat.

4. Serve hot or chilled.

CHINESE

Sweet Yam Paste

A tasty dessert of mashed yam, boiled gingko nuts and pumpkin cubes.

Gingko nuts	115 g (4 oz), peeled and bitter shoot removed
Water	as required
Sugar	220 g (8 oz)
Pumpkin	220 g (8 oz), diced into 2-cm (1-in) cubes
Yam	900 g (2 lb), diced into 5 x 1-cm (2 x ½-in) cubes
Sugar	12 Tbsp
Lard	6 Tbsp
Shallots	3, peeled and sliced thinly

1. Wash gingko nuts. Boil with half of the sugar in 2 Tbsp water over low heat for 45 minutes until sugar is absorbed into nuts. Add water a little at a time while cooking. Cool and cut gingko nuts into half, removing centre fibre if any.

2. Cook pumpkin cubes in remaining sugar and 2 Tbsp water over low heat in a heavy-bottomed saucepan. Cook until sugar is absorbed. Add a little water at a time while cooking to prevent sugar from burning. Set gingko nuts and pumpkins aside.

3. Steam yam pieces over rapidly boiling water until very soft. Use a blender to blend half of the yam, 2 Tbsp lard and half of the castor sugar until paste is smooth. Remove to a bowl and repeat with remaining yam, lard and remaining sugar.

4. Heat another 2 Tbsp lard in a wok and fry sliced shallots until very lightly browned. Add yam paste and stir-fry over low heat for 30 seconds. Remove to a shallow serving bowl. Place cooked pumpkin cubes around sides of the bowl and gingko nuts over the yam.

5. Serve hot.

Peanut Crème

Blended peanuts and rice boiled with sugar and water is a perfect dessert to end off a meal.

Peanuts	625 g (1 lb 6 oz), shelled
Rice	2 Tbsp, washed and drained
Water	2 litres (64 fl oz / 8 cups)
Sugar	310 g (11 oz)

1. Roast peanuts until light brown. Remove skin.

2. Using an electric blender, blend rice and half of the peanuts with 435 ml (14 fl oz / 1¾ cups) water until very fine. Add 2–3 Tbsp of water if necessary to keep the mixture moving and rotating. Pour into a bowl and set aside.

3. Repeat process using the other half of the peanuts with another 435 ml (14 fl oz / 1¾ cups) water.

4. Place blended peanuts, sugar and remaining water in a heavy-bottomed aluminium saucepan. Bring to the boil over a moderate heat. Lower heat and simmer for 5 minutes, stirring continuously. Remove from heat.

5. Serve hot or chilled.

FILIPINO

Young Coconut Pie

Here, a rich, buttery pastry encases a sweet, creamy filling made from young coconut. Serve as a dessert or tea-time snack with coffee.

Young coconut	1, about 450 g (1 lb), flesh scooped out and water reserved
Milk	250 ml (8 fl oz / 1 cup)
Single (light) cream	300 ml (10 fl oz / 1¼ cups)
Sugar	85 g (3 oz)
Egg yolks	5
Plain (all-purpose) flour	55 g (2 oz)
Vanilla essence	1 tsp
Screwpine leaves	3, knotted
Egg wash	1 egg yolk mixed with 1 Tbsp fresh milk

PASTRY

Plain (all-purpose) flour	280 g (10 oz)
Sugar	3 Tbsp
Salt	½ tsp
Vegetable shortening	70 g (2½ oz)
Butter	85 g (3 oz), cubed
Egg	1
Iced water	4 Tbsp

1. Prepare pastry. In a mixing bowl, combine flour, sugar and salt. Cut in shortening and butter until mixture resembles coarse meal.

2. Crack egg into mixture and stir lightly to combine. Gradually add water and using a fork, mix until dough starts to come together. Using your fingertips, knead dough until smooth. Roll into a ball, cover with plastic wrap and refrigerate for 30 minutes.

3. In a saucepan, combine coconut water, milk, cream, sugar, egg yolks, flour, vanilla essence and screwpine leaves over medium heat, stirring constantly until mixture thickens. Remove from heat and set aside to cool. Add coconut flesh, mix well and set aside.

4. Preheat oven to 200°C (400°F). Divide dough into 2 parts, one 3 times bigger than the other. Roll out bigger portion to line a 23-cm (9-in) pie dish. Using a fork, prick base and sides of dough. Bake for 20 minutes or until pastry is light brown. Remove from heat and keep oven heated. Pour in coconut mixture, spreading evenly.

5. Roll out remaining dough into a 24-cm (9½-in) long sheet. Cut into a 1-cm (½-in) wide strip and place over filling, creating a lattice design, if desired. Lightly brush with egg wash, then return pie to oven to bake for 25 minutes or until golden brown.

6. Serve warm.

Filipino Créme Caramel

There are many versions of this Filipino dessert, which is practically a staple at tea-time and festive gatherings. This is a classic version that features the distinct flavour and aroma of lemon and vanilla.

Sugar	170 g (6 oz)
Water	90 ml (3 fl oz / ⅜ cup)
CUSTARD	
Eggs	5
Egg yolks	15
Sweetened condensed milk	450 ml (15 fl oz / 1⁴⁄₅ cups)
Milk	450 ml (15 fl oz / 1⁴⁄₅ cups)
Water	450 ml (15 fl oz / 1⁴⁄₅ cups)
Vanilla essence	1 tsp
Lemon or lime zest	2 tsp

1. In a saucepan, melt sugar over low heat, stirring constantly with a wooden spoon until melted and dark brown. Pour in water and increase heat to medium. Stir until sugar dissolves completely. Remove from heat and pour syrup into a 27-cm (10½-in) flan mould. Set aside for caramel to cool completely.

2. Preheat oven to 190°C (370°F).

3. In a bowl, crack eggs and add egg yolks and condensed milk. Whisk until well blended. Add milk, water and vanilla and whisk lightly until just combined. Strain and pour on top of cooled caramel syrup, then stir in lemon or lime zest. Cover and seal with aluminium foil.

4. Place mould on a deep baking tray and fill tray with water until it reaches 1-cm (½-in) up the sides of mould. Bake for 1 hour 45 minutes–2 hours, or until créme caramel is firm to the touch. Remove from heat and discard aluminium foil. Set aside to cool completely before placing in the refrigerator to chill for 1 hour.

5. To unmould, run a sharp knife along the edges of créme caramel. Place a serving plate on top of mould and invert mould. Gently remove mould and ease créme caramel out. Garnish as desired.

6. Serve chilled.

Corn Pudding

Corn pudding, known as *maja blanca* or *tibok tibok*, originates from Pampanga, a district in the Central Luzon region. It is traditionally made with carabao milk.

Wilted banana leaf	1, large
Thick coconut milk	1 litre (32 fl oz / 4 cups)
Sugar	180 g (6½ oz)
Corn flour (cornstarch)	115 g (4 oz)
Canned creamed corn	125 g (4½ oz)
Ripe jack fruit	85 g (3 oz), finely chopped
Butter	125 g (4½ oz), melted
Yellow food colouring	¼ tsp

COCONUT MILK NUGGETS
Thick coconut milk   500 ml (16 fl oz / 2 cups)

1. Prepare coconut milk nuggets. In a wok, heat coconut milk over medium heat and bring to the boil. Reduce heat to low and simmer, stirring occasionally to prevent burning, until oil separates and coconut milk starts to curdle and solidify. Continue cooking until coconut milk is golden brown. Remove from heat and strain. Set aside and reserve oil.

2. Prepare a 18 x 27-cm (7 x 10½-in) rectangular pan. Trim banana leaf to fit and line pan. Lightly grease leaf with reserve coconut oil.

3. In a medium bowl, combine 360 ml (12 fl oz / 1½ cups) coconut milk and corn flour and whisk until smooth. Set aside.

4. In a frying pan, combine remaining coconut milk and sugar. Bring to the boil over medium heat. Add coconut milk and corn flour mixture and stir continuously with a whisk until smooth and lightly thickened.

5. Add creamed corn, jack fruit, butter and food colouring and cook until mixture has a firm, thick consistency. Remove from heat, pour into prepared pan and level with a palette knife or spatula. Set aside to cool completely before refrigerating for 1 hour.

6. Slice pudding and sprinkle with coconut milk nuggets Serve chilled or at room temperature.

INDIAN

Cream of Jackfruit and Sago

In Kerala, the jackfruit is a most versatile fruit. Young jackfruit is used in savoury dishes while ripe jackfruit is made into jam or used in desserts like this one.

Jackfruit	1 kg (2 lb 3 oz), stones discarded
Sago	30 g (1 oz), soak for 20 minutes then drained
Water	700 ml (23⅓ fl oz / 2⅘ cups)
Salt	¼ tsp
Dark brown sugar	480 g (1 lb 1 oz)
Cardamom	10 pods, pound into powder
Coconut milk	500 ml (16 fl oz / 2 cups)
Ghee (clarified butter)	½ Tbsp

GARNISH

Ghee (clarified butter)	2 tsp
Fresh coconut slivers	114 g (4 oz), coconut flesh cut into slivers, fried in hot ghee until golden brown and drained
Cashew nuts	10, chopped

1. Dice jackfruit into small pieces and place in a saucepan with sago. Add water to cover jackfruit and sago completely. Bring to the boil then reduce to moderate heat.

2. When jackfruit is soft, add salt and brown sugar. Cook for a further 10 minutes. Stir in powdered cardamom.

3. Carefully pour in coconut milk and simmer gently. Add ghee and simmer for 20 minutes for flavours to infuse.

4. Meanwhile, prepare garnish. Heat ghee then add coconut and cashew nuts. Fry to a golden brown. Drain and use to garnish cream of jackfruit.

5. Serve hot or chilled.

INDIAN

Green Mung Payasam

Payasams are sweet desserts served after an Indian meal.

Green (mung) beans	100 g (3½ oz), soaked overnight and drained
Water	2 litres (64 fl oz / 8 cups)
Sago pearls	30 g (1 oz), soaked in cold water
Brown sugar	300 g (11 oz)
Coconut milk	300 ml (10 fl oz / 1¼ cups)
Cardamom	10 pods, powdered and sifted
Salt	2 tsp

1. Cook beans in water until beans are soft but not mushy. Drain beans and reserve water.

2. Pour cooked beans into a saucepan. Add brown sugar and stir well. Cook over medium heat for 10 minutes then add 250 ml (8 fl oz / 1 cup) reserved liquid from boiling beans. Top up with water if necessary to cover beans. Continue to cook over medium heat to allow beans to absorb the flavour of the brown sugar.

3. Add drained sago and more water if necessary to cover beans. Continue to cook until sago is translucent.

4. Add salt, then coconut milk and cardamom powder. Simmer over low heat until payasam is thick, stirring occasionally to keep sago from sticking to the bottom of the pan.

5. Serve hot or chilled, with a little dollop of coconut cream (optional).

Indian Bread and Butter Pudding

Replete with the sweetness of peaches, this simple pudding is inexpensive and easy to prepare.

Sliced bread	300 g (11 oz)
Butter	as needed
Peach syrup (from canned peaches)	125 ml (2 fl oz / ½ cup)
Canned peaches	250 g (9 oz), drained weight, sliced

CUSTARD

Eggs	3
Sugar	150 g (6⅓ oz)
Milk	300 ml (10 fl oz / 1¼ cups)
Cream	90 ml (3 fl oz / ⅜ cup)
Cinnamon powder	½ tsp
Vanilla essence	1 tsp
Crushed nuts	
Vanilla ice cream	

1. Butter bread slices and cut in half to get triangles.
2. Line a baking or casserole dish with buttered bread slices.
3. Drizzle peach syrup over bread and arrange peach slices on top. Set aside.
4. Beat eggs lightly with a whisk then add sugar and whisk until sugar is dissolved.
5. Add milk, cream, cinnamon powder and vanilla essence. Whisk to mix well.
6. Pour mixture over bread and peaches. Use a spoon to gently press bread down, so bread is covered in mixture. Set aside for 10 minutes.
7. Bake in a preheated oven at 180°C (350°F) for 30 minutes. Sprinkle nuts over and serve warm with vanilla ice cream.

Steamed Jackfruit Turnover

Known as *ada*, this fragrant dessert is subtly perfumed with cardamom.

Jackfruit	500 g (1 lb 1½ oz), stones discarded and minced
Grated coconut	300 g (11 oz)
Dark brown sugar	300 g (11 oz)
Cardamom powder	1 tsp
Salt	½ tsp
Water	125 ml (4 fl oz / ½ cup)
Banana leaves	

BATTER

Plain (all-purpose) flour	500 g (1 lb 1½ oz), sifted
Water	300 ml (10 fl oz / 1¼ cups)
Salt	a pinch
Ghee (clarified butter)	1 Tbsp

1. Cook jackfruit, grated coconut, dark brown sugar, cardamom powder, salt and water in a wok over medium heat until mixture is thick with a jam-like consistency.

2. Prepare batter. Combine flour, water and salt to get a thick batter. Add ghee and mix until smooth. Leave for 10 minutes.

3. Place some batter on a banana leaf and spread it out over the center of the leaf. Place a generous spoonful of jackfruit jam on batter then fold leaf over and place in a steamer for about 10 minutes. Repeat until ingredients are used up.

4. Unwrap and serve hot or cold.

INDONESIAN

Fried Coconut Cakes

The combination of glutinous rice flour and plain flour ensures that the texture of these coconut cakes are light but also firm enough to hold their shape.

Glutinous rice flour	250 g (9 oz)
Plain (all-purpose) flour	125 g (4½ oz)
Coconut flesh	250 g (9 oz), from medium-ripe coconut, roughly chopped
Coconut juice	250 ml (8 fl oz / 1 cup)
Salt	a pinch
Cooking oil	for deep-frying

PALM SUGAR SYRUP

Palm sugar	250 g (9 oz)
Water	100 ml (3½ fl oz / ²/₅ cup)
Ginger	20 g (⅔ oz), peeled sliced and bruised.

1. Combine both flours, coconut flesh and juice and salt in a large bowl and knead into a soft, smooth, elastic dough.
2. Shape 1 heaped Tbsp dough into an oval-shaped dumpling. Repeat until ingredients are used up.
3. Deep-fry dumplings in medium-hot oil until golden, then remove and drain on absorbent paper.
4. Prepare palm sugar syrup. Combine all ingredients in a heavy saucepan and simmer until thick. Remove from heat and strain, discarding ginger.
5. Serve dumplings with syrup.

INDONESIAN

Coconut Almond Pudding

This dessert can be prepared in advance and kept refrigerated, making it perfect for a dinner party.

Coconut juice	500 ml (16 fl oz / 2 cups)
Young coconut flesh	200 g (7 oz), finely sliced
Sugar	30 g (1 oz)
Almonds	100 g (3½ oz), blanched, peeled and sliced
Cinnamon	2 sticks, each about 7.5-cm (3-in) long
Nutmeg	½, finely grated
Screwpine leaf	1, washed and cut into 5-cm (2-in) lengths
Sweetened condensed milk	2 Tbsp
Salt	a pinch
Corn flour (cornstarch)	2 Tbsp, dissolved in 4 Tbsp water

1 Combine coconut juice and flesh, sugar, almonds, cinnamon, nutmeg and screwpine leaf in heavy saucepan. Bring to the boil over low heat.

2 Add condensed milk and salt. Return to the boil.

3 Stir in corn flour paste and simmer for 1 minute, stirring continuously. Remove from heat when mixture thickens.

4 Divide mixture among individual serving glasses and refrigerate until set.

5 Serve chilled and garnished, if desired, with cinnamon sticks and sprigs of mint.

INDONESIAN

Fried Mung Bean Balls

The sesame seeds coating the mung bean balls become very fragrant when fried, making this dessert irresistible and a wonderful treat.

Rice flour	100 g (3½ oz)
Tapioca (cassava) flour	55–70 g (2–2½ oz)
Coconut milk	130 ml (4 fl oz / ½ cup)
Salt	a pinch
White sesame seeds	70 g (2½ oz)
Cooking oil	for deep-frying
FILLING	
Green (mung) beans	100 g (3½ oz), soaked in water overnight and drained before use
Sugar	55 g (2 oz)
Coconut milk	100 ml (3½ fl oz / ⅖ cup)
Screwpine leaf	1, washed and cut into pieces
Salt	a pinch

1. Combine both flours, coconut milk and salt in a large bowl. Mix into a smooth dough. Set aside.
2. Prepare filling. Combine all ingredients in a heavy saucepan, bring to the boil and simmer until beans are soft. While simmering, check liquid level frequently and add water, if necessary.
3. When beans are soft and all the liquid has evaporated, transfer to a stone mortar or blender and grind into a very smooth paste. Divide paste into 20 g (⅔ oz) portions.
4. Divide dough into 40 g (1⅓ oz) portions, then use your hands to pull or press each one out into an evenly thick round about 7-cm (3-in) in diameter.
5. Place a portion of bean paste on the centre of each round, gather edges and shape into a ball.
6. Roll balls in sesame seeds until evenly coated, then deep-fry in preheated oil at 160°C (325°F) until golden brown. Drain well and serve.

INDONESIAN

Dumplings in Sweet Ginger Soup

The starchiness of this rich combination of toppings and dumplings is balanced by the aroma and flavour of ginger in the sweet soup.

SWEET GINGER SOUP
Water	1 litre (32 fl oz / 4 cups)
Ginger	100 g (3½ oz), peeled, sliced and bruised
Sugar	100 g (3½ oz)
Salt	a pinch
Coconut milk	500 ml (16 fl oz / 2 cups)

SWEET DUMPLINGS
Glutinous rice flour	160 g (5¾ oz)
Tapioca flour	45 g (1½ oz)
Water	160 ml (5½ fl oz)
Sugar	40 g (1⅓ oz)
Green food colouring (optional)	2 drops

GARNISHING
Green (mung) beans	55 g (2 oz), cooked
Cooked sago	25 g (⅘ oz)
Cooked glutinous rice	55 g (2 oz)
White sliced bread	55 g (2 oz), diced

1. Prepare sweet ginger soup. Combine water, ginger, sugar and salt in a heavy saucepan. Bring to the boil, reduce heat and simmer until liquid is reduced by half.
2. Add coconut milk, return to the boil and simmer for 5 minutes, then remove from heat. Leave to cool to room temperature.
3. Prepare dumplings. Combine all ingredients in a large bowl and mix into a smooth, soft dough.
4. Shape dough into small dumplings and simmer in salted water until dumplings float. Drain and plunge into iced water.
5. Divide dumplings among 4 individual serving bowls. Top with a little of each garnishing ingredient, ladle ginger soup over and serve.

JAPANESE

Rice Ball Skewers

You can find this popular dessert at any traditional confectionery shop in Japan—it remains a perennial favourite of both the young and old.

Japanese rice flour (*jo shin ko*)	250 g (9 oz)
Sugar	1 Tbsp
Warm water	220 ml (7⅓ fl oz)
Bamboo skewers	10, soaked in water for 5 minutes and drained

SWEET SOY SAUCE (*MITARASHI ANN*)

Water	100 ml (3½ fl oz / ⅖ cup)
Dark soy sauce (*koikuchi shoyu*)	70 ml (2⅓ fl oz)
Mirin	1 Tbsp
Sugar	90 g (3 oz)
Potato flour (potato starch)	15 g (½ oz), mixed with 1 Tbsp water

1. Prepare rice balls. Combine rice flour and sugar in a mixing bowl. Add warm water and stir to mix well. Knead to form a medium-soft dough. Divide dough into 5–6 equal portions. Roll into balls and flatten into circles.

2. Line the bottom of a preheated steamer with a piece of wet muslin cloth. Place dough circles into steamer. Cover and steam over high heat for about 15 minutes until cooked.

3. Remove and transfer steamed dough circles into a wet grinding bowl (*suri bachi*). Using a wet pestle, pound and mash dough circles together to obtain an elastic and soft dough. Divide and shape cooked dough into balls, each weighing about 15 g (½ oz).

4. Skewer 3 rice balls on a bamboo stick. Repeat until ingredients are used up. Preheat a metal grill over a gas hob until red-hot. Grill each stick of rice balls for 3 seconds on each side until rice balls are seared with brown grill marks. Repeat until all rice balls are grilled. Set aside.

5. Prepare sweet soy sauce. Combine water, soy sauce, mirin and sugar in a small saucepan.

6. Heat and bring to the boil. Stir in potato flour mixture and cook until sauce has thickened and turned glossy. Remove from heat.

7. Dip each stick of rice balls into sweet soy sauce to coat evenly. Serve warm.

Agar–agar, Glutinous Rice Balls and Red Bean Paste with Syrup

Comprising a mouth-watering selection of textures, this dessert of chewy glutinous rice balls, smooth red bean paste and crunchy agar-agar cubes, laced with brown sugar syrup, is a real winner, and definitely my favourite. For an extra treat, serve with tea ice cream.

GLUTINOUS RICE BALLS
Glutinous rice flour   150 g (5⅓ oz)
Water   130 ml (4 fl oz / ½ cup)

AGAR-AGAR
Water   600 ml (20 fl oz / 2½ cups)
Agar-agar (*kanten*)
  stick   1, 7 g (⅓ oz)

BROWN SUGAR SYRUP
Muscovado (dark
  brown) sugar   100 g (3½ oz)
Water   50 ml (1⅔ fl oz / ¼ cup)

RED BEAN PASTE
Japanese red beans   500 g (1 lb 1½ oz), washed and drained
Japanese sugar
  or castor (superfine)
  sugar   430 g (15⅓ oz)
Salt   ½ tsp

GARNISHING
Canned mandarin
  orange slices   to taste
Canned cherries   to taste

1 Prepare red bean paste (page 21). Prepare glutinous rice balls. Place glutinous rice flour and water into a mixing bowl. Combine well to form a smooth dough with a slightly sticky texture.

2 Pinch off small portions of dough and roll into 2-cm (¾-in) balls. Press the centre of each ball of dough with a finger to flatten into a disc with a slight indent. Bring a large pot of water to the boil and add glutinous rice discs. When they float to the surface, drain and transfer to a bowl of iced water. This prevents the sticky discs from clumping together.

3 Prepare agar-agar. Pour water into a medium saucepan and soak agar-agar stick for 20 minutes until soft. Bring to the boil for about 5 minutes, until agar-agar dissolves completely.

4 Strain with a fine sieve. Pour strained mixture into a four-sided tin lined with cling film. Leave at room temperature to set for 1 hour, then refrigerate for another hour. When chilled, remove carefully and cut into small cubes.

5 Prepare brown sugar syrup. Combine muscovado sugar and water in a small saucepan. Simmer over medium heat, skimming off any foam that rises to the surface, until sugar dissolves. Remove from heat. Pour into a serving jug and set aside to cool. To serve, place small portions of red bean paste, glutinous rice discs and agar-agar cubes into individual serving bowls.

6 Garnish with mandarin orange slices and cherries to taste. Accompany with jug of brown sugar syrup for adding to taste.

Pancakes with Red Bean Paste

Traditionally made up of red bean paste sandwiched between two pancakes, *dora yaki* takes its name from *dora*, the little percussion instrument of a gong that the snack resembles.

Plain (all-purpose) flour	100 g (3½ oz)
Baking powder	½ tsp
Eggs	2
Castor (superfine) sugar	90 g (3 oz)
Honey	1 Tbsp
Mirin	1 Tbsp
Water	2 Tbsp
Cooking oil for pan-frying	
Candied chestnuts	8, cut into small pieces
RED BEAN PASTE	
Japanese red beans	500 g (1 lb 1½ oz), washed and drained
Japanese sugar or castor (superfine) sugar	430 g (15⅓ oz)
Salt	½ tsp

1. Prepare red bean paste (page 21).
2. Weigh cooled red bean paste to obtain 240 g (8½ oz) as filling for pancakes.
3. Divide into equal portions of 30 g (1 oz) each, and arrange on a baking tray.
4. Cover with cling film. Set aside.
5. Sift flour and baking powder together twice. Set aside.
6. Beat eggs and sugar in a separate bowl until mixture is very pale and thick.
7. Add honey, mirin and water. Combine well to obtain a smooth mixture.
8. Using a rubber spatula spoon, gradually fold flour into egg mixture to obtain a smooth batter.
9. Cover with cling film. Set aside at room temperature for about 20 minutes.

JAPANESE

10. Heat a little oil in a non-stick pan over low heat. Remove from heat and rest bottom of pan on a piece of damp cloth.
11. Pour in about 3 Tbsp batter, then swirl pan to obtain an 8-cm (3¼-in) circle.
12. Return pan to heat and cook over low heat for 1 minute, until bubbles appear on surface of pancake and underside is brown.
13. Turn pancake over and pan-fry other side for a few seconds until brown.
14. Remove cooked pancake and repeat to make more pancakes until batter is used up. There should be about 16 pancakes in total.
15. Top half the pancakes, each, with a portion of red bean paste and some candied chestnut pieces. Sandwich with remaining pancakes.
16. Serve warm or at room temperature.

JAPANESE

Candied Sweet Potatoes

The origins of this dessert can be traced back to a shop, located in front of Tokyo University nearly a century ago, that sold these candied potatoes.

Japanese sweet potatoes	400 g (14⅓ oz), scrubbed, rinsed and left unpeeled
Cooking oil	for deep-frying
Sugar	5 Tbsp
Water	2 Tbsp
Japanese dark soy sauce	1 tsp
Toasted black sesame seeds	1 tsp

1. Cut sweet potatoes lengthways into 1.5 x 1.5 x 6-cm (¾ x ¾ x 2½-in) strips. Soak in water for 10–15 minutes. Drain.
2. Cook sweet potatoes in the microwave oven on high, or steam over high heat for 5 minutes. Remove and pat dry. Set aside.
3. Heat oil to 160–170°C (325–330°F). Deep-fry sweet potatoes for 2–3 minutes, until light brown.
4. Remove and drain thoroughly on absorbent paper. Set aside.
5. Combine sugar, water and soy sauce in a non-stick frying pan over medium heat.
6. Stir continuously until sugar has dissolved completely. Continue to cook for another 2–3 minutes until bubbles appear on the surface, and sauce has thickened and turned glossy. Remove from heat.
7. Coat sweet potatoes with sauce evenly. Transfer to a serving plate. Sprinkle black sesame seeds on top and serve immediately.

KOREA

Sweet Rice Cake

Steamed glutinous rice cake coated in soy bean powder.

Glutinous rice flour	500 g (1 lb 1½ oz), sifted
Sugar	85 g (3 oz)
Salt	1½ Tbsp
Water	625 ml (20 fl oz / 2½ cups)
Soy bean powder	10 Tbsp
Honey (optional)	

1. Mix flour with sugar, salt and water to form a paste.
2. Line steamer with a clean muslin cloth. Pour flour paste onto cloth and steam for 45 minutes.
3. Spread soy bean powder on a large plate. Remove cake from muslin cloth and place onto powder to coat.
4. Slice coated cake and serve hot or chilled, drizzled with honey, if desired.

KOREAN

Cinnamon Punch with Dried Persimmon

Cinnamon and ginger punch with dried persimmons make a refreshing dessert.

Ginger	55 g (2 oz), peeled and thinly sliced
Water	2 litres (64 fl oz / 8 cups)
Cinnamon sticks	30 g (1 oz)
Brown sugar	170 g (6 oz)
Dried seedless persimmons	3, medium, calyx discarded
Pine nuts	

1. Put ginger and water in a large saucepan. Bring to the boil, then lower heat and simmer for 20–30 minutes.
2. Add cinnamon sticks and return to the boil.
3. Strain water through a fine sieve. Discard ginger and cinnamon sticks. Stir in sugar.
4. Bring water to the boil to dissolve sugar. When sugar has melted, leave liquid to cool.
5. Place persimmons into ginger and cinnamon liquid. Leave for 2 hours.
6. Cut persimmons into smaller pieces then place into cooled cinnamon and ginger liquid. Serve garnished with pine nuts.

Sugar-coated Tapioca Rings

These tapioca rings are made by deep-frying mashed tapioca dough rings and coating them in sugar.

Tapioca	600 g (1 lb 5⅓ oz)
Salt	1 tsp
Plain (all-purpose) flour	200 g (7 oz), sifted
Granulated sugar	600 g (1 lb 5⅓ oz)
Cooking oil	1 litre (32 fl oz / 4 cups)
Water	375 ml (12 fl oz / 1½ cups)

1. Peel and boil tapioca with salt until tender. Mash into a smooth paste.
2. Add plain flour and knead until dough is soft. Add 250 g (9 oz) granulated sugar.
3. Divide dough into 30 equal portions. Shape into 7.5-cm (3-in) rings and arrange them on a tray sprinkled with flour to prevent dough from sticking to tray.
4. Heat cooking oil in a pan and deep-fry tapioca rings until golden brown. Drain and leave aside to cool.
5. Boil remaining granulated sugar in water for about 10 minutes until thick and sticky. Put in fried tapioca rings. Coat rings well with sugar. Place on dish and serve.

STRAITS CHINESE

Sesame Puffs

These semi-circular puffs with a sweet sesame and peanut filling make a delightful snack at any time of the day.

Plain (all-purpose) flour	300 g (11 oz)
Salt	a pinch
Butter	150 g (5⅓ oz)
Egg yolks	2, 55 g (2 oz) each
Egg white	1, about 55 g (2 oz)
Iced water	2 Tbsp
Egg	1, about 55 g (2 oz), slightly beaten for glazing

FILLING (COMBINED)

Peanuts	85 g (3 oz), toasted and finely ground
Sesame seeds	45 g (1½ oz), toasted
Sugar	55 g (2 oz), or to taste

1. Sift plain flour and salt into a mixing bowl. Rub butter into flour until it resembles bread crumbs.

2. Beat egg yolks, egg white and water together with a fork. Pour into flour and butter mixture and mix into a soft dough. Allow dough to rest for 30 minutes.

3. Roll dough to 0.3-cm (⅛-in) thickness and cut into 7.5-cm (3-in) rounds with a pastry cutter.

4. Place 1½ tsp filling in the centre of each pastry round. Fold one side of the dough over the other to enclose filling. Press edges to seal and pinch surface with pastry pincers to make a pattern.

5. Place on an ungreased baking tray. Bake in a preheated oven at 170°C (338°F) for 10 minutes. Glaze with beaten egg and continue baking for another 10 minutes until golden brown.

6. Remove and leave to cool before storing in an airtight container.

Nyonya-style Pancakes

These mini pancakes are known as *apam* and are made from coconut juice, coconut milk, sugar and screwpine leaves.

Plain (all-purpose) flour	300 g (11 oz)
Baking powder	1¼ tsp
Salt	⅛ tsp
Coconut juice	200 ml (7 fl oz / ¾ cup)
Palm sugar	200 g (7 oz), finely crushed
Demerara or pale brown granulated sugar	3⅓ Tbsp
Screwpine leaves	3, shredded and knotted
Egg	½, about 30 g (1 oz), lightly beaten
Coconut milk	400 ml (13 fl oz / 1⅗ cups), extracted from 500 g (1 lb 1½ oz) grated coconut and 400 ml (13 fl oz / 1⅗ cups) water

1. Sift flour, baking powder and salt into a mixing bowl. Make a well in the centre. Set aside.
2. Combine coconut juice, palm sugar, demerara or pale brown granulated sugar and screwpine leaves in a saucepan. Bring to the boil. Remove syrup from heat and strain. Set aside until lukewarm.
3. Gradually pour syrup into flour mixture and blend with a hand whisk.
4. Add egg and continue mixing. Stir in coconut milk and blend to a smooth consistency.
5. Heat *apam* mould and its cover separately over a medium stove until hot. Lower heat and grease mould lightly.
6. Pour batter to fill three-quarters of mould. Cook over a low heat, uncovered, until bubbles appear on the top and the sides of *apam* turn golden. Cover mould for 20 seconds to cook the top of *apam*. *Apam* is cooked when it is firm and not sticky to the touch.
7. Remove cover and replace it on stove to keep it hot. Transfer mould to a heatproof working surface. Loosen the sides of *apam* with a toothpick. Fold each *apam* into half before taking out. Serve immediately.

THAI

Water Chestnut Cake with Coconut Cream Topping

A crunchy dessert of crunchy water chestnut cake with a rich coconut cream topping.

Screwpine leaves	30, for making leaf cases
Arrowroot flour	5 heaped Tbsp, sifted
Water	750 ml (24 fl oz / 3 cups)
Sugar	220 g (8 oz)
Water chestnuts	12, peeled and finely diced

COCONUT CREAM TOPPING

Coconut milk	625 ml (20 fl oz / 2½ cups)
Rice flour	2 Tbsp, sifted
Corn flour (cornstarch)	1 Tbsp, sifted
Salt	½ tsp

SCREWPINE LEAF JUICE

| Screwpine leaves | 10 |
| Water | 3 Tbsp |

1. Make screwpine leaf cases. Make four cuts at regular intervals along one side of leaf, up to the spine. Fold at these notches to create a square case. Trim off any excess leaf. Repeat until leaves are used up and set aside.
2. Prepare screwpine leaf juice. Cut screwpine leaves crosswise into 2.5-cm (1-in) lengths. Pound leaves, add water and squeeze to extract juice. Strain juice through a muslin cloth.
3. Combine arrowroot flour, screwpine leaf juice, water and sugar in a pan and cook until thick, translucent and shiny. Add in chestnuts and mix well. Pour into screwpine leaf cases until they are half-full. Set in the refrigerator for about 30 minutes.
4. Meanwhile prepare the coconut cream topping. Cook coconut milk with rice flour, corn flour and salt until thick.
5. Fill screwpine leaf cases with coconut cream topping and leave aside to cool before serving.

THAI

Red Rubies

A brightly coloured dessert of diced water chestnuts covered in a translucent coating, and served in sweetened coconut milk.

Water chestnuts	300 g (11 oz), peeled and finely diced
Red food colouring	1 tsp, dissolved in 250 ml (8 fl oz / 1 cup) water
Tapioca flour	55 g (2 oz), sifted
Corn flour (cornstarch)	2 Tbsp, sifted
Water	1.2 litres (40 fl oz / 5 cups)

COCONUT SYRUP
Sugar	150 g (5⅓ oz)
Water	250 ml (8 fl oz / 1 cup)
Screwpine leaves	2, shredded and knotted
Coconut milk	300 ml (10 fl oz / 1¼ cups)

1. Soak water chestnut cubes in coloured water until they turn red.
2. Combine tapioca flour and corn flour. Roll water chestnut cubes in flour to coat. Shake off excess flour.
3. Bring water to the boil. Add coated water chestnut cubes and boil for 3 minutes. Remove and rinse under running water. Drain well.
4. Wrap cooked water chestnut cubes in thin muslin cloth and set aside.
5. Meanwhile, prepare coconut syrup. Boil sugar, water and screwpine leaves. Remove and set aside to cool. Add coconut milk and stir well.
6. To serve, top water chestnut cubes with coconut syrup.

THAI

Coconut Bananas

A sweet dessert of boiled bananas served with warm coconut cream.

Bananas	6–9
Water	500 ml (16 fl oz / 2 cups)
Sugar	350 g (12 oz)
Coconut cream	125 ml (4 fl oz / ½ cup)
Salt	½ tsp

1. Peel bananas. If they are large, cut in half across, but if they are small, leave whole.
2. Mix water with sugar, and bring to the boil, stirring. Simmer for 5 minutes. Add bananas and cook for 5 minutes. Drain.
3. Bring coconut cream to the boil with salt. Reduce heat and stir until liquid thickens.
4. Serve bananas with warm coconut cream.

VIETNAMESE

Sweet Yam Dessert

Similar to but starchier than the mango and sticky rice of Thai fame, this dessert is easy to prepare and a solid way to wrap up any meal.

Water	2 litres (64 fl oz / 8 cups)
Glutinous rice	250 g (9 oz), washed and soaked in water for 1–2 hours
Salt	½ tsp
Sugar	300 g (11 oz)
Yam	500 g (1 lb 1½ oz), washed, peeled and cut into bite-sized cubes
Screwpine leaves	4, washed, dried and tied together to form a bunch, or ½ tsp vanilla essence
Coconut milk	300 ml (10 fl oz /1¼ cups)

1. Bring water to the boil. Add glutinous rice and cook for 20 minutes or until liquid is not visible from the top.
2. Add salt and half the sugar. Cook until both are completely dissolved.
3. Add yam, remaining sugar and screwpine leaves. Do not stir. Cook over low heat for 15 minutes or until yam cubes are cooked.
4. Mix in coconut milk, then remove from heat and leave to cool. Serve in small bowls at room temperature.
5. Alternatively, coconut milk can be served separately alongside dessert. Separately bring coconut milk to the boil, then add a solution of corn flour mixture and water to thicken.

Peanut and Sago Dessert

With green beans, peanuts, sago and shredded black fungus, this dessert has a delightful variety of soft and crunchy textures.

Green (mung) beans	300 g (11 oz), soaked in water for 1 hour or until softened then rub off and discard skins
Peanuts	100 g (3½ oz), soaked in water for 1 hour and drained
Water	2 litres (64 fl oz / 8 cups)
Sugar	200 g (7 oz)
Sago	55 g (2 oz), soaked in water for 1 hour or until softened
Black (woodear) fungus	55 g (2 oz), soaked in water until soft, then finely shred
Coconut cream	200 ml (7 fl oz / ¾ cup)
Screwpine leaves	4, washed and dried, or ½ tsp vanilla essence
Salt	½ tsp

1. Steam skinless green beans for about 5 minutes or until cooked through, but not soggy.

2. Put peanuts in a pot. Add sufficient water to cover, then boil for about 20 minutes or until softened. Drain peanuts well, then transfer to a bowl. Add sugar and mix.

3. Bring 2 litres (64 fl oz / 8 cups) water to the boil in a large pot. Add soaked sago and cook for 10 minutes or until sago becomes clear.

4. Add all remaining ingredients and return to the boil, then turn off heat.

5. Serve hot or chilled.

VIETNAMESE

Tapioca Cake

As delicate as much of Vietnamese cuisine, this cake is mildly fragrant from the coconut cream and not overbearingly sweet.

Tapioca	1 kg (2 lb 3 oz), washed, peeled and cut into small pieces then blended until fine and pasty
Coconut cream	200 ml (7 fl oz / ¾ cup)
Condensed milk	3 tsp
Vanilla essence	½ tsp
Sugar	100 g (3½ oz)
Salt	½ tsp
Butter	55 g (2 oz)

1. Put tapioca paste into a cloth bag or fine strainer. Squeeze firmly to drain out excess liquid. Use about 650 g (1 lb 7 oz) of tapioca paste to make cake. Reserve and refrigerate any remainder for future use.

2. Put tapioca paste into a large bowl. Mix in coconut cream, condensed milk, vanilla essence, sugar, salt and half the butter.

3. Melt remaining butter and use it to grease the base of a 20–25-cm (8–10-in) round metal cake tin.

4. Bake in a preheated oven at 180°C (350°F) for about 15 minutes or until surface is golden brown.

5. Remove cake from oven and leave to cool. Turn out cooled cake, then slice and serve.

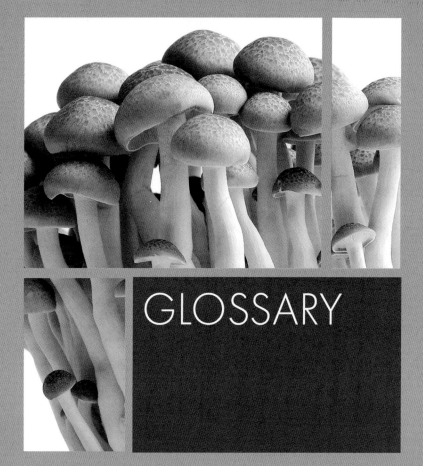

GLOSSARY

FRESH PRODUCE

Aubergines

Aubergines

Also known as eggplants or brinjals, aubergines come in many varieties that vary in size, colour and shape, ranging from long tubes to small, round pea-like shapes, and deep purple, green and striped varieties. Their neutral flavour and ability to take on the flavour of other ingredients makes it a versatile and popular ingredient in Asian cooking. Aubergines can be used in stews, stir-fried dishes, grilled with salt or made into dips. Choose firm, heavy aubergines that have smooth, shiny skins with no discolouration.

Bamboo Shoot

Bamboo Shoot

The tender, young shoots of the bamboo plant, bamboo shoots are harvested when they first appear at the base of the bamboo plant. The bamboo shoot is covered with dark coloured leaves which should first be peeled off before use. Inside, the flesh is cream-coloured. Fresh bamboo shoots must be boiled for at least an hour before it is ready for use. After boiling, leave the shoots to soak in water until required. Bamboo shoots are available fresh, canned, pickled or sour.

Calamansi Limes

The calamansi is a variety of the lime fruit. Round, small and green or greenish-yellow, it has an extremely sour taste, whether young or ripe. In the Philippines, it is favoured for making refreshing drinks or cordials. Its zest is used to give desserts a refreshing zing, and its juice is typically used as part of a dipping sauce, salad dressing or is simply sprinkled over food.

Calamansi Limes

Chillies

Chillies are an essential spice and flavouring ingredient in many Asian dishes. The main chillies used in Asian cooking are large red or green chillies, and bird's eye chillies. Large chillies are by far the mildest and are mainly used as a vegetable or for flavouring. They are also typically seeded before use, making them even milder as the fieriness of chillies comes from the seeds. Bird's eye chillies are the smallest and also the most potent. Mostly used raw and served as a condiment, these tiny chillies are fiery-hot, and are served raw as garnish or a condiment. The general rule of thumb is that the smaller the chilli, the spicier it is. Deseeding chillies, whether fresh or dried, will also help make dishes less spicy. Use sparingly or with much care. When buying chillies, they must be firm to the touch, shiny and smooth-skinned, and the stem should be green. It is best to use chillies that were recently harvested and if possible, do not refrigerate for long periods as this will change the chilli's crisp, clean flavour. Always wear gloves when handling chillies and thoroughly wash hands and all surfaces that came into contact with the chillies afterwards.

Chillies

Bird's Eye Chillies

Glossary 345

Chinese Cabbage

Also known as napa cabbage, elongated heads of Chinese cabbage consist of tightly packed leaves, each of which is frilly and very faint green along the edges and has a wide white ridged stem at the centre.

Chinese Lettuce

Also known as leaf or curled lettuce, Chinese lettuce comes in small bunches resembling bouquets. Although iceberg lettuce leaves can be a substitute, Chinese lettuce leaves are said to have a higher nutritional value than those of iceberg lettuce simply because of their darker, rich green colour.

Coconut

The coconut is a key ingredient in Asian cooking. Many vegetable and meat dishes, as well as cakes and desserts, use coconut for flavouring. In many Western countries, freshly shredded coconut is now available vacuum-packed in Asian stores and some supermarkets. If freshly grated coconut is unavailable, desiccated coconut moistened with coconut milk can be used as a substitute.

Coconut cream or milk should not be confused with coconut juice, also called coconut water. The latter is a translucent liquid that is inside the coconut and most refreshing when drunk on a hot day. Coconut cream or milk is a white liquid traditionally derived by squeezing grated coconut flesh. Coconut cream is, as its name suggests, thicker than coconut milk.

To obtain coconut cream and milk by hand, combine 300 g (11 oz / 2 cups) freshly shredded coconut with 250 ml (8 fl oz / 1 cup) warm water, then stir the mixture thoroughly and leave to cool before passing through double muslin cloth or a potato shredder and squeeze as hard as possible to extract the maximum amount of liquid. Refrigerate the squeezed liquid for 30 minutes. During this time, the cream will separate from the milk and rise to the top. This makes it easy to skim off the coconut cream. The milk, on the other hand, is typically used to cook stews. Good quality coconut milk and cream are easily available in most Asian stores.

Coriander Leaves (Cilantro)

Also known as Chinese parsley, coriander is fully edible, from its leaves to its stems and roots. Coriander leaves are commonly used to garnish dishes as well as to flavour foods. When storing coriander, first pat dry with absorbent paper or kitchen towel, then wrap in clean absorbent paper or keep in an airtight container. Refrigerate and use as needed. Coriander can be kept for up to a week, depending on the freshness of the herb.

Fiddlehead Ferns

Also known as ostrich ferns, fiddlehead ferns are the unfurled fronds of a young fern of an edible variety. In certain rural areas of the Philippines, fiddlehead grows in abundance, particularly along the banks of streams at local villages. Filipinos consume them as a simple salad, flavoured with fermented anchovies (*bagoong isda*), fish sauce (*patis*) and calamansi. Choose fronds that are tender, unblemished and a deep, shiny green colour.

Gingko Nuts

Gingko nuts are almond-shaped nuts that are commonly used as either a savoury stuffing or in sweet dessert soups. When peeled, they are a pale, yellow colour, with a smooth texture. Their flavour is distinctively buttery and bitter-sweet. The bitter shoot located in the core of the nuts should be removed before use.

Green Papaya

Papaya is a tropical fruit that grows in most countries in Asia. It contains papain, an enzyme which behaves as a meat tenderiser. Green or unripe papaya has a sourish, sharp taste and a crunchy texture. It can be eaten raw as a salad tossed with lime juice and other raw vegetable ingredients, or cooked in soup. Green papayas can also be made into pickles.

Ladies Fingers

Ladies fingers or okra are used extensively in Asian cooking. Slender and slightly fuzzy to the touch, they release a sticky, gelatinous substance when cooking, which gives a slimy texture and serves as a thickening agent. Ladies fingers should be consumed cooked; either boiled, as a salad ingredient or in stews and stir-fried dishes.

Lotus Root

Lotus roots are actually the rhizomes or stems of the lotus plant from which the roots grow. The stems are also sliced into thin rounds and pickled with vinegar to accentuate the sweetness of the vegetable. When cooked, starch is released, bringing out the root's faint, natural sweetness and nutty quality. Choose roots that are firm with smooth, unblemished skin.

Lotus Seeds

Dried lotus seeds require considerable preparation before use. For a start, they will need to be soaked in water for some hours or quickly parboiled to slightly soften. The brown skins and the green cores, which are bitter, need to be removed, if either or both are attached. While the brown skins can be simply rubbed off, there are two ways to remove the green cores — either split each seed in two and brush it off or poke a bamboo toothpick or cocktail stick through the centre of the seed to push the core out. The latter method has the advantage of leaving the seeds whole. In recent years, however, fresh, skinless lotus seeds have become available in some supermarkets. Although they, too, have the green cores attached, they require no soaking or parboiling before use. Canned lotus seeds may need the least preparation but their mushy softness leaves much to be desired.

Mushrooms
Straw Mushrooms

Straw mushrooms have been named as such because they are cultivated in straw. You can buy them either fresh or canned, but fresh ones have to be scalded before use. After scalding, they can be stored in the refrigerator for only a few days.

Dried Chinese Mushrooms

There are two varieties of dried Chinese mushrooms–the winter mushroom and the flower mushroom. The former is thick and greyish-black in colour while the latter is paler in colour and more expensive. Before cooking, soak them in water for at least 30 minutes to soften. Reserve the stems for flavouring stocks, especially for strict vegetarian cooking. Remove the stems, wash, dry and grind with a pepper mill or an electric blender until fine for the stock. To store for a long period of time, ensure that they are well dried before blending and store in the refrigerator in an air-tight container.

Honshimeji Mushrooms

Honshimeji mushrooms is a popular variety of Japanese mushroom that grow in bunches under the Japanese oak and beech trees in the autumn. Cooked in clear soups and hotpots, these mushrooms are rather mild in flavour, but are highly regarded for their meaty texture. Before using, trim about 2.5 cm (1 in) of the spongy portion from the bottom, then rinse the mushrooms briefly under cold tap water, and gently separate into individual stems.

Purple Yam

Purple yam or *ube*, as it is known in Tagalog is a tuberous root distinguished by its bright purple colour. In Filipino cuisine, it is used to make sweet desserts such as ice cream, puddings, cakes and jams. It is particularly valued for its attractive colour. *Ube* is also available in powdered form.

Shallots

Shallots belong to the same family as onions, and range from purplish-red to brown in colour. They should be peeled before use, and are either thinly sliced or ground and used in almost all dishes, whether as part of the dish or as a garnish. Crisp-fried shallot slices make a deeply aromatic and flavourful garnish for just about any dish. Ready-made crisp-fried shallots are available in Asian stores and while they save considerable time, the ready-made variety is also less tasty than home-made shallot crisps. Indonesian shallots appear similar enough to shallots sold in the West but they are usually smaller and also much softer in flavour. If shallots are unavailable, use red Spanish onions instead.

Lotus Root

Lotus Seeds

Purple Yam

Straw Mushrooms

Honshimeji Mushrooms

Dried Chinese Mushrooms

Shallots

Glossary 349

Sour Star Fruit

Known to Malay-speakers as *belimbing buluh*, this small green, elongated fruit is a relative of the more famous yellow star fruit but it is extremely sour and is used predominantly in cooking. Sour star fruit (right), when added in small quantities, imparts a tartness to the dish. It is sometimes also known as sour finger carambola. If sour star fruit is unavailable, replace with segments of lime.

Taro

Taro is a tuberous root that is widely cultivated and used in Asia. Taros have a brownish-yellow skin that should be removed completely before use in cooking, as it contains calcium oxalate crystals that cause throat irritation and swelling in the mouth. However, these crystals are neutralised upon cooking. Taro flesh is pearl-white in colour and crunchy in texture. It is a versatile vegetable that can be boiled and steamed. In Filipino cooking, they are used in soups and stews.

Water Chestnuts

This edible dark brown tuber has crunchy cream-coloured flesh that is rather bland but has a slight sweetness. Choose water chestnuts with a firm texture. Water chestnuts can be eaten raw or cooked. Peel off the skin before using. If the fresh variety is unavailable, substitute with canned water chestnuts. The canned version is ready-peeled. Water chestnuts are commonly used in Asian cooking to add a pleasant crunch to stir-fried dishes, snacks and desserts. Store in the refrigerator for up to a week.

Watercress

A pungent-tasting vegetable, not unlike rocket (arugula) leaves, watercress works well in conjunction with other ingredients with forward flavours. Delicate tastes and aromas are likely to be lost alongside watercress.

White Radish

Also known as daikon, this is the root of a plant belonging to the mustard family. White radishes are elongated and are usually larger in diameter than the common orange carrot. Radishes are available all year round. Choose radishes that are firm to the touch. Peel off the skin and trim off the caps and root ends as you would carrots before using.

Yuzu

This citrus fruit is about the size of a tangerine. It has thick, brightly coloured zest with a sharp, refreshing fragrance. Yuzu is used almost entirely for its aromatic zest. Small pieces are grated, or finely shredded, and added to soups, salad, pickles as well as desserts. Its juice is used to make a citrusy vinegar for salad dressings.

SEASONING AND SAUCES

Distilled Vinegar

Also known as white vinegar, distilled vinegar is a clear liquid made from distilling alcohol. It contains an ingredient known as acetic acid, which acts as a tenderiser and preservative. Filipinos use distilled vinegar to add a piquant taste to some of their dishes.

Fermented Anchovy Sauce

Fermented anchovy sauce or *budu* originates from the state of Kelantan in eastern Malaysia. Like fish sauce, it is made from a mixture of fermented fish, but is given its distinctive, dark reddish brown colour from the addition of tamarind and palm sugar. *Budu* can be used as a seasoning ingredient or as part of a dipping sauce. If *budu* is unavailable, prawn paste is a good substitute.

Fermented Black Beans

Fermented black beans or black bean sauce is sold in small plastic packets. Made from salted and fermented black soy beans, they have a very strong flavour so it is best to use sparingly. Before using, soak them in water for 5–10 minutes then rinse and drain thoroughly. Fermented black beans are used in both meat and seafood dishes.

Fermented Prawns (Shrimps)

Fermented prawns, or *bagoong alamang* as it is known in the Philippines is one of the most common varieties of dried prawn (shrimp) pastes. Blended from a combination of tiny prawns and salt, it has a strong, pungent taste and aroma. Unlike some varieties of prawn paste, it has a chunky consistency due to the fact that the prawns retain their shape and texture. *Bagoong alamang* features heavily in many Filipino dishes, and is such a well-loved product that it is eaten in almost every way possible. Filipinos mix it with plain rice, sometimes with other condiments. There are several varieties of *bagoong alamang* with sweet or salty flavours.

Dried Prawn (Shrimp) Paste

Dried prawn (shrimp) paste is an essential ingredient in Southeast Asian cooking. Made from fermented prawns, it has a distinctively pungent smell and strong, salty flavour. Depending on where it is made, prawn paste varies in texture, saltiness and colour. In Thailand and Vietnam, prawn paste is known as *kapi* and *mam tom* consecutively. Sold either in blocks or paste form, colour ranges from a pinkish-grey to dark brown. In Malaysia, Singapore and Indonesia, prawn paste is known as *belacan* or *terasi*. It is recognisable by its rich brown colour. There is also another type of sweet prawn paste that is black in colour and made from a mixture of fermented prawns, salt, sugar, flour and water. Known as *hae ko* or *petis udang*, it has a texture similar to that of molasses, and is an essential ingredient in making the sauce for *rojak*, a type of Asian salad. Unless otherwise stated, prawn paste should be grilled or toasted before use. Store prawn paste in air-tight containers away from heat and moisture.

Fish Sauce

Fish sauce is made from a brew of fermented fish or prawns (shrimps), and ranges in colour from light brown to dark brown. Just like prawn paste, taste and colour varies across countries. Salty, pungent and strong-flavoured, fish sauce is commonly used in Southeast Asia to enhance the flavour of dishes. Vietnamese fish sauce may be similar enough to Thai fish sauce in the larger scheme of things but is nevertheless quite distinct in taste. Vietnamese fish sauce is said to be more tangy than its Thai counterpart, which is more salty. For the uninitiated, fish sauce can be unpalatably fishy, although this is sometimes also a question of quality. Generally, better quality products are less fishy. The fishiness of fish sauce can be tempered with any or a combination of the following: lime juice, vinegar or sugar. In fact, simply diluting the sauce with some water often helps. When a recipe calls for a considerable amount of fish sauce, add it to the dish in small amounts, adjusting it to taste as you go. It is far more problematic to counter the effects of too much fish sauce in a given dish.

Distilled Vinegar

Dried Prawn (Shrimp) Paste

Fermented Anchovy Sauce

Fish Sauce

Fermented Prawns (Shrimps)

Fermented Black Beans

Glossary 353

Korean Hot Chilli Paste

This is a special type of chilli paste from Korea. It cannot be replaced with other types of chilli paste otherwise the taste of the dish will be different. It is commonly used in Korean cooking and is easily available from Korean supermarkets.

Korean Preserved Prawns (Shrimps)

These preserved prawns are different from the preserved prawns used in other types of Asian cooking. They are larger in size and very much sweeter than the common Asian variety. As such, they cannot be used as substitutes for each other. Preserved prawns are commonly used in Korean cooking and are thus readily available from Korean supermarkets.

Maltose

Also known as malt sugar, this thick golden-colored syrup is available bottled from Asian supermarkets. It has a thick consistency like honey, but it is not as sweet. It is used to add sweetness to dishes.

Mirin

Mirin is an extremely sweet sake made from a brew of glutinous rice and rice malt. It is that is light golden in colour. Used extensively in Japanese cooking, it imbues a dish with a subtle, sweet flavour, an attractive glaze, and also goes well with soy sauce in many simmered dishes.

Wasabi

Also known as Japanese horseradish, wasabi is a member of the cabbage family. The root of the plant is used as a spice. Wasabi has a pungent flavour and radish-like aroma. It grows naturally, along the beds of mountain streams flowing through river valleys in Japan. Although grating the fresh roots renders the best wasabi paste, they are rather rare, even in Japan. Instead, wasabi is more ready available in the form of powder and paste. In Japanese cuisine, wasabi paste is always served together with soy sauce to accompany sushi and sashimi.

Sesame Oil

Extracted from toasted white sesame seeds, two varieties of this oil exist. One is lighter in color and the other is darker in color. In this book, the darker variety is used. It has a rich brownish color and a strong fragrance. It is generally used to enhance the flavour of dishes in Asian cooking. High in polyunsaturated fats, sesame oil is a healthy cooking oil.

Tamarind Pulp

Tamarind pulp is the flesh of the tamarind fruit. The tamarind tree grows abundantly in Southeast Asian countries, and is valued for its acidic, sourish fruit. The pulp imparts a fragrant, tangy flavour to soups, gravies and dishes. Tamarind pulp is brown in colour and is available in packet form, from the market and supermarket. To use, the required amount of tamarind pulp is first soaked in water for about 10 minutes. The liquid is then strained of any fibre and seeds to obtain the sour juice.

DRY INGREDIENTS, HERBS AND SPICES

Annatto Seeds

Annatto seeds come from the achiote plant, which is indigenous to the Caribbean and Central America. Primarily used as a colouring agent, they have a sweet and slightly peppery flavour, with a hint of nutmeg. The red colouring can be extracted through infusing and squeezing the seeds in water, or frying them in hot oil, after which the seeds are discarded and the oil used. Choose seeds that are a vibrant, brick-red colour.

Black (Woodear) Fungus

These hard, curly-edged pieces of dried fungus expand with soaking in water. Almost invariably, first-time users will overestimate the amount they soak to derive what they really need. Should that happen, drain the soaked fungus of water well and store in a covered container in the refrigerator. It can be kept for up to a week.

Bonito Flakes

Shaved from smoked blocks of skipjack tuna, bonito flakes or *katsuo boshi* are one of the key ingredients, used especially for making the basic stock, *dashi*, in Japanese cooking. At the supermarket, there are several kinds of bonito flakes available. Large flakes called *hana katsuo*, are used for preparing *dashi*, while small flakes called *kezuri bushi* are used as a garnish for dishes. For optimum freshness, store them in the freezer.

Candlenuts

These roundish nuts, are a creamy yellow in colour and are brittle and waxy in texture. Used as a binding agent, candlenuts also impart a faint flavour to the dish to which they have been added. As candlenuts are mildly toxic, they should not be consumed raw, and must be toasted or cooked before consumption. If unavailable, replace with macadamia, raw peanuts without the shell and skin or raw cashews.

Cardamom Seeds

Cardamom seeds are small, green and aromatic. The pods, from which are usually added whole to dishes for flavour as without the pods, the seeds are very pungent. In Indian cooking, cardamom is used in making *garam masala* and other curry powders.

Chana Dhal

Chana dhal is yellow in colour and looks somewhat like split peas. It has a sweet, nutty flavour, and is used in Indian curries or ground into flour to make the batter for a number of Indian breads.

Chinese Red Dates

Also known as Chinese dates or jujubes, red dates can be used to make herbal teas, and are added to soups and teas for flavour and sweetness. They are sold in dried form at Chinese medical and herbal shops.

Cinnamon

Cinnamon is the inner bark of a tropical evergreen tree. The bark is harvested during the rainy season then dried into long quills, which are either cut into lengths and sold as cinnamon sticks, or ground into powder. Cinnamon is widely used in sweet dishes, but also makes an interesting addition to savoury dishes such as stews and curries.

Cloves

Cloves are the dried, unopened flower buds of the tropical evergreen clove tree. They are sold either whole or ground and can be used to flavour dishes. However, they tend to lose their flavour if left in storage for too long. Test the freshness in water: if fresh, it will sink or float upright; stale ones will lie on the surface.

Glossary 357

Coriander Seeds

Although not really seeds, these tiny fruit are commonly referred to as seeds to distinguish them from coriander (cilantro) leaves in recipes. In Indian cooking, both the fresh coriander leaves and seeds are used. When lightly roasted, the seeds impart a lovely flavour and aroma to vegetables and meat curries. However, use sparingly and roast lightly or the finished dish will have a bitter aftertaste.

Cumin

In Indian cooking, cumin are usually added to the hot oil at the start of the cooking so that the oil is infused with its flavour. It is also dry-toasted and ground then sprinkled on yoghurt, snacks and salads. When roasting and grinding cumin, it is best to roast and store just a little at a time as the ground cumin loses its fragrance easily. Warm cumin water is said to be a great digestive after a spicy meal.

Curry Leaves

Curry leaves have an unmistakable aroma and flavour. To release their essence, they are added to hot oil. Commonly found in Indian grocery shops, they can be used as garnish, chopped and added to salads, yoghurt or lassi drinks, or thinly sliced and added to meat cutlets, patties and omelettes. Dried curry leaves can be used as a substitute if fresh leaves are unavailable.

Dried Anchovies (large)

These dried anchovies are significantly larger than the common dried anchovies available in Chinatowns the world over. The smallest can be at least 5-cm (2-in) long. They are used to flavour soups and stocks and discarded thereafter. You can use the more common but smaller dried anchovies if these are not available, although the flavour will not be as robust or satisfying.

Dried Anchovies (small)

These small dried anchovies are commonly available in markets and supermarkets. They are not as strong in flavour as the large dried anchovies, but as they are easily available, they are often used in recipes that call for dried anchovies.

Dried Prawns (Shrimps)

Dried prawns are tiny prawns that have been completely peeled, salted and sun-dried. They are valued for the smoky, briny, salty-sweet flavour they impart to dishes, pastes and sauces. They can be used whole, chopped or finely ground. Simply rinse or if preferred, soak in water for 10–15 minutes to remove the salty flavour.

Dried Red Chillies

These come in different sizes and varying strengths of spiciness. The long crinkled ones are not as spicy as the short, smooth ones. Dried red chillies need to be soaked in hot water to soften before use.

Fennel Seeds

Fennel seeds are often confused with cumin because they look somewhat similar. Fennel seeds are slightly bigger and greenish in colour while cumin is brown. Fennel is also sweeter and can be eaten after a meal as a mouth freshener. Roast fennel in a dry pan, grind into a powder and sprinkle on meat dishes just before dishing out for additional fragrance.

Fenugreek Seeds

Fenugreek seed is a spice that is integral in Indian cooking. They have a very bitter taste and a unique smell. Just a pinch makes a difference to fish curries and yoghurt-based dishes. Fenugreek seeds also have medicinal properties. For an upset stomach, stir the seeds in a cup of boiling water and strain before drinking.

Five-spice Powder (not pictured)

Five-spice powder is made from a combination of star anise, cinnamon, clove, fennel and Szechuan peppercorn. It is readily available at supermarkets. You only need a small amount to season toasted and braised poultry or meat and to reduce the strong flavour of beef, lamb and fish.

Galangal

This rhizome looks like ginger, but it can be distinguished from the former by its faint pinkish colour. Galangal has a distinctive peppery taste that is best when fresh. It lends a unique flavour to the dish when used in cooking. The flesh is cream-coloured. Slice off the required amount and peel off the skin before using. The remaining root can then be stored for later use. Simply slice off the dried portion.

Garlic)

The Asian varieties of garlic is very much similar to Western garlic, except that the cloves are usually smaller. Their flavour is also slightly less pungent and sharp. Try to purchase young garlic with firm heads that are free of bruises. To peel garlic easily, crush each clove lightly with the flat blade of a heavy knife or cleaver first. This makes it very easy to remove the skin.

Ginger

Ginger is a fragrant spice that has a thin brown skin and bright yellow flesh. Young rhizomes are milder in taste as compared to mature ones. When buying the ginger roots, look out for plump and firm ones. Ginger must always be peeled before use. It is usually sliced, finely chopped, pounded or ground and used in savoury dishes.

Ginseng

Also known as Korean ginseng, this is one of the most popular medicinal herbs in the world. It has been used for thousands of years to promote good health and is popularly used to lower cholesterol, increase energy levels and stimulate the immune system. Ginseng is easily available from Chinese medical stores as well as some health food stores.

Green (Mung) Beans

Green beans are the sources of bean sprouts commonly seen in Asian cooking. They are most often bought whole and dried, which means that they require soaking before use. The skins of the beans loosen when soaking and some people discard these skins, while others do not in view of their nutritional value. Green beans can also be bought skinless and split. Without their outer covering, they are a bright light yellow and cook easily.

Salam Leaf

The *salam* leaf is widely used in Indonesian cooking to flavour soups, stews, sauces, fish and meat dishes. Although it is similar to the bay leaf in use and appearance, they come from a completely different plant species and should not be used as a substitute for each other. *Salam* leaves are sometimes labelled "Indonesian bay leaves" by some suppliers.

Japanese Red Beans

Rich in protein and fibre, Japanese red beans, or adzuki beans are regarded as a very nutritious food in Japan. Although used in both savoury and sweet dishes, red beans are predominantly used in making Japanese sweets, such as stuffed glutinous rice cakes and glutinous rice balls.

Korean Chilli Powder

This chilli powder is unique in Korea. It is of a higher grade than other types of chilli powder and should preferably not be replaced if possible. If unavailable, however, you can use other types of chilli powder, but the amounts to be added to the recipe will vary. Adjust to taste when using other types of chilli powder.

Lemon Basil

True to its name, this delicate spice has a very pleasant lemon-basil flavour. Known to the Malay-speakers as *daun selasih* or *kemangi*, it is most commonly used in fish-based dishes where the fish is wrapped in banana leaves and cooked by steaming or grilling. If used in stove-cooked dishes, lemon basil (above) should be bruised to release its fragrance and then added towards the end of cooking to best retain the clean, lemon fragrance. Regular basil can be used as a substitute.

Lemongrass

This is a very important herb in Thai cooking. With long thin light green-grey leaves and a bulbous base, only the lower 10–15 cm (4–6 in) portion of the herb is used in cooking. Fragrant and aromatic, lemongrass imparts a distinctive lemony flavour dishes. To use, trim off the base and peel off the tough outer layers to reveal the tender centre. Bruise to release its flavour when the herb is used whole, or slice finely.

Lesser Ginger

Also known as Chinese keys or *krachai*, lesser ginger comes in bunches of slender, short tuberous roots. They range in colour from yellow to light brown and have a distinct aromatic flavour. Omit it from the recipe if it is unavailable.

Mustard Seeds

These tiny black seeds are an essential spice in South Indian cooking. They are tempered with a dose of hot oil, mustard seeds, curry leaves and sometimes a dried red chilli. Mustard seeds have a slightly bitter aftertaste and this quality makes them perfect for adding to pickles.

Nutmeg

The nutmeg is the hard kernel of the fruit of an evergreen tree native to the Moluccas of the Spice Islands. Avoid using ground or powdered nutmeg, as much of its pungency would have been lost. Instead, grate whole nutmeg to use. This aromatic and sweet spice is usually used with strongly flavoured meats such as pork, duck and lamb.

Palm Sugar

Made from the sap of coconut or palm trees, this natural sugar varies in colour from dark to light brown. It is less sweet than cane sugar and has a distinctive fragrance and flavour. Palm sugar has a soft texture and may melt easily depending on where it is stored. Store in a cool dark place in an air-tight container. Palm sugar usually comes in a cylindrical block or in rounds. If unavailable, substitute with brown sugar.

Sesame Seeds

These tear-drop shaped seeds are mainly used to garnish and flavour dishes. They have a distinct flavour which is enhanced when roasted. In Asian cooking, white sesame seeds are toasted without oil and left to brown slightly. They are then added as a garnish after the dish is cooked. Vary the amount added to your personal preference.

Sago

Sago comes from the sago palm, an evergreen plant native to Asia. Sago pearls are made from the starch of the sago palm. In the preparation process, the starch is washed in water, strained through a sieve and dried on a hot surface. When cooked, sago pearls turn translucent and sticky, and can be used to make dessert or shells for savoury fillings.

Salted Cabbage

Salted cabbage is made by salting and pickling green stem vegetables. It should be washed thoroughly and soaked in water before use to remove excessive saltiness. It is most commonly used in duck soup but it can also be fried with meat.

Screwpine Leaves

Commonly known in Southeast Asia as *pandan* leaves, screwpine leaves impart a unique and subtle fragrance that somehow makes a world of difference in lifting the dish, usually desserts, out of stodginess. The leaves are usually washed and knotted together before use. Often, a knot of 5–6 leaves will suffice in scenting a stock pot of ingredients, although the amount can be increased or decreased to taste.

Seaweed

Hijiki

Hijiki seaweed is a black algae that grows around the coast of Japan, and is available in dried, narrow and curly strands. Like wakame seaweed, soak it to rehydrate before use. It is often combined with deep-fried bean curd (*abura age*) in simmered vegetable dishes.

Kelp (*Konbu*)

An essential ingredient for preparing dashi stock, kelp is a seaweed with a fresh, intense aroma of the sea and is rich in calcium, calcium and fibre. It grows in the northern seas off the Japanese coast, and Hokkaido is its biggest producer. Kelp is available in various grades and sizes in the market, ranging from 5–30 cm (2–12 in) in width. Choose kelp that is thick and a glossy dark green in colour. Dried kelp is usually covered with a fine white powder that is a by-product of the drying process. Do not wash or rinse, but simply wipe with a piece of damp cloth before using. Kelp will last for several months refrigerated.

Nori

Laver or *nori* sheets are sun-dried sheets of a film-like marine algae, that is greenish-brown in colour. They have a slight smoky flavour and are used for wrapping sushi rice or adding to soups. Toast lightly before use to obtain a crisp texture and accentuate their aroma. *Kizami nori* refers to nori strips that are often added to soups, or rice dishes as a garnish.

Wakame

An orangey-brown algae that grows on rocks in the sea during winter and summer, *wakame* seaweed is sold, dried or salted. Used in soups, salads and simmered vegetable dishes, dried, cut wakame is easily available at Japanese supermarkets today. Always soak the dried seaweed in water to rehydrate before using.

Sour Plums

These are marble-sized, light-brown plums that have been pickled in vinegar and salt. They are usually used when steaming fish to add a sour tang, or to make refreshing drinks.

Thai Sweet Basil

Also known as sweet basil, this aromatic herb is used widely in Thai cooking. Whenever possible, use the herb fresh, as it does not retain its flavour when dried. When choosing sweet basil, choose leaves with a fresh green colour that show no sign of wilting. Add the whole leaves to dishes or slice them finely. To store, place the herb stem-down in a glass of water and refrigerate. Fresh Thai sweet basil will keep for up to a few days.

Torch Ginger Bud

As its name suggests, this plant belongs to the ginger family. The tightly closed buds are light pink in colour and have a sweet, tangy fragrance. Shave or thinly slice the bud and add it to salads for both colour and flavour.

Turmeric

Turmeric is a rhizome that is valued for its aromatic and spicy fragrance. It is used extensively in the preparation of curries, pickles and marinades. It is also used to spice and colour foods, and is available in powdered form.

Deep-fried Bean Curd

Fermented Red Bean Curd

Fermented Soy Bean Cake

Firm Bean Curd

Silken Bean Curd

Preserved Soy Beans

SOY PRODUCTS

Deep-fried Bean Curd

Also known as *abura age*, this thin, rectangular-shaped bean curd is highly versatile, and can be added to many dishes including stir-fries, simmered dishes and soups. Rich in vegetable protein, it can also be slit open to form pockets for stuffing with sushi rice or vegetables. Suitable for vegetarians, it is readily available, frozen or fresh, at Japanese supermarkets. Always blanch in boiling water before use to remove any excess oil.

Fermented Red Bean Curd

Fermented bean curd comes in two main types: white and red. The white variety is usually served and eaten alongside plain rice or congee, while the red variety is more commonly cooked and used to flavour dishes. These knobs of bean curd fermented in rice wine are pungent and can be an acquired taste. In fact, fermented bean curd pieces have such a strong smell and taste that they are also known as bean curd cheese.

Fermented Soy Bean Cake

Malay speakers know this product as *tempe*, which was first made in Indonesia. Applauded as an inexpensive source of protein, *tempe* is made by subjecting skinned soy beans that have been pre-boiled to quick fermentation—a special variety of mould is introduced to the boiled soy beans when they have thoroughly cooled and then left for three days. Unlike its famous soy cousins, sweet and salty soy sauces, *tempe* is not preserved and is, therefore, easily perishable. Fresh *tempe* has a yeasty, mushroom-like aroma but when sliced and fried, it develops a nutty, almost meaty flavour.

Firm Bean Curd

Bean curd, made from soy beans, comes in many forms. Soft bean curd is sold as white squares or rectangles of curd immersed in water. There is also a circular type that is sold in plastic tubes, known as Japanese *tau fu*. They should be able to keep for a few days. Bean curd cubes that have been fried in oil are called *taufu pok*. Bean curd can be made into yellowish translucent sheets called bean curd sheets or *foo pei*. It is commonly used for wrapping meat and vegetable fillings. Make sure you buy the soft and flexible sheets because the brittle ones are inappropriate for wrapping. Dried soy bean sticks (*foo chok*) are yellow in colour. They are often used in mixed vegetable dishes. They have to be soaked in warm water prior to use. Soft salted bean curd cubes (*lam yee*) are kept preserved in a brine and wine solution with chillies. They have a distinctive flavour and complements porridge very well.

Hot Bean Paste (not pictured)

Also known as chilli bean paste or *dou ban jiang*, hot bean paste is a salty and spicy paste that is made from fermenting broad beans, soy beans, chillies, salt and spices together. It is often added to stir-fried dishes, rice and noodles for flavour and spiciness. It is available in bottled form.

Preserved Soy Beans

Preserved soy beans are rather salty and have a unique flavour. They are added to dishes when cooking or used to make tasty sauces. The beans can be used whole or mashed to make a paste. When preserved soy beans are used in a dish, salt is commonly omitted or significantly reduced.

Silken Bean Curd

There are basically two types available: soft bean curd and silken bean curd. Soft bean curd is processed from soy bean milk mixed with a coagulant, that is then left to set in moulds lined with cotton cloth; this allows any excess water to drain away. The bean curd is therefore, firm in texture, and also has a visible cloth mark on its side when set. Silken bean curd, on the other hand, is processed with thick soy bean milk, and set in moulds lined with silk. Hence the water content is retained, resulting in a bean curd with a smoother and softer texture.

Soy Bean Paste

Used in soups, marinades and dipping sauces, soy bean paste or *miso* is one of the most important seasoning ingredients in Japanese cuisine. As the paste is rich in protein, it was a precious and nourishing food in the olden days, when food was scarce.

The variety of soy bean paste differs from region to region, and are mainly categorised into three grades, according to the dominant ingredient that they are made with. Soy bean pastes made with rice are red, light brown or white in colour, and tend to have a mild flavour. Soy bean pastes made with barley are red or light brown in colour and have a medium flavour. Pure soy bean pastes are dark red or black in colour and have the richest and most salty flavour among the three. Another way of categorising soy bean pastes is by colour: white (*shiro miso*), red (*aka miso*) or dark (*kuro miso*).

A popular variety of soy bean paste is *shinshu miso*, a white soy bean paste made with rice, that hails from central Japan. I believe that the type of soy bean paste to use in any dish, is entirely one of personal tastes and preferences. As soy bean paste will lose its aroma if overcooked, add it to a dish only towards the end of cooking time. Always store any unused soy bean paste in tightly-covered containers in the fridge, to minimise the loss of flavour.

Soy Bean Powder

Also known as soy flour or *kinako*, soy bean powder is made from finely ground soy beans. This dark cream-coloured flour is high in protein and is commonly used in desserts and other confections in Japan and Korea. It is relatively tasteless on its own and can be mixed with sugar for sweetness.

Soy Sauce

Soy sauce is one of the essential everyday seasonings in Asian cooking, providing the dishes with both a pleasant flavour and colour. Depending on which country it is made in, soy sauce differs in flavour and colour. The most common types of soy sauce available are light soy sauce and dark soy sauce. Used in dipping sauces or to season dishes, Chinese light soy sauce is generally saltier than dark soy sauce, which has a thicker consistency and is slightly sweet. Japanese soy sauce or *shoyu* taste slightly sweeter, due to the type of grains it is brewed with. It is not recommended that Chinese soy sauces be used as a substitute for *shoyu*. Indonesian soy sauces consist of sweet and salty varieties—*kecap manis* and *kecap asin*.

Soy Sauce

Soy Bean Paste

Soy Bean Powder

Glossary 369

RICE, NOODLES AND FLOURS

Black Glutinous Rice

Black glutinous rice is typically used for making desserts and it is interesting to note that black glutinous rice grains are only black on the outside and are white at the centre. Short and stubby, the black rice grains are considerably more expensive than the white variety and is seldom used in home cooking.

Dried Egg Noodles

Made from a combination of wheat flour, egg and water, dried egg noodles come in thin or medium thickness. They are also available fresh. Before use, dried noodles should be soaked in water until slightly softened.

Dried Sweet Potato Noodles

As its name suggests, these noodles are made from the sweet potato. They are commonly used in Korean cooking and are available from Korean supermarkets. Long and thin, these noodles resemble angel-hair pasta but differ in colour. When boiled or cooked, these noodles become translucent. If unavailable, use glass vermicelli.

Glass Noodles (not pictured)

Also known as transparent noodles, cellophane noodles, jelly noodles or mung bean vermicelli, these thin, dried noodles can be softened in warm water before use or simply placed in boiling water to cook until tender. Glass noodles do not have much flavour of their own. As such, they take on the flavour of the gravy or soup they are cooked in most readily.

Glutinous Rice Cake

Also known as *mochi*, glutinous rice cake is made from steamed and pounded glutinous rice, rice cakes are available in rectangular blocks, or circular shapes, and are usually eaten grilled, fried or lightly boiled. A traditional food, rice cakes are cooked in soups, and eaten by the Japanese to celebrate the New Year on the first of January. It is believed that the sticky and elastic qualities of the rice cakes symbolise long life and wealth. Ready-made rice cakes are easily available at Japanese supermarkets today, and if unopened, can be kept refrigerated for several months.

Rice Cakes, Slices and Rolls

Made of rice flour, water and salt, these rice cakes are available from the frozen section of Korean supermarkets. They have a firm chewy texture and take on the flavour of the dish readily. The Chinese also have a variety of rice cakes similar to these, but the taste and texture are slightly different.

Rice Papers

A quintessentially Vietnamese condiment, round rice papers are sold as dried, white discs sealed in plastic packets. The rice papers need to be softened with water before use. Liquid turns the white discs into translucent sticky sheets that require careful handling, an experience similar to trying to use overly sticky cling wrap or to undoing a long, mangled strip of sticky tape. The rice papers, however, are remarkably resistant to tears even when dampened.

Black Glutinous Rice

Dried Egg Noodles

Dried Sweet Potato Noodles

Glutinous Rice Cake (Mochi)

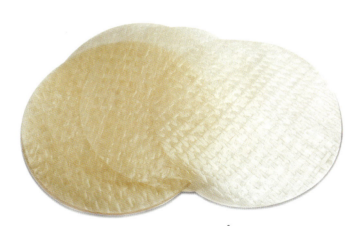

Rice Cakes, Slices and Rolls

Glossary 371

Rice Vermicelli

Rice vermicelli is most commonly available dried, although some Asian markets sell them fresh. Fresh rice vermicelli has a sticky quality that the dried variety, even after reconstitution, does not possess. If the fresh rice vermicelli is required in a roll or in a dish where its stickiness is required, then it is advisable to substitute with Indian string hoppers (*putu mayam*) or thick round rice (*laksa*) noodles. In the event that the fresh rice vermicelli is meant for a noodle dish, then dried rice vermicelli can be substituted. The rule of thumb is to quarter the weight of fresh vermicelli called for in a recipe and then let that figure be the amount of dried vermicelli required for reconstituting.

Soba

Made from a combination of buckwheat and wheat flour, soba noodles are rich in protein. Korean soba noodles tend to be more chewy than the Japanese variety. Soba noodles retain their texture when boiled. The are also eaten cold, served with a dipping sauce.

Somen

Somen refers to very fine noodles made from wheat flour. The noodle dough is stretched very thinly with the aid of vegetable oil into fine strands, and air-dried. Cold somen noodles are often served during the summer months in Japan.

Spring Roll Wrappers

These are thin dough wrappers available fresh or frozen. Defrost the frozen wrappers before use and cover with a damp cloth to prevent them from drying out.

Tapioca Flour (not pictured)

Tapioca flour is commonly used to make Asian dessert and snacks. It is also used as a thickening agent for gravies, sauces and soups, much like corn flour (cornstarch). If tapioca flour is not available, substitute with corn flour.

Udon

Udon refers to thick wheat noodles that are made from combining wheat flour with salted water. The noodles can be round or flat, and come in a variety of widths. Udon is available fresh, frozen or dried.

Water Chestnut Flour

Obtained from ground dried water chestnuts, this flour is used as a thickening agent, much like corn flour (cornstarch). It is available in Asian supermarkets and health food stores. If unavailable, substitute with potato flour or corn flour.

Wheat Noodles

These are thin, pale noodles made of wheat flour. They are usually sold dried. They are easily reconstituted when boiled in water, but do not overcook. If unavailable, substitute with other Asian wheat noodles.

Wheat Noodles

Glossary 373

INDEX

A
aubergines 33, 36, 45, 260, 268, 345

B
bamboo shoots 41, 71, 77, 190, 215, 228, 286, 345
bean curd
    deep-fried bean curd 44, 79, 148, 364, 366–367
    fermented soy bean curd 25, 28, 367–368
    firm bean curd 85, 93, 146, 176, 182, 368–369
    silken bean curd 71, 93
    soft bean curd 33, 71, 102
bell pepper 22
black glutinous rice 308, 370–371
black (woodear) fungus 86, 221, 302, 342, 356, 357
bonito flakes 19, 44, 48, 79, 178, 356–357

C
calamansi lime 136–137, 172–173, 345
candlenuts 14–16, 18, 87, 98, 101, 119, 176, 182, 205–207, 235, 237, 241, 264
Chinese cabbage 50, 74, 260,
Chinese lettuce 218, 220, 300–303, 305, 346–347
Chinese red dates 69, 210, 240, 294, 356
Chinese rice wine 19, 21, 102, 286
Chinese sausage 21
cinnamon 10, 13, 114–115, 140, 294, 322, 325, 334, 356, 357
cloves 115, 119, 141, 213,
coconut 96, 261, 263, 265, 274, 276, 277, 280, 299–300, 302,
coriander leaves 50, 135, 141, 160–161, 170, 184, 185, 216, 220, 229, 232, 234, 242–243, 245, 252, 255, 276–278
coriander seeds 14–16, 18, 20, 119, 177, 194, 204–205, 235, 237, 241, 264, 356–357
cumin 13, 16, 18–19, 36–37, 39–40, 58, 109, 111–114, 204, 213, 234, 235, 241, 261–263, 271, 276, 292, 358–359
curry leaves 13, 36, 37–38, 40, 109–110, 139, 141–142, 203, 213, 232–233, 261, 263, 292, 358–359, 363

D
distilled vinegar 190, 230–231, 257–258, 288, 352–353
dried anchovies 84–85, 180, 358–359
dried prawns 59, 90, 93, 158, 161, 359
dried prawn (shrimp) paste 14–17, 19, 24, 32, 58, 90–91, 118–119, 144, 158, 205, 242, 277, 352–353
dried red chillies 13, 35, 38, 175, 203, 233, 242, 261, 263, 358–359
dried sweet potato noodles 179, 370–371

F
fennel seeds 241, 358–359
fenugreek seeds 261, 263, 358–359
fermented anchovy sauce 35, 352–353
fish sauce 52, 56, 58, 59–60, 62, 72–75, 88–90, 92, 118, 126–127, 137, 159–161, 171, 173, 183–184, 188–190, 214–216, 218, 242, 244, 246–247
five-spice powder 24, 64

G
galangal 14–18, 24–25, 28, 58, 76–77, 88–89, 101, 119, 205–206, 229, 235–237, 241, 274, 276–277, 360–361
garlic 5–6, 10, 12, 14, 18–20, 24–26, 28, 30, 32–33, 37, 39–41, 49–54, 56–62, 66, 96, 98–99, 101, 103, 105–109, 111–113, 118–119, 122, 124, 127, 166–168, 171, 177, 180, 184, 186, 189–190, 196–197, 212, 226, 228, 230–237, 239–245, 247, 254–257, 260–261, 263, 264, 271–272, 277, 279–281, 283, 360
ginger 27, 29, 32–34, 41–42, 44, 48–50, 52, 55, 57, 64, 68, 72–73, 76, 81–82, 84, 98–99, 102, 104, 110, 114, 116, 119, 122, 125, 127, 133, 135, 137, 141, 144, 150–151, 162–163, 170, 175, 190, 195, 203, 208, 213, 228, 233–234, 237–239, 246, 255–257, 264, 270–271, 287, 306, 324, 326–327, 332, 334, 360–361
gingko nut 104, 109, 267, 314–315
gingseng 238, 240, 360–361
glass noodles 59, 77, 127, 166–168, 171–174, 177, 179, 181, 183–184, 186, 188–190, 296
glutinous rice 99
glutinous rice cake 333
glutinous rice flour 107
green (mung) beans 326–327, 342, 360
green papaya 66, 71, 73, 348–349

H
hot bean paste 254, 368

J
Japanese red bean 19, 329, 330, 360, 362

K
kelp 19, 44, 48, 78–81, 147–148, 151, 178, 360, 362
Korean soy bean paste 85, 368

L

ladies fingers 33, 208, 268, 348, 349
lemongrass 14–20, 42, 66, 72, 76, 77, 88–90, 100–101, 115–116, 119, 130, 132, 144, 177, 194–195, 205–206, 217–218, 220, 224–225, 235, 237, 241–242, 244–245, 251–253, 264–265, 273–274, 276–277, 362–363
lemon basil 42, 76, 96, 118, 120, 177, 250, 363
lotus root 47, 123, 141, 171, 348–349

M

maltose 103, 180, 270, 354–355
mirin 12, 44–47, 120–123, 147, 151, 155, 178, 208, 238, 271, 328, 330
mushrooms
    dried Chinese mushrooms 29, 102, 135, 172–173, 178, 226, 286, 296, 348, 349
    straw mushrooms 162, 189, 305, 348
    button mushrooms 102, 169, 174, 279
    honshimeji mushrooms 148, 348–349
mustard greens 166–167, 170,
mustard seeds 37–38, 40, 142, 203, 362

N

noodles
    dried egg noodles 172, 186, 370–371
    fresh flat rice noodles 91
    fresh yellow noodles 88
    rice vermicelli 182, 185, 190, 218, 300, 370–371, 326, 354, 362–363
nutmeg 14, 119. 176, 237, 325, 362–363

P

palm sugar 15–16, 18–19, 24, 25, 28, 59, 96, 101, 115, 196, 204–205, 234, 237, 242, 252, 279, 297–298, 308–309, 311–312, 324, 352, 363
polygonum leaves 58, 60, 62, 63, 190, 363
preserved soy beans 182, 185, 187, 191, 226, 244, 273, 300

R

rice cakes 80, 144, 146, 156–157, 204, 260, 333, 370–371
rice papers 218, 220, 282, 300, 302, 370–371

S

sago 320, 321, 327, 342, 363
salam leaves 14–15, 18–20, 43, 66–67, 76, 96–98, 100–101, 119, 130, 132, 194–196, 224–225, 235, 250, 264, 360–361
salted cabbage 68, 364
screwpine leaves 11, 42, 72, 130, 136, 140, 364–365
seaweed 12, 79, 81, 152, 178, 360, 364–365
sesame oil 29, 31, 45, 47, 51, 53–54, 78, 86, 102–103, 120, 122, 124, 127, 134–135, 155, 157, 167, 179–181, 209–211, 238–239, 244, 255, 287, 294–296
sesame seeds 49, 153, 155, 156, 179, 209, 212, 272,
shallots 10, 14–21, 26, 42, 96, 130–135, 140, 144–145, 158, 161–162, 242, 253, 255, 260, 264–266, 274, 277–278, 281, 283, 297–298, 302
soba 178, 181, 370–371
sour plums 68, 364
sour star fruit 17, 67, 75–76, 218, 220, 264,
soy bean paste 185, 187, 191, 366–367
soy sauce 48, 69, 80–83, 102, 131, 133–135, 139, 143, 145–148, 151–153, 155, 157, 161, 198, 212, 254, 256–258, 267, 269–271, 287, 294, 296, 300, 354, 367–369
spring onion 29, 42, 44, 49–52, 54, 74, 77–78, 82, 84, 88, 97–98, 102, 104, 109, 116, 166–168, 170, 173, 176, 178, 184, 187–190, 208–210, 215–217, 228, 246, 350–351

T

tamarind pulp 10, 14, 15, 75, 185, 205, 213, 242, 261, 263–264, 281, 354–355
taro 32, 75, 163, 302, 350–351
Thai sweet basil 90, 126, 159, 215, 276–277, 364
turmeric 12, 14–16, 177, 262–265, 274, 276, 364–365

W

wasabi 125, 152–153, 178, 181, 354–355
water chestnut 314, 338–339, 350–351
watercress 281
white radish 47–50, 52, 75, 78–80, 84, 121, 217–218, 269, 295–296, 350–351

Y

yuzu 80

WEIGHTS AND MEASURES

Accuracy in measuring and weighing ingredients is essential for successful cooking, particularly so with light desserts and cakes where incorrect amounts of ingredients could spoil the dish altogether.

The measures used in this cookbook are in metric and the American standard measuring cups and spoons. The measuring cups are easily obtainable in sets of four: 1 cup, $1/2$ cup, $1/3$ cup and ¼ cup. The cup is equivalent to 250 ml (8 oz). The spoons are also easily available in sets of four: 1 Tbsp, 1 tsp, $1/2$ tsp and $1/4$ tsp.

It must be remembered that when measuring dry ingredients, always fill the measure to overflowing and without shaking it, level off with the straight edge of a knife, unless otherwise specified in the recipe.

LIQUID AND VOLUME MEASURES

Metric	Imperial	American
5 ml	$1/6$ fl oz	1 tsp
10 ml	$1/3$ fl oz	1 dsp
15 ml	$1/2$ fl oz	1 Tbsp
60 ml	2 fl oz	$1/4$ cup (4 Tbsp)
85 ml	$2\,1/2$ fl oz	$1/3$ cup
90 ml	3 fl oz	$3/8$ cup (6 Tbsp)
125 ml	4 fl oz	$1/2$ cup
180 ml	6 fl oz	$3/4$ cup
250 ml	8 fl oz	1 cup
300 ml	10 fl oz ($1/2$ pint)	$1\,1/4$ cups
375 ml	12 fl oz	$1\,1/2$ cups
435 ml	14 fl oz	$1\,3/4$ cups
500 ml	16 fl oz	2 cups
625 ml	20 fl oz (1 pint)	$2\,1/2$ cups
750 ml	24 fl oz ($1\,1/5$ pints)	3 cups
1 litre	32 fl oz ($1\,3/5$ pints)	4 cups
1.25 litres	40 fl oz (2 pints)	5 cups
1.5 litres	48 fl oz ($2\,2/5$ pints)	6 cups
2.5 litres	80 fl oz (4 pints)	10 cups

DRY MEASURES

Metric	Imperial
30 grams	1 ounce
45 grams	$1\,1/2$ ounces
55 grams	2 ounces
70 grams	$2\,1/2$ ounces
85 grams	3 ounces
100 grams	$3\,1/2$ ounces
110 grams	4 ounces
125 grams	$4\,1/2$ ounces
140 grams	5 ounces
280 grams	10 ounces
450 grams	16 ounces (1 pound)
500 grams	1 pound, $1\,1/2$ ounces
700 grams	$1\,1/2$ pounds
800 grams	$1\,3/4$ pounds
1 kilogram	2 pounds, 3 ounces
1.5 kilograms	3 pounds, $4\,1/2$ ounces
2 kilograms	4 pounds, 6 ounces

LENGTH

Metric	Imperial
0.5 cm	$1/4$ inch
1 cm	$1/2$ inch
1.5 cm	$3/4$ inch
2.5 cm	1 inch